HISTORY
OF RUSSIA

Sergei Mikhailovich Soloviev

The
Academic International Press
Edition
of
Sergei M. Soloviev

History of Russia From Earliest Times

G. EDWARD ORCHARD
General Editor

Contributing Editors

HUGH F. GRAHAM

JOHN D. WINDHAUSEN

ALEXANDER V. MULLER

K.A. PAPMEHL

RICHARD HANTULA

WALTER J. GLEASON, JR.

WILLIAM H. HILL

G. EDWARD ORCHARD

LINDSEY A.J. HUGHES

NICKOLAS LUPININ

GEORGE E. MUNRO

DANIEL L. SCHLAFLY, JR.

ANTHONY L.H. RHINELANDER

SERGEI M. SOLOVIEV

History of Russia

Volume 10

The Reign of Ivan the Terrible

*Kazan, Astrakhan, Livonia,
the Oprichnina and the Polotsk Campaign*

Edited, Translated and With an
Introduction by

Anthony L.H. Rhinelander

Academic International Press
1995

The Academic International Press Edition of S.M. Soloviev's
History of Russia From Earliest Times in fifty volumes.

Volume 10. *The Reign of Ivan the Terrible. Kazan, Astrakhan,
Livonia, the Oprichnina and the Polotsk Campaign.*
Unabridged translation of the text of Chapters III, IV and V of
Volume 6 of S.M. Soloviev's *Istoriia Rossii s drevneishikh vremen*
as found in Volume III of this work published in Moscow in 1965,
with added annotation by Anthony L.H. Rhinelander.

ISBN: 0-87569-144-7

Composition by Ethel B. Chamberlain

Printed in the United States of America

ACADEMIC INTERNATIONAL PRESS
Box 1111 • Gulf Breeze FL 32562-1111 • USA

CONTENTS

Correspondence with Ivan—Ivan's Proud Response—Psychological Impact of Kurbsky's Departure—Ivan Abandons Moscow—Oprichnina Set Up—Metropolitan Philip—Death of Prince Vladimir—Executions at Novgorod—Traitors Executed—Ivan's Testament of 1572—Grand Prince Simeon.

WEIGHTS AND MEASURES

Linear Measure

Verst: 500 sazhen, 1166 yards and 2 feet, .663 miles, 1.0668 km
Sazhen: 3 arshins, 7 feet, 2.133 m
Arshin: 16 vershoks, 28 in (diuims) 72.12 cm
Chetvert: 1/4 arshin
Fut: 12 diuims, 1 foot, 30.48 cm
Vershok: 1.75 in, 4.445 cm, 1/16 arshin
Diuim: 1 inch, 2.54 cm
Desiatina: 2400 square sazhens, 2.7 acres, 1.0925 hectare
Chetvert (quarter): 1/2 desiatine, 1.35 acre (sometimes 1.5 desiatinas or ca 4.1 acres)

Liquid Measure

Stof: Kruzhka (cup), 1/10 vedro, ca 1.3 quarts, 1.23 liters
Kufa: 30 stofy
Vedro (paid): 3.25 gallons, 12.3 liters, 10 stofy
Bochka (barrel): 40 vedros, 121 gallons, 492 liters
Chetvert (quarter): 1.4 bochka, 32.5 gallons

Weights

Berkovets: 361 lbs, 10 puds
Pud: 40 funts, 36.113 lbs (US), 40 lbs (Russian), 16.38 kg
Funt: 96 zolotniks, .903 lbs, 14.4 ozs, 408.24 grams
Grivenka: 205 grams
Korob (basket): 7 puds, 252 lbs
Rad: 14 puds, 505.58 lbs
Chetvert (grain measure) 1/4 rad, 3.5 puds, 126.39 lbs, ca 8 bushels
Chetverik (grain measure dating from 16th century): 1/8 chetvert, 15.8 lbs
Zolotnik: 1/96 lb, 4.26 grams

Money

Chervonets (chervonny): a gold coin minted in the first half of the 18th century
    worth about 3 rubles
Muscovite Denga: 200 equals 1 ruble
Novgorod Denga: 100 equals 1 ruble
Ruble: 100 copecks, 200 dengas
Altyn: 6 Muscovite dengas, 3 copecks
Grivna: 20 Muscovite dengas, 100 grivnas equals 1 ruble, 10 copecks
Poltina (Poltinnik): 50 copecks, 100 dengas
Polupoltina (-nik): 25 copecks, 50 dengas
Poltora: 1 1/2 rubles
Peniaz: 10 equals one grosh (Lithuania)
Kopa grosh: 60 groshas, one Muscovite poltina
Chetvertak: silver coin equal to 25 copecks or 1/4 rubles (18–19th centuries)
Copeck: two Muscovite dengas
Foreign Denominations: 1 efimok or 1 thaler (Joachimsthaler)-about 1 ruble, 1
    chervonets or chervonnyi—a ducat, about 3 rubles
Levok—Dutch silver lion dollar

Note: Weights and measures often changed values over time and sometimes held
    more than one value at the same time. For details consult Sergei G.
    Pushkarev, *Dictionary of Russian Historical Terms from the Eleventh Century
    to 1917 (Yale,* 1970).

PREFACE

This book is an unabridged translation of Volume 6, Chapters 3-5, of the Soviet edition of Soloviev's *Istoriia Rossii s drevneishikh vremen* (History of Russia from Earliest Times) re-published in Moscow in 1959-1966; its location in the original edition (St. Petersburg, 1851-1879; 29 vols.) is Volume 6, pages 7-185; in the Moscow edition it is found in Book III, pages 455-610. We have divided the original three chapters into four: Soloviev originally combined both the eastern campaigns against the Tatars and the Western campaigns against the Livonians into one, the first, chapter; as the two are quite distinct it made sense to divide them into two separate chapters. The other two chapters remain as in the original.

Soloviev's pages are featureless and interminable, one long and complex sentence treading Indian file after another. To make the text easier to follow, long paragraphs and sentences have been broken into shorter ones. The main consideration has been to make his history as readable as possible consistent with accuracy. An effort has been made to find English-language equivalents for all the technical terms that Soloviev employs (ranks, offices, titles, legal, administrative, and so on) in order to smooth the flow of the narrative for the general reader and to avoid cluttering the pages with untranslated words. The exception involves Russian words which have become common in English—boyar, tsar, cossack, khan. The translator remains acutely aware of the inevitable shortcomings that may remain.

Most of the subtitles are based on the descriptive topic headings clustered at the beginnings of the chapters in the Russian edition. These headings have been moved into the body of the text as subtitles to mark the transition from one subject to another. In some cases new subtitles have been added, but Soloviev's arrangement of the material has not been altered.

Remarks in parentheses in the text are Soloviev's, as is the italicization of words or phrases for emphasis. Explanatory or interpretive information has been supplied by the translator in footnotes placed at the end of the book; where it appears in the text of the translation, it is enclosed in brackets. The general policy followed in annotating has been to identify prominent personalities at first mention and to give explanations and elucidations of obscure or uncommon terms and passages, assuming that the usual reader will have relatively little familiarity with Russian history. Most of Soloviev's own notes are not included; their highly specialized archival, documentary, and bibliographic nature would be of value only to specialists who would prefer to consult the original Russian text. Most of the notes added by the editors of the Soviet edition also have been excluded since they too are technical in nature, primarily supplying fuller bibliographic citations than Soloviev's notes. When the author's notes and those of the Soviet editors are included, they are so designated. All other notes are those of the present translator. In the notes the reader is frequently referred to entries in the *Modern Encyclopedia of Russian and Soviet History* (MERSH), a reliable and up-to-date reference source readily available in most university libraries.

Russian personal names are preserved in their Russian form except for Alexander, Alexis, Michael, Nicholas, Catherine, and Peter, which English usage has made familiar with respect to Russian historical figures. The names of important ecclesiastics have been recast into Latin or Greek equivalents, especially for the earlier period of Russian history. This applies to prominent individuals; less prominent figures get their Russian forms. Certain other names and terms have been anglicized for the sake of clarity and because they are used widely, such as Casimir, Sophia, Danzig, boyar, rubles, versts, and Dnieper.

The editors of the edition published in the USSR frequently added patronymics and other names, and these have been retained without brackets; patronymics appearing in the original edition also have been kept. Plural forms for names and terms which might be confusing have been anglicized—Vologdians rather than Vologzhane, Voguls and not Vogulichi, the Dolgorukys not Dolgorukie, and so on; in a few cases the Russian plural form is used when it is common. The final "-iia" in feminine personal names has been shortened to "-ia"—"Maria" and "Evdokia" instead of "Mariia" and "Evdokiia." Most Slavic surnames show gender, and this has been preserved. An "-a" at the end of a word usually signifies a female: thus Golovkin's wife or daughter would be Golovkina.

Non-Russian names, locations, terms, ranks and so on are spelled according to the language native to the person or particular to the city, region or culture where this can be determined. Confusion arises at times because the text is not clear about nationalities. An example is Lithuania where at least three languages intermingle. In such cases the context rules; the Russian rendering is the last resort. Individuals whose ancestors were non-Russian but whose family had been in Russian service for generations are named by the Russianized spelling of the family name. Turkish, Tatar, Persian, and other names and terms usually are spelled in the original according to accepted scholarly forms. In some instances, if not otherwise ascertainable, they are transliterated from the Russian as given by Soloviev. The names of geographical locations conform to commonly accepted English usage—Podolia, Moscow, Copenhagen, Saxony, and so on.

With respect to transliteration, the translation follows a modified version of the Library of Congress system, omitting diacritical marks and ligatures, and rendering an initial "Ia-" and "Iu-" as "Ya-" and "Yu-" ("Yasnaia" and "Yury") and occasionally the initial "E-" as "ye" (Yermak, Yevlev); the suffix "-yi" or "-ii" as "y" ("Dmitry Poliansky" instead of "Dmitrii Polianskii"); and the form "-oi" has been replaced by "-oy" ("Donskoy" instead of "Donskoi"). The soft sign, indicated by an apostrophe in some transliteration systems, is usually dropped altogether ("tsar" instead of "tsar'"), although in some cases an "i" has been inserted in place of a hard or a soft sign: "Soloviev" instead of "Solov'ev."

All dates, as in Soloviev's original text except where otherwise specified, are according to the Julian calendar, in use in most of Western Europe in the sixteenth century until 1582; this in spite of the fact that the Russians themselves at the time figured dates from the creation of the world, which they reckoned to be 5,508 years before the birth of Christ. By the sixteenth century A.D. the Julian calendar was ten days behind the solar calendar. Pope Gregory XIII reformed it in 1582 and the "Gregorian" calendar soon came into general usage throughout Catholic Europe; Protestant Europe (except England) adopted it in 1700, England in 1750. Oddly, the Russians under Peter I adopted the Julian or "Old Style" rather than the current Gregorian calendar, which was not adopted in Russia until 1918.

A table of weights and measures is included at the front of this volume for the convenience of the reader. The source of the maps and illustrations in each case is as noted.

For providing secretarial assistance, xeroxing and word-processing facilities, funds for photographic reproduction, and intellectual support I am indebted to St. Thomas University, Fredericton, New Brunswick, Canada.

I dedicate the work to my Russian History students.

Anthony Rhinelander

INTRODUCTION

The present volume of Sergei Soloviev's *History of Russia from Earliest Times* concerns one of Russia's most important, most dramatic and least understood periods.

Whether or not sixteenth-century Russia belonged culturally to Western Europe is still debated among historians. Until relatively recently misconceptions about the period were rife. Westerners and Russians alike were wont to picture Ivan as a representative of Russia's essential barbarism, a result of centuries of arbitrary Mongol domination not overcome until Peter the Great managed to turn dark, brutal, medieval Muscovy into dazzling, modern Russia. Some popularizing historians still do so, but recent evidence has shown a different reality. It appears that many vital issues in the West at the time were also vital issues in Russia during Ivan's half-century reign.[1] It is a useful exercise to attempt to see sixteenth-century Russia in the context of sixteenth-century Europe.

West Europeans were discovering the world and founding empires in the sixteenth century—empires which for better or for worse shaped our modern world. Under Ivan IV the Russians also founded an empire, the legacy of which long will be with us despite the recent collapse of its Soviet descendant.

The political history of sixteenth-century Europe is the history of efforts to secularize, centralize and professionalize. The same holds true for Russia. Ivan demanded reforms that would make his government more effective. Secularization meant bypassing the political authority of a backward-looking church. Centralization meant eradicating the vestiges of aristocratic autonomy and drastically rearranging old patterns of loyalty and service. Professionalization meant creating a new class of technocrats with the professional expertise to fulfill the new goals. That the class became a dynamic new aristocracy to challenge the old has been a basic social phenomenon of the modernizing world. That the Terrible Tsar was brutal in his impatience to effect these changes does not deny their relevance to the creation of the modern political world.

One of the most striking features of sixteenth-century Europe is the vastly increased tempo of economic life. The increase is evident in Russia too. There was brisk trade with the East and West, the tsar became Russia's biggest merchant, and a bustling artisan and trading quarter called Kitay quarter emerged outside the Kremlin walls, the precursor of the "German Quarter" in the next century. Cities grew enormously. Ivan's Moscow was one of the contemporary world's largest urban conglomerations. Muscovites evidenced an eagerness to apply new scientific discoveries as techniques to increase power and productivity. Historians agree that Ivan's desire to open wide the conduit to the West's economy and technology was one of the most compelling reasons leading him to undertake his exhaustive campaign to found a Russian port on the Baltic Sea.

In the West the full bloom of humanistic culture in the sixteenth century crucially shaped modern life. In this regard too the argument for Russia's being a part of the West under Tsar Ivan is strong. Written remains from the period are fewer than we have a right to expect, mainly because of invasion and widespread destruction both in the latter part of Ivan's reign and the turbulent period of civil unrest that followed. Nevertheless they show how in public life the richness of vernacular Russian rapidly was ousting the inflexible and inaccessible Church Slavonic. The tsar himself was an enthusiastic writer. Widely-read, delightfully catholic in tastes, flamboyant in style, stunningly sarcastic, he is a spectacle of the rebirth of secular man. On his initiative Russia's first printing press, the indispensable tool of European humanism, was set up near the Kremlin. With his encouragement the energetic master printer Fedorov undertook an ambitious program of publication. Another press was established in the village of Alexandrov in the "dark" days of the oprichnina. It is not outlandish to imagine that, given prolonged peace, the Russian literary language would have found its Shakespeare when English did, rather than two hundred years later; that Russian universities would have flourished when Czech or German or English ones did, rather than many generations later.

Architectural remains of the sixteenth century are also scarce but even more remarkable. Unlike the literary remains they are impervious to charges of forgery. Like the new brilliance of Renaissance architecture in the West, the Russian architectural creations of the sixteenth century astound the observer: the sheer imaginative exuberance of the Intercession (Vasily the Blessed) cathedral in Moscow's Red Square, built between 1555 and 1560 on Ivan's orders to commemorate the conquest and Christianization of the Kazan Tatars (see illustration, p. 28); the soaring grace of the other tent-roofed churches in Muscovy: the Ascension church in Kolomenskoe (see illustration, p. 89), the Transfiguration church at Ostrov, the Intercession church in Medvedkovo, the St. Sergius church in the Kremlin, no longer standing; the imaginative experiments adapting other traditional, pre-Christian features of wooden architecture of Northern Russia, such as the onion gable or the *kokoshnik*.[2] Sometimes these experiments succeeded, as in the perfectly proportioned Old Church in the Virgin-on-Don monastery; sometimes they did not, as in the striking but ponderous church of St. John the Baptist at Diakovo. All these structures nevertheless became symbols of Russian man's new-found belief in himself, his creativity, his artistry. Again, given a long period of peace, we have every reason to believe that this aspect of newly emerging Russian national culture would have blossomed and borne fruit so that, for example, Russian architecture in the eighteenth century would have presented the world with its own interpretation of neo-classical architecture instead of making the Western, artificial and totally un-Russian copy that was St. Petersburg.

Indeed the Western forms that overwhelmed Russian culture from the late seventeenth century onward, although often brilliant, were essentially artificial. It is hard to deny that Emperor Peter, with at least as much brutality as his predecessor Tsar Ivan, practically destroyed old Russian culture in his mania to adopt Western modes of thought and communication, cleaving the folk from the elite for centuries to come, perhaps forever. Centuries passed after Ivan before Russian intellectuals and artists once again tried to tap their real cultural roots; some would say they have yet to do so.

The extraordinary promise of sixteenth-century Russia was unfulfilled. Ironically, the explanation rests on much that was improbable, even accidental. Ivan's usually far-sighted statesmanship, for example, make it improbable that he should have overestimated, as he did, the resources of his fledgling state. Was it perhaps the accidental and inhuman physical suffering that, as we know from modern examination of his remains,[3] he underwent as he grew older and his spine gradually fused, which made him irrationally continue the Livonian war? In his rage he flew in the face of all reasoned argument to settle for an early armistice, to consolidate the real gains that his forces made early on in the war, and so lost all.

Certainly it was an accident that Ivan's only capable son and heir should have died before becoming tsar, thus depriving the autocratic state of its most essential link to the past and future. The unbroken chain of inheritance of the Muscovite throne, from Prince Daniel in the thirteenth century to Ivan IV in the sixteenth, was one factor that more than any other allowed Moscow to emerge as the "gatherer of the Russian lands" and the capital of the Russian nation. Even if Ivan IV actually did not kill his son and successor Ivan Ivanovich as popular myth would have it, it is still an historic accident of great consequence that the twenty-seven-year-old heir died in 1581. An Ivan V, secure as Muscovy's legitimate ruler after Ivan IV died in 1584, probably would have done much, conceivably everything, to restore the stability and security so desperately needed after the ruinous Livonian war. The men in the various ranks of the tsar's service probably would have worked together for the nation instead of being divided and against it. The forces of modernization probably once again would have gathered momentum. The accident shattered the promise. Civil war is the enemy of civilization. Russia slid back into conservative, medieval Muscovy.

But accident and irony are the pepper and salt of history. At any given point a particular society can follow many possible paths. Though each path is explicable, the choice is not predetermined. It is instructive to see how often the actual choice appears to depend on pure circumstance, on accidents of time and place in human existence. The fact remains that from the vantage point of the mid-sixteenth century the probable direction of Muscovy's development was a seventeenth-century Russia as "modern" as any Western country: highly centralized, managed by its rulers as a "well-ordered police state" for the welfare and prosperity of its citizens, professional, secular, culturally active.

Soloviev's history is a relatively straightforward narration of these crucial events of empire, government, religion, economy, society, knowledge and culture. Although the sense of importance and immediacy of these events is not always evident, Soloviev's account is generally reliable and his work of lasting encyclopedic value. Perhaps most important, he included many and long quotations from the original documents. It is this constant reference to and inclusion of sources that makes Soloviev historiographically significant and indeed still useful to the modern student of Russian history.

The present volume was written over a century ago, and historians have added much since then to our understanding of the period of Ivan the Terrible. George Vernadsky became the doyen of twentieth-century Russian historians, first within the famous Kondakov group of scholars in post-revolutionary Prague and later at Yale University from 1927 until his death in 1973. He argued that Russian history best can be understood as "Eurasian," that is, as a legacy of East as well as West, and made major contributions in English to the modern understanding of Ivan and his times with the fourth and fifth volumes of his multivolume and incomplete *History of Russia.*[4] The present-day reader is still recommended to these works, although a more recent and more general account of the history of the period has been written by Robert Crummey.[5] The best contemporary Russian historian to have added to our understanding of Ivan and his times is Ruslan G. Skrynnikov; his readable and highly recommended history of Ivan the Terrible, first published in 1975, has been translated into English.[6] One aspect of Ivan's reign, his correspondence with Andrei Kurbsky, the cultured Russian aristocrat and general who defected to Poland from Ivan's camp, is available in English, edited and translated by the late J.L.I. Fennell.[7] This fascinating and illuminating literary exchange, long accepted as a major source for Ivan's life and rule, was brought into question when Edward L. Keenan of Harvard University[8] argued that the entire correspondence was a seventeenth-century forgery. When the dust of the ensuing and major battle among historians of Russia finally settled (for some it has yet to settle), the authenticity of the correspondence emerged tattered but credible. Historian Charles Halperin has written a good guide to the controversy, a controversy almost as fascinating as the correspondence itself.[9] Ivan's extraordinary personality naturally attracted both approval and disgust over the centuries. The common folk appear to have made him a hero.[10] Two of Russia's greatest historians of the nineteenth century, Vasily Kliuchevsky and Sergei Platonov, both argued at length about the influence of Ivan's personality on the formation of the Russian state. Soviet Marxist historians had a particularly difficult time dealing with Ivan's personality.[11] Even post-Marxist historians have difficulty with the issue, inclined as they are to blame Ivan IV and his police actions for the Soviet dictatorship; a good example of this interesting if un-historical approach is the controversial work of the Russian émigré Alexander Yanov.[12]

Still, no definitive scholarly account of Ivan and his times exists. It may never appear, given both the scarcity of evidence and the passions aroused by Ivan, but at least we can say that Soloviev in these chapters of his great *History* began the process. With his passion for archival research, he was the first to set an examination of the period onto a scholarly, disinterested, "scientific" footing.

Soloviev referred to a number of unpublished archival sources in this section of his work. These included the Synodal Archival Collection, or Synodal Chronicles collected and held in Soloviev's time by the Archeographical Commission. Soloviev gave special thanks in his notes to one M.A. Korkunov of the Commission for helping him to use this archival collection, now located in the Manuscript Division of the State Historical Museum in Moscow. He consulted the Morozov and Alexander Nevsky Chronicles now located in the Manuscript Division of the Saltykov-Shchedrin Library in St. Petersburg, the St. Cyril of Beloozero Chronicle now held in the archive of the St. Petersburg branch of the Historical Institute of the Academy of Sciences, the *Life of Gennady of Kostroma* now held in the Manuscript Division of the Moscow Public Library, and various diplomatic documents held in Soloviev's time in the Archives of the Ministry of Foreign Affairs but now located in the Russian State Archive of Ancient Acts. The latter included the Nogay archival deposit and the Polish, Swedish and Danish deposits.

He also used many published primary materials in such works as Marcin Bielski,[13] Sigismund von Herberstein,[14] Alessandro Guagnini,[15] Christian Kelch,[16] the source commonly known as *The Tsar's Book,*[17] the *Ancient Russian Library,*[18] the Nikon Chronicle,[19] the source known through its compiler as the *Lvov Russian Chronicle,* [20] Hakluyt's travel accounts concerning Russia,[21] and various collections of state documents.[22]

Soloviev used Kurbsky's narrative in the form edited by N.G. Ustrialov.[23] He also was able to avail himself of the recently started compilation of Russian chronicle sources,[24] as well as collections of documents pertaining to Muscovy's western neighbors, Lithuania and Livonia.[25] Light is thrown on Ivan's proposed reforms of the 1550s by the Kozhanichkov edition of the resolutions of the Hundred Chapters Council.[26]

The published secondary works that Soloviev consulted included: M.M. Shcherbatov, *Russian History from Earliest Times* (7 vols., St. Petersburg, 1770-1791), A.I. Mankiev, *The Core of Russian History* (Moscow, 1784), G. Ewers and M. Engelhardt,*Contributions to the Understanding of Russia and its History* (Dorpat, 1816), N.M. Karamzin, *History of the Russian State* (12 vols., St. Petersburg, 1818-1829). E.G. Geijer, *History of Sweden* (Hamburg, 1834); J. Hammer, *History of the Ottoman Empire* (Pest, 1834), N.S. Artsybashev, *Narrative about Russia* (Moscow, 1838), Michal Balinski, *Historical Letters* (Warsaw, 1843), and the *Life of Prince Andrei Mikhailovich Kurbsky in Lithuania and Volhynia* (Kiev, 1849).

It is Soloviev's place in Russian historiography that makes it so important for his famous work to be known to an English-reading audience. That audience long has known the great creations of modern Russian fictional literature of the nineteenth century. Now it may know also one of that century's greatest creations of modern Russian historical literature.

The present volume of Soloviev's great work opens with the preparations for the final assault on the Tatar khanate of Kazan. Safa-Girey was the ruling khan. A member of the powerful Girey family from the Crimean khanate, he first became khan of Kazan in 1524 when he took over from his uncle Sahib-Girey, whose election as khan of Kazan in 1521 broke a period of relative peace and active economic relations between the states of Muscovy and Kazan. His "Crimean" rule—he was the brother of the Crimean khan—represented a more belligerent stance against the Russians as the Crimean Tatars responded to the urgings of the Turks to hold the northern Muslim line against infidel Christianity. According to some historians this period represents a new phase in the struggle between the Russians as represented by Muscovy and the Tatars as represented by the Crimean and Kazan khanates for mastery of the vast and strategic Eurasian steppe.[27]

Muscovy's relations with the Crimea were, in diplomatic terms, far more important than those with Kazan. The struggle between the Russians and the Crimean Tatars, which dragged on into the eighteenth century, until the incorporation of the Crimea into the empire in 1783, reflected the struggle between the Russian and Turkish imperial designs, which themselves continued into the nineteenth century. Nevertheless during the 1530s and 1540s relations with Kazan dominated the thinking of the Muscovites, partly because they were injected with the enmity of Crimean politics and partly because the Tatars of Kazan were more familiar and therefore less formidable to Muscovite Russians. Kazan was also much further from Turkey than the Crimea. In terms of the growth of the Russian empire, particularly its annexation and exploitation of the vast Siberian lands to the east, Muscovy's struggle with Kazan was a crucial stage in the history of Russian imperialism, even though it was centuries before Russians became conscious of the importance of that realm to their empire.

Because Vasily III's army could not force Kazan's surrender the grand prince was compelled to recognize Safa-Girey as Kazan's legitimate ruler and for the time being accept the special relationship between Kazan and the Crimea. In 1532 Vasily had a chance to increase his control over Kazan when Safa-Girey, following a turn in domestic Kazan politics, was expelled by the khanate's powerful ruling council and replaced by a pro-Muscovite khan, Yan Ali;[28] but Vasily III died in 1533, leaving a relatively unstable regency for his three-year-old successor Ivan IV.

The Crimean party re-established its control of Kazan politics. In 1535 Yan Ali was assassinated and Safa-Girey was invited back as khan of Kazan, much to the discomfiture of Ivan's mother, the regent Elena, and the boyars in Moscow. Yet by 1545 the adolescent and precocious Ivan began to assert his authority. He adopted a new offensive stance against

Kazan.[29] His actions stirred up the Kazan political beehive once again, and by the end of 1546 Safa-Girey again was expelled by the pro-Muscovite, anti-Crimean faction. Ivan was only too happy to re-install his puppet khan, Shah Ali, on the Kazan throne, but the restoration was short-lived. Shah Ali soon was expelled and Safa-Girey once again placed on the throne, taking appropriate action to punish and discourage the pro-Muscovite party.

In January 1547 Grand Prince Ivan officially became Tsar Ivan, assuming a title formerly reserved for the Tatar khan.[30] By this act Ivan publicly challenged the Tatars to mortal combat. He immediately went on the offensive. Safa-Girey's troops barely defended themselves against a Russian winter attack in 1547–1548; Safa-Girey himself lost a skirmish against Russian cavalry and was forced to flee into the Kazan citadel.

When word arrived in 1549 that Safa-Girey had died the Muscovites realized that the stalemate was broken and their chances in the struggle much improved. Scenting victory, whether by diplomatic intervention in Kazan politics or outright military conquest or both, Tsar Ivan concentrated all his attention and resources on the conquest.

SWEDEN

WHITE SEA

FINLAND

BALTIC
SEA

L.
Ladoga

L.
Onega

Pustazersk

Arkhangelsk
Kholmogory

Reval
Narva
Dorpat
LIVONIA
Riga
W. Dvina
Rusa
Opochka

Ivangorod
Oreshek

Kirilov Monastery
(Beloozero)

Ustiug

MUSCOVY

Pskov
Novgorod
Yazhelbitsy
Ustiuzhna
Vologda

Khlynov

Kostroma
Yaroslavl
Uglich
Volga

PRUSSIA
Kovna
Polotsk
Troki
Wilno
Grodno
Krevko
Drogichin
Minsk
Melnik
Novgorod Litovsk
Brest
Pinsk
Slutsk

Toropets
Torzhok

M U S C O V Y

Tver
Trinity
Monastery
Mohaisk
Viazma
Moscow
Smolensk
Kolomna
Mstislavl
Serpukhov
Kazimov
Oka R.
Riazan

Vladimir
Nizhni Novgorod
Vasilsursk
Murom
Kazan
Kama R.

Vitebsk

Turov
Vladimir-in-Volynia
Lutsk
LITHUANIA
Ostrog
Kiev
Kamenets
Vinnitsa
Khotin
Braslav
Cherkasy
Iasi
Ochakov
Belgorod

POLAND

Briansk
Starodub
Chernigov
Putivl
Belaia Tserkov
Kanev
Mishurin Rog

Mtsenk
Elets
Novgorod Severisk
Rylsk
Kursk
Glinsk

Dnieper R.
Don R.

TATARS

Donets R.

ASTRAKHAN
Astrakhan

Volga R.

Yaik R.

Prath R.
Bug R.
Dniester R.
Danube

CRIMEAN

SEA of AZOV
Bakhchisarai
Kaffa
Kerch
Taman
Temriuk
Azov

CIRCASSIANS

BLACK SEA

Constantinople

CASPIAN

SEA

Russia in the Sixteenth Century

History of Russia

Volume 10

The Reign of Ivan the Terrible

*Kazan, Astrakhan, Livonia,
the Oprichnina and the Polotsk Campaign*

I

KAZAN, ASTRAKHAN, AND CRIMEA

UNSUCCESSFUL CAMPAIGN AGAINST KAZAN

The death in 1549 of Safa-Girey, the ruling khan of Kazan,[1] disorganized his Crimean party and aggravated domestic disorders. The situation was ideal for the designs of the nineteen-year-old tsar of Muscovy. The Tatars hastily proclaimed as khan the two-year-old Utemish, son of Safa-Girey, but the fact remained that the very relationship between Kazan and Muscovy was altered. While Ivan was in his minority the Kazan Tatars could maintain their independence. Now that Ivan was of age, however, he manifested his intention to pursue an active policy towards Kazan. It was not an opportune moment to have an infant khan on the throne. The embarrassed Tatar leaders sent envoys to the Crimean khanate requesting aid, but cossacks loyal to Muscovy intercepted and killed the emissaries and forwarded their credentials to Moscow.

In July 1549 the Kazan Tatars sent Ivan a written request for peace in the name of Khan Utemish-Girey. The tsar replied that the Tatars would have to send plenipotentiaries to negotiate. None arrived, so on November 24 Ivan and his brother Prince Yury[2] set out for Kazan, entrusting the protection of Moscow in his absence to his cousin Prince Vladimir Andreevich.[3] When Ivan reached the city of Vladimir he officially launched the campaign.

It is worth noting that among other things the tsar considered it necessary to summon Metropolitan Makary.[4] The church leader obeyed the summons, journeying to Vladimir, where he urged the Russian commanders to put aside considerations of precedence[5] for the duration of the campaign and to settle accounts after the war was over.

The tsar reached Kazan in February 1550. An attack on the city was unsuccessful. Large numbers were killed on both sides, and the battle immediately was followed by an early thaw. Strong winds blew, rains poured down, streams turned to torrents, rivers flooded their banks. Ivan remained at Kazan for eleven days but finally was forced to turn back. It was the second campaign against Kazan that he personally undertook, both ending unsuccessfully. This time Ivan was determined not to return empty-handed.

FOUNDING OF SVIIAZHSK FORTRESS

Ivan's father[6] founded the fortress of Vasilsursk [in 1523].[7] Following his example, Ivan now laid the foundation for a fortress at the point where the Sviiaga emptied into the Volga and called it Sviiazhsk. Crown Secretary Ivan Vyrodkov[8] set off to the Uglich district with some junior boyars,[9] to the estates of the Ushaty princes, to cut timbers for the churches and town walls of Sviiazhsk and transport them on barges down the Volga. In the spring another commander, the boyar Khan Shah Ali,[10] set out with more barges to secure provisions for the town. He went with two of the chief commanders, the boyar Yury Bulgakov of the Golitsyn-Patrikeev family[11] and the boyar Daniel Romanovich of the Zakharin-Yuriev family, brother of the tsaritsa.[12] They were accompanied by some of the five hundred Kazan Tatar refugees currently residing in Moscow.

Prince Peter Obolensky-Serebriany[13] was ordered to conduct a raid from Nizhny Novgorod against Kazan's trading quarter. Cossacks were stationed at every crossing of the Kama, Volga and Viatka rivers so that Tatar warriors might not enter or leave Kazan. Serebriany carried out his orders to the letter. He appeared suddenly in Kazan's trading quarter, killed many people, took some captives and freed a number of Russian captives.

On May 24, 1550, Shah Ali arrived at the Sviiaga with the other commanders. They immediately went to work to make a clearing in the forest where the new town was to be. When a hill site was cleared, they first held a service and sprinkled holy water on the spot and carried crosses around the site of the fortified wall. Then they proceeded to enclose the town and laid the foundation for the church, which was to commemorate both the Nativity of the Virgin and St. Sergius the Miracle Worker.[14] The timbers brought down the Volga sufficed to fortify only half the hill. The commanders and junior boyars with their men rapidly completed the other half, so that everything was finished in four weeks.

NATIVE TRIBES SUBDUED

The construction of Sviiazhsk had immediate results.[15] The highland Cheremiss tribes, seeing a new Russian town in their territory, approached Shah Ali and the Russian leaders with a petition that the tsar reward them, forgive them, allow them to live near Sviiazhsk and not wage war on them. If it pleased the tsar, would he also lighten their tribute[16] and grant them a charter by which they might henceforth abide?

The tsar granted their request, issued them a charter with a gold seal, and suspended their tribute for three years. To Shah Ali and the Russian commanders Ivan sent a sack of gold coins to distribute as rewards, and an order that they administer the oath of allegiance to the entire highland native population. They also were ordered to send into action against the Kazan Tatars the Cheremiss, accompanied by junior boyars and pro-Muscovite Kazan princes who were to observe whether the natives served the tsar faithfully.

The Russian leaders delivered the oath of allegiance to the Cheremiss, Chuvash and Mordvinian natives, saying, "You have given your oath to the tsar. Go, therefore, show your faithfulness to the tsar by doing battle against his enemies." They gathered in large groups and were sent across the Volga to the plains side. When they arrived at the Field of Arsk outside the city the Kazan and Crimean Tatars rushed out to meet them and fighting began in earnest. When the Tatars brought out cannon and handguns and began firing, the Cheremiss and Chuvash fell back and fled. The Tatars killed about a hundred and captured some fifty more. The Russian commanders concluded that the highlanders served faithfully, and allowed them to return to their side of the river.

Over the course of the summer some five or six hundred of these tried-and-true highlanders journeyed to Moscow, where the tsar rewarded them. He feasted their princes, chieftains and cavalry leaders at his own table and presented them with gifts of armor and horses, furs and money.

KAZAN SUBDUED

The construction of Sviiazhsk and defection of the highland tribes produced a quick reaction within Kazan. It strengthened the anti-Crimean faction. The chronicles tell us that the Kazan Tatars began to quarrel with the Crimean Tatars. Some Chuvash from Arsk even came armed to fight the Crimeans. "Why do you not surrender to the tsar?" they shouted. They got as far as the khan's palace but eventually were defeated by the Crimean Tatar leader Ulan Kashchak and his supporters.

Their success nevertheless did not greatly improve the fortunes of the Girey. One after another the Kazan princes and nobles deserted to the Russians. So the Crimeans, mindful of how Kazan betrayed them during the Muscovites' first attack, gathered together and went on a rampage, plundering everything within reach. About three hundred left Kazan, leaving their women and children behind. They fled up the Kama river as far as Viatka but there they were routed by the commander of Viatka, named Ziuzin, and many were drowned. He dispatched forty-six captives, including Ulan Kashchak, to Moscow where, according to the chronicler, they were executed for their cruelty.

The flight of the Crimeans delivered Kazan to the pro-Russian party. Emissaries from Kazan arrived in Moscow to petition the tsar not to place them in captivity but to grant them Shah Ali as their ruling khan. As for the present khan, Utemish-Girey, the tsar might take him away along with his mother Siuiunbek. Ivan replied that he would so favor the land of Kazan if they would hand over the khan, his mother, and the remaining Crimeans with their children, and incidentally set free all Russian captives.

Alexis Adashev[17] set out for Sviiazhsk to advise Shah Ali that the tsar granted him the khanate of Kazan. His rule would include the plains side and the Arsk region but exclude the highland side, which would remain under the governance of Sviiazhsk, since the tsar conquered it before granting the Kazan Tatars their petition. These conditions deeply upset Shah Ali, but the boyars told him frankly that the decision could not be altered. They said the same to the Kazan dignitaries when they also protested against breaking up their traditional territory.

SHAH ALI AS KHAN OF KAZAN

In August Shah Ali was installed in Kazan. True to the conditions imposed upon him, he set about freeing all Russian slaves, numbering altogether about sixty thousand.[18] At first the domination and violence of the Crimeans gave strength to the pro-Russian faction. Now the burdensome conditions imposed by the Russian tsar provoked greater dissatisfaction and strengthened the opposite faction. Khan Shah Ali and his Kazan dignitaries considered the removal of the highland bank intolerable. Kazan suffered real privation from the freeing of the Russian slaves. Indeed the boyar Ivan Khabarov[19] and Crown Secretary Vyrodkov, who remained with the new khan, sent word to the tsar in September that not all the slaves were freed, and that Shah Ali, although aware of the fact, closed his eyes to it for fear of an uprising.

Moscow nevertheless could not retract its stipulated conditions or bear the idea of Russians languishing in captivity under a subject government, or that the Russian town of Sviiazhsk might become an island in foreign territory. Moderation and benevolence, it was hoped, would gradually make Shah Ali and the Kazan Tatars forget their privations.

The boyar Prince Dmitry Paletsky[20] and a crown secretary named Ivan Klobukov were sent to Kazan with presents. They took clothing, plate and money for the khan, his wife, and for the princes of Kazan and Gorodets. For the khan and the members of his government they took service commendations. In return for all this they were instructed to demand the emancipation of all slaves, declaring that the tsar would not tolerate the thought of Christians in bondage. They were to remind Shah Ali of the oath of allegiance he swore to the tsar and to his father Grand Prince Vasily III, and to hold him to his contract. He must free all Russian captives and bind Kazan as tightly to the tsar and to himself as Kasimov,[21] so that during his rule and afterwards things remain unalterable and blood forever cease to flow.

Paletsky delivered these instructions to Kazan. Subsequently a large legation came to Moscow from Kazan with a petition from Shah Ali, begging the tsar to cede the highland side. If he did not wish to cede the entire area, let him at least turn over to Kazan some of the tribute from the area. They further petitioned the tsar graciously to promise the khan and the whole Kazan land that he would keep the peace. Ivan gave answer that not a penny[22] from the highland area would he turn over to Kazan. As for making promises, he would do that as soon as they set free every last slave in Kazan.

Khabarov and Vyrodkov returned from Kazan to report that the Tatars, rather than freeing their Russian slaves, were chaining them up and hiding them in underground caves. Furthermore, Shah Ali was not punishing those found keeping slaves, justifying his actions by saying he feared a disturbance. In other matters, he was informed that certain Tatar princes were holding conclave with the Nogay.[23] He wished to let the tsar know that he was investigating the situation.

TATARS' HATRED OF SHAH ALI

In November Shah Ali learned that the Tatar princes indeed communicated with the Nogay and were plotting to kill him and Prince Paletsky. The khan unearthed the pact, intercepted some documents, and slaughtered seventy of the conspirators as they were feasting. The rest scattered. He sent word to the tsar not to let the large Kazan legation leave Moscow since they were party to the conspiracy.

This piece of news compelled the tsar to consider adopting a different method of dealing with Kazan. He sent Adashev to Shah Ali with the following message. "Shah Ali sees for himself the treachery of the men of Kazan. From the beginning they have lied to the Muscovite tsars. They killed Shah Ali's brother Yan Ali. Several times they drove Shah Ali away. Now they wish to kill him. *He must immediately fortify the city with Russian soldiers.*"

When he received this message, Shah Ali replied, "I cannot remain in Kazan any longer. I have enraged the inhabitants. I promised them to solicit the tsar and grand prince for the return of the highland side. If the tsar were to grant me the highland side I could remain in Kazan, and so long as I lived Kazan would remain bound to the tsar. If the highland side is not to be mine, I must flee back to the tsar."

"If you are going to flee to the tsar anyway," Paletsky and Adashev responded, "surely you can garrison the city with Russian soldiers." Shah Ali disagreed. "I am a Muslim," he said, "and I do not wish to act against my own faith, but neither do I wish to betray the tsar, for I have nowhere to go except to him. Prince Dmitry, give me your solemn word that the grand prince will not let me perish here. Let him assign me to Kasimov, which would be more useful. I have come to know the evil people here, and I abandon them to cannon, musket and powder. Let the tsar come here himself to carry on his own business."

Paletsky and Adashev set out for Moscow. They left a detachment of musketeers to protect Shah Ali and ordered its commander Ivan Cheremisinov to keep the tsar informed. When Paletsky arrived at the Sviiaga, Chapkun and Burnash, two Kazan Tatar princes who lived there, told him about some rumors circulating among the people. In the spring, apparently, the people of Kazan were going to revolt against the tsar, for they disliked Shah Ali. Thus the tsar should press his plans as rigorously as possible. "We," said the princes, "have given our pledge to the tsar, and according to that pledge we must inform him now that when the Tatars revolt, as surely they must, we will not be able to control these highlanders."

So things went in the year 1551. Matters were coming rapidly to a head. Kazan could not be left for long in such a position. Hatred for Shah Ali reached new heights after his bloody banquet. To attempt to sustain a hated khan any longer by force was inadvisable. To advance large forces to Kazan without waiting for the first move by the inhabitants would mean hastening a bloody catastrophe and exposing to very real danger the lives of Shah Ali and his Russian musketeer bodyguards, giving the men of Kazan a perfect pretext to rebel. To attempt to capture the city suddenly,

without warning the khan, was impossible. Anyway, the khan did not wish
to betray Islam. It was the Kazan Tatars themselves who offered the Muscovite tsar a compromise.

REQUESTS TO REPLACE SHAH ALI

As we have seen, some of Shah Ali's chief enemies were those very
dignitaries sent to Moscow. Only the fact that they were part of a legation
saved them from the fate that befell their comrades at the khan's banquet.
Furthermore not all of Shah Ali's enemies in Kazan perished. Malevolents
yet remained, and Shah Ali had promised to destroy them. It is no wonder
that such men, fearing daily for their lives, would want to replace Shah Ali
some way or another. In order to do so they established contact with the
emissaries detained in Moscow and acted through them. The Tatars'
hatred for Shah Ali, coupled with their inability to get rid of him, as well
as the impracticability of waging a war against Muscovy, led them to a new
proposal. They would accept complete subjugation to Ivan if he removed
Shah Ali.

Thus in January 1552 these emissaries appeared before Ivan, announcing they had received instructions from the Kazan land to petition the tsar
to remove Shah Ali. They begged him to give them one of his boyars as
viceroy, to rule them as in Sviiazhsk. If the tsar did not grant their wishes
the people of Kazan would switch their loyalties and find themselves a
ruler from some other land.

The tsar ordered one of his boyars, Prince Ivan Vasilievich Sheremetev,[24]
to confer with them and find out why the people of Kazan disliked their
khan. Sheremetev also was to determine how the khan might be removed,
what sort of viceroy they wanted, and how they were to be trusted. The
emissaries told him that Shah Ali killed and robbed them and forcibly
seized their wives and daughters. If the tsar granted the wishes of the Kazan
land and removed the khan, as a token he should allow one of the three
hundred Tatar princes, noblemen and cavalrymen now in Moscow to
return to Kazan. All of Kazan would swear allegiance to the tsar, admit his
viceroys and turn over the entire city. They would live in the city or the
trading quarter, wherever he ordered them to, and the same would apply
to the inhabitants of all the villages. The khan's revenues would be collected for the tsar, the tsar could distribute as he saw fit the possessions of
the childless princes who were killed, and all the people would be at his
mercy to do with as he wished. If Kazan did not comply, the tsar might put

all the Tatars in Moscow to death. If Shah Ali was reluctant to leave Kazan, the tsar merely had to remove his musketeers and he would certainly flee on his own.

IVAN AGREES TO REPLACE SHAH ALI

In February, Adashev again was sent to Kazan to remove Shah Ali. He took with him one of the Tatar emissaries and a charter for the people of Kazan in which the agreement concluded with the tsar in Moscow was spelled out. Adashev told Shah Ali to admit Muscovite soldiers into the city. He could request whatever he needed from the tsar and would receive it all. Shah Ali answered as before that he would not destroy a Muslim city. He could not remain in Kazan, so he would leave for Sviiazhsk. The Tatars requested another khan from the Nogay.

Shah Ali shipped several cannon and sent muskets and powder on to Sviiazhsk. He left Kazan on March 6 as if he were going on a fishing trip to the lake.[25] He took with him all five hundred Muscovite musketeers and many Tatar princes, nobles and townsmen. Once outside the city he said to the Tatars accompanying him, "You wanted to kill me, and you petitioned against me to the tsar and grand prince to have me removed, saying that I did vile things to you. You asked to be given a viceroy. The tsar and grand prince has ordered me to leave Kazan, so I go to him now. I am taking you with me, and we shall sort things out there."

Shah Ali arrived at Sviiazhsk with eighty-four of these princes and nobles. The same day the boyar Prince Simeon Ivanovich Mikulinksy[26] sent two cossacks to Kazan with documents proclaiming that, in accordance with the petition of the Kazan princes, the sovereign tsar was removing Shah Ali and assigning him, Prince Mikulinksy, to be their viceroy. They were to come to Sviiazhsk to take an oath of allegiance. Once they did so, Mikulinsky would come to them. The Tatars replied that they were grateful for the tsar's favor and were willing to fulfill the tsar's requests entirely, if only Prince Mikulinsky would send them the Tatar princes Chapkun and Burnash, whom they would welcome. The following day Chapkun and Burnash were sent to Kazan with Cheremisinov, who sent back word to Mikulinsky that the entire Kazan countryside was eager to swear allegiance to the tsar and that the most important inhabitants were leaving for Sviiazhsk.

These dignitaries indeed arrived on the following day, along with Chapkun and Burnash, and took their oaths. They in turn received assurances from Mikulinsky and his comrades that all trustworthy men of

Kazan would receive rewards. Thereafter Mikulinsky sent Cheremisinov with an interpreter to Kazan to administer the oath to the rest of the inhabitants and to see if any devilment remained, for which purposes he sent along Chapkun, another Kazan Tatar prince and eight junior boyars. They were to occupy the houses the princes promised to vacate, and to see that all remained quiet when the Russian regiments entered the city. During the night Cheremisinov sent word to Mikulinsky that all was peaceful. He and his men took over the courtyard of the khan's palace. The villagers, after taking their oaths, returned to their villages. Cheremisinov requested light transports with provisions and a cossack squadron, as he felt they would prove useful for whatever might take place in the palace courtyard.

As requested, the viceroy sent off a train of seventy cossacks with seventy-two muskets. The boyars Mikulinsky, Sheremetev and Obolensky-Serebriany also hastened to Kazan. Prince Ivan Vasilievich Romodanovsky[27] led the rearguard regiment and with him went all those Tatars whom Shah Ali brought out of Kazan. On the way they met various princes who begged the boyars to be allowed to enter the city, for which favor they would all become the tsar's servants and be completely at his mercy. When they reached Kazan, the junior boyars came out of the city to the commanders and told them that everyone was pleased with the tsar's favor and that Cheremisinov was continuing to administer oaths.

BOYARS REFUSED ENTRY

Everything went perfectly until the commanders gave leave to two Tatar princes, Islam and Kebiak, and a Tatar nobleman named Alikey to enter Kazan. Once inside Kazan these three closed the city gates and announced to the citizens that the Russians surely would destroy them all, as Tatars in the town were saying and as even Shah Ali himself said. When the boyars approached Kazan, Cheremisinov and Prince Kulaley met them at the Bulak river declaring, "Up to now we have seen no mischief, but now that those princes you brought are here, they have been spreading evil rumors and the people are confused. All the princes have left the city with us except for Chapkun, who alone remains." The boyars went around to the Royal gate. The doors were open, and people were running about on battlements. Just then Ulan Kudaikul, Prince Liman and some other Tatar princes came up to the Russian leaders, begging them not to be upset that troublemakers were stirring up the populace; if they would be patient, things soon would quieten.

The boyars sent the Tatar princes Kudaikul and Burnash into the city to deliver the following message to the inhabitants. "Why are you breaking your promises? Just yesterday, and even today, you pledged your allegiance, and now suddenly you break your pledges! We give you our solemn word that we shall do you no harm." Indeed the Russian soldiers caused no harm whatever to the commercial folk in their quarter, leaving them in their houses undisturbed with all their belongings. "The people fear beatings and will not listen to us," was the reply the emissaries brought back. Many were the arguments and speeches, but all in vain. The boyars, seeing they were getting nowhere, gave orders to seize Kudaikul and Liman as well as all the princes and horsemen whom Shah Ali brought out. The Kazan inhabitants then seized the junior boyars who had been sent ahead with the commanders' transports.

After remaining outside Kazan for a day and a half, the commanders returned to Sviiazhsk. They left orders not to disturb Kazan's trading quarter so as not to break their side of the bargain, but the men of Kazan, after requesting a new khan from the Nogay, immediately opened hostilities. They crossed over to the highland side to turn its inhabitants away from Muscovy. The highlanders destroyed the detachment and captured two princes. They delivered them to the Russian commanders, who ordered the prisoners executed.

GREAT CAMPAIGN OF 1552

Ivan received the news on March 24 and immediately dispatched his brother-in-law Prince Daniel Romanovich to the aid of his commanders in Sviiazhsk. He ordered Khan Shah Ali to his khanate of Kasimov. In April he summoned a council to consider taking conclusive action against Kazan.

Several different opinions were voiced in the council. It was suggested that the tsar send commanders to Kazan but remain personally in Moscow, for the fighting would be against not only the Kazan Tatars but also the Nogay and the Crimeans, but experience showed how inconclusive were previous campaigns against Kazan. Ivan announced his determination to set out on campaign immediately. It was decided to send ahead a large reserve force by boat with supplies for the tsar and the whole army. The tsar himself, when the time came, would travel by land.

The same month some bad news arrived from Sviiazhsk. Mikulinsky wrote that the highlanders were agitated; many were plotting with the Kazan Tatars and there was little law and much disobedience everywhere.

Worst of all, scurvy broke out in the Russian army. Many junior boyars, musketeers and cossacks died. Others lay sick. At this news, the tsar ordered Prince Alexander Gorbaty[28] and Prince Peter Shuisky[29] to move on to Sviiazhsk without delay.

The princes soon reached the town but the news they sent back to Moscow was even more disconcerting. All the highland tribes deserted back to Kazan. They were now marching on Sviiazhsk and raiding the commanders' livestock. The commanders sent cossacks to face them but the Tatars routed the cossacks, killing seventy and taking their guns. Meanwhile the disease did not slacken but continued to strike down many. Prince Mikhail Glinsky sent cossacks from the Kama river in boats to forage along the Sviiaga, but all were slaughtered by Tatars, who showed their captives no mercy. They also slaughtered all the junior boyars who went on ahead to Kazan with the commanders' transport and were seized by the inhabitants. Finally Kazan accepted a khan from the Nogay, an Astrakhan crown prince named Ediger Mahmed.

Moscow refused to give up. It was decided to use religious means to raise the spirits of the army in Sviiazhsk, the more so because falling morale combined with physical sickness to cause serious deterioration.[30] Relics of the holy fathers were carried from the Annunciation to the Dormition cathedral. They were used to bless some holy water, which was then sent to Sviiazhsk with Timothy, archpriest of the Archangel cathedral, "a handsome man, learned in the holy scriptures." Together with the holy water, Timothy took along a testament from Metropolitan Makary for the army.

Just then Shah Ali arrived from Kasimov and tried to tell Ivan not to begin the campaign until wintertime, for they could certainly expect invasion by other enemies during the summer. Furthermore the land of Kazan was well fortified by nature, being surrounded by forests, lakes and swamps, and was easier to attack in winter. Ivan replied that he already had sent off the commanders and a great many soldiers on boats, together with heavy artillery and all the supplies. Besides, though the forests and waters of Kazan were indeed great fortresses, the Lord made impassable places passable and crooked paths straight.

Ivan entrusted Tsaritsa Anastasia with all matters of charity, such as pardoning those disgraced by the tsar and freeing prisoners from the dungeons. On June 16 he set out for Kolomna. He dined in the village of Kolomenskoe, whence he aimed to reach Ostrov for the night.

CRIMEAN KHAN INVADES

On the way he was overtaken by a courier, a village cossack from Putivl, with news that a large number of Crimeans were invading the borders. The cossack did not know if the khan himself or one of his sons was leading the invading force, but it was across the North Donets river.

The tsar was greatly disturbed but continued his journey to Kolomna, arriving on June 19. Another courier arrived with news that many Crimeans were indeed on the move and were approaching Riazan and Kolomna. The tsar ordered his regiments to the riverbank. The main regiment he stationed by Kolychevo, the vanguard by Rostislavl, and the left wing by the Golutvin monastery.[31] It was announced that if the Crimean khan arrived the tsar intended to challenge him directly.

On June 21 a courier rode in from Tula. The Crimeans reached Tula, but evidently in small number and led by one of the khan's sons. The tsar dispatched Princes Peter Mikhailovich Shcheniatiev,[32] Andrei Mikhailovich Kurbsky,[33] Ivan Ivanovich Pronsky,[34] Dmitry Ivanovich Khilkov[35] and Mikhail Vorotynsky[36] to Tula. The following morning he was preparing to follow when he received news that only about seven thousand Crimean Tatars had reached Tula and had turned back after attacking the suburbs. Ivan decided to remain where he was and let his commanders proceed without him; but on the twenty-third, just as he was sitting down to dinner, another courier arrived from Tula with news that the khan himself had arrived and was approaching the city. He had heavy artillery and Turkish janissaries. Ivan, who never missed a service, ordered vespers to be read promptly. He then ordered all his generals to cross the Oka as quickly as possible. He himself hurried to Kashira where the crossing was to be carried out.

A new courier galloped up. The khan was no longer at Tula. On June 22 the Crimeans had reached Tula and attacked the city all day, bombarding it with flaming cannon balls. When a number of dwellings caught fire the khan ordered the janissaries to attack, but the Russian commander in Tula, Prince Grigory Temkin,[37] repulsed the assault with the small force at his command. The next morning the khan had ordered preparations for a renewed attack when word arrived that the Russian tsar was approaching the city. The people of Tula, spying dust clouds in the distance from atop the city walls, shouted out, "Merciful God has come to our aid! The Orthodox tsar is coming!" and threw themselves at the Tatars. It was not just the soldiers and men who charged out of the city, but the women and children too. Many Tatars were killed in this sortie, among them the khan's brother-in-law.

Three hours later, continued the courier, Ivan's commanders arrived at the town. The khan fled to the steppes. The Russians gave chase, caught up to the Crimeans at the Shivorona river,[38] and there overcame them. They freed many Russian prisoners and captured the khan's wagons and camels. Tatar captives told the full story. The khan had attacked Muscovy after word came to the Crimea that the Russian tsar was at Kazan with all his men, but at Riazan they had captured village cossacks who told them the tsar was at Kolomna awaiting the khan in order to challenge him face to face. The khan then had wanted to return to the Crimea but his princes said to him, "If you wish to save face, the Russian tsar has a city on the plain named Tula, which lies far from Kolomna, separated from it by a mighty fortress, the forests." The khan had listened to their advice and had gone to Tula.

ON TO KAZAN

Ivan, hearing of this turn of events, returned to Kolomna. His commanders joined him there from Tula on July 1 to report that, according to some village cossacks, the khan was retreating headlong, covering sixty or seventy versts a day at the expense of many horses. The tsar was relieved to have averted the Crimean menace.

He summoned his cousin Prince Vladimir, the boyars and all the commanders to plan their route to Kazan. They decided to travel by two separate routes. The tsar himself would go through Vladimir and Murom. The commanders would travel through Riazan and Meshchera so as to shield the tsar from unexpected Nogay attack. They would meet on the plain beyond Alatyr,[39] but when the time came for the expedition to begin, some junior boyars from Novgorod begged the tsar to release them from further service in the campaign. They had been in service in Kolomna since springtime. Some had gone after the Crimean Tatars and participated in those battles. To endure a yet longer journey and remain away for such a length of time was too much! The request distressed Ivan, for to grant it would disable his undertaking before it really began. He finally devised an effective solution. He ordered a re-enlistment of all serving men, announcing that all who decided to continue with their tsar would be rewarded and would feast with him at Kazan. Any who refused might stay at Kolomna. Hearing the proclamation, everyone answered as with one voice, "We are ready to go with the tsar! He is our provider whether here or there. As God counsels him, so he will direct us."

On July 3 Ivan left Kolomna with his cousin Prince Vladimir. In the city of Vladimir he received the welcome news from Sviiazhsk that the outbreak of scurvy was subsiding. In Murom he received more heartening news. Princes Mikulinsky and Daniel Romanovich did battle with the highlanders and overpowered them. As a result the highland tribes the length of the Sviiaga and along the Volga renewed their allegiance to the tsar.

On July 20 the tsar departed Murom. His army marched through dense forest and over open ground. Everywhere they found abundant food, every variety of edible plants and elk that practically came up to be slaughtered, according to the chronicler. There was plenty of fish in the rivers, an abundance of fowl in the forests. The Cheremiss and Mordvinians, frightened by the march of such a sizeable army, sought the tsar and threw themselves on his mercy. They brought bread, honey and meat, which they either sold or gave away, and helped construct bridges over the rivers.

At the Sura river messengers from the commanders and from the highlanders at Sviiazhsk met the tsar. They announced that Princes Peter Ivanovich Shuisky and Daniel Romanovich had subdued the remaining highland tribes. Now all highlanders promised allegiance and were inscribed in the township of Sviiazhsk. Ivan invited the envoys from the highlanders to dine with him. He announced that he forgave their people's perfidy, and commanded them to build bridges across the rivers and clear the narrow passages along the road.

Beyond the Sura the tsar joined forces with the commanders marching from Riazan and Meshchera. On August 13 they reached Sviiazhsk, which looked like home to them after such a long and difficult journey. They had their fill of game, fish and Cheremiss bread, and they looked forward to the supplies from home being brought by boat. Besides, a crowd of merchants gathered with various goods so that practically anything was obtainable.

Ivan set up his tents in the meadow by the town. He held a conference with Prince Vladimir, Shah Ali, the boyars and his commanders as to how he should carry on from there. It was decided to proceed directly to Kazan and to send a message to its inhabitants indicating that, if they agreed to become his subjects peacefully, the tsar would welcome them. Shah Ali was to write to his relative Ediger Mahmed, the new khan of Kazan, to request him to leave the city and come to visit the tsar. He need not be afraid, for the tsar would welcome him. Ivan himself sent letters to the

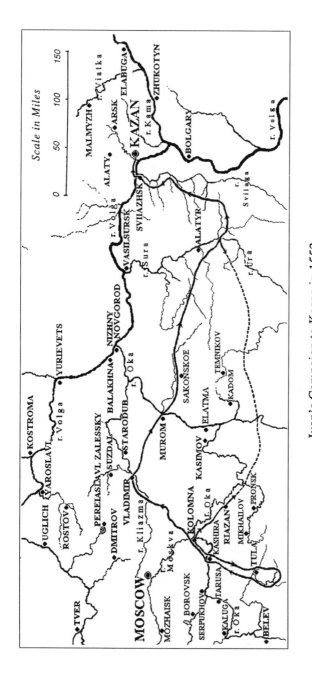

Ivan's Campaign to Kazan in 1552

Source: V. Trofimov, *Pokhod pod Kazan* (Campaign at Kazan) Kazan, 1890.

chief mullah and to the whole Kazan land saying that if they would bow down to him he would forgive them.

On August 16 the armies began to ferry over the Volga [from Sviiazhsk] to take up position on the Kazan side. On the eighteenth the tsar himself crossed the Volga. On the twentieth he crossed the Kazanka[40] and there received Ediger Mahmed's answer—a curse against Christianity, against Ivan, against Shah Ali, and a challenge to the battlefield. Ivan gave orders to unload the cannon from the boats and to prepare everything for the march on the city. Just then Kamay, a Kazan nobleman, came over to the tsar's side with seven horsemen. He recounted how some two hundred men wanted to join the tsar's service but that when the Tatar leaders learned about it they slaughtered nearly all of them. As for Kazan, he told how Khan Ediger Mahmed and his dignitaries refused to submit to the tsar and were leading the whole place into trouble. The city had large stores of provisions. A separate Tatar force under the leadership of Prince Yapancha was gathered well away from the city in the stronghold at Arsk so as not to allow the Russians onto the Arsk plain.

The tsar convened his council. He related Kamay's information and they discussed how to advance upon the city. It was decided that the tsar and Prince Vladimir would take a stand at the Khan's meadow, with Shah Ali across the Bulak river. The main regiment, the vanguard, and Prince Vladimir's own retinue[41] was positioned on the Arsk plain. The right wing with the cossacks was situated across the Kazanka. The rearguard regiment was at the mouth of the Bulak with the left wing upstream. Orders were issued to prepare protective gabions [huge earth-filled wicker baskets set on rollers] for the entire army, one for every ten men. Each was ordered to prepare one log for a stockade. Strictest orders were given that no one move to attack the city without the express command of the tsar or his commanders.

By August 23 the regiments took up their assigned positions. Ivan walked out into the field facing the city and ordered his banner unfurled. On the banner was a copy of the icon "not made by human hands,"[42] and above it the cross which Grand Prince Dmitry Donskoy had at the Don.[43] Offering a prayer, the tsar summoned Prince Vladimir, his boyars, his commanders and the warriors of his own regiment. "The time has come," he said, "for our great deed! With one accord you must be prepared to sacrifice yourselves for piety, for the holy churches, for the Orthodox Christian faith, for the fraternal kinship of our ruling house, and for those Orthodox Christians who have endured a long captivity, suffering at the

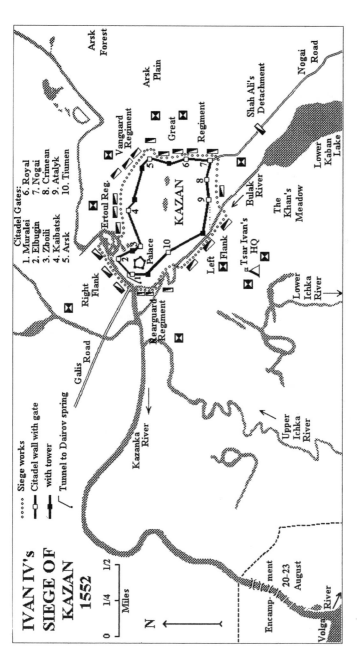

IVAN IV's SIEGE OF KAZAN 1552

Miles
0   1/4   1/2

N

Siege works
Citadel wall with gate
with tower
Tunnel to Dairov spring

Citadel Gates:
1. Muralei   6. Royal
2. Elbugin   7. Nogai
3. Zboli   8. Crimean
4. Kaibatsk   9. Atalyk
5. Arsk   10. Tiumen

Arsk Forest

Arsk Plain

Vanguard Regiment

Great

Regiment

Shah Ali's Detachment

Nogai Road

Lower Kaban Lake

Ertoul Reg.

KAZAN

Palace

Bulak River

The Khan's Meadow

Left

Flank

Tsar Ivan's HQ

Right Flank

Rearguard Regiment

Galis Road

Lower Ichka River

Kazanka River

Upper Ichka River

Encamp- ment 20-23 August

Volga River

Source: V. Trofimov, *Pokhod pod Kazan* (Campaign at Kazan) Kazan, 1890

hands of these heathen of Kazan. Let us remember the words of Christ, that there is nothing greater than to lay down your own life for your friend. Let us bow down with pure hearts to Christ our Creator. Let us beg Him for the deliverance of poor Christians—may He keep us from falling into the hands of our enemies. Be not sparing of your lives, for you are carrying out a sacred task. If we die, it will not mean death but new life. We shall all die sooner or later, but if we are not prepared to die now, how will we ever banish these heathen? I myself have accompanied you here. Better that I die here than live to see Christ execrate me for my sins, allowing Christians entrusted to my keeping to be tortured by the heathen of Kazan! If our merciful God shows us His mercy and grants us His succor, gladly shall I bestow great rewards on you all. Whosoever happens to suffer death, let him know now that I shall be glad to watch over the welfare of his wife and children all their days."

"We see thee, O tsar, firm in the true faith," Prince Vladimir answered, "unsparing of yourself for the sake of Orthodoxy, a living affirmation of our belief. Therefore must we all with one accord be willing to die in facing these godless sons of Hagar.[44] Lead on, O tsar, to the business at hand! May the blessing of Christ be upon you, may He grant your supplication and turn back our enemies!" Then Ivan, looking up at the icon of Christ, said in a loud voice for all to hear, "Savior! Onward in Thy name!"

KAZAN UNDER SIEGE

One hundred fifty thousand soldiers with one hundred fifty cannon lay siege to Kazan. It was defended only by earth-filled wooden walls, but crouching behind those walls were thirty thousand hostile soldiers. Skirmishes between besiegers and besieged began on September 23. The Russians usually proved themselves superior, demonstrating unprecedented orderliness. Only those soldiers specifically ordered to fight did so. Not a soul in the other regiments dared move.

Ivan's firmness at the very start of the siege underwent a severe trial. At one point a terrible storm flattened the tents, including the tsar's own. Many of the boats on the Volga were wrecked and supplies lost. The soldiers grew discouraged but not the tsar. He sent orders for more supplies from Sviiazhsk as well as from Moscow. He declared his firm intention to winter at Kazan if necessary. Day and night he rode around the city, inspecting places most suitable for fortified positions.

The siege works proceeded without break, supervised by Crown Secretary Vyrodkov.[45] Gabions were set up and supplied with cannon.

Where it was impossible to build gabions they constructed stockades, so that Kazan was surrounded on all sides by Russian fortifications. Couriers could neither enter nor leave the city. The Tatars made continual sallies, desperately attacking the gabions and their defenders. They attacked, they fought hand-to-hand, but always they were pressed back into the city. Many were killed in the uninterrupted bombardment of the city. The musketeers and cossacks, protected by the gabions, picked off with well-aimed shots the Tatars who appeared on the battlements.

Abruptly the besiegers' attention was diverted. From the forest on the Arsk plain a vast host of the enemy poured out and fell upon the Russian regiments. Although the Russians repulsed their attackers, inflicting many casualties, they themselves suffered just as many losses. Captives informed them that it was the doing of the Tatar commander Yapancha, operating from the hiding place about which the Kazan nobleman Kamay told them earlier. Thenceforward Yapancha gave the Russians no peace. A large banner was flown on the highest tower in the city, giving the signal to Yapancha in the forest to attack the Russians from behind. At the same time the Tatars charged out of the gates to attack the Russians' fortifications from their side. The continual sallies from the city, the raids from the forest and the lack of food began to exhaust the army. Food supplies fell until there was not enough bread to fill a soldier. Besides, practically every night he had to go without sleep in order to protect the cannon, his life and his honor.

On August 30 Obolensky-Serebriany and Gorbaty were sent off to destroy the forest raiders. Yapancha's band, some mounted and some on foot, streamed out of the forest to meet him. The Tatars suffered a decisive defeat. The victorious Russians pursued the survivors for a distance of fifteen versts before managing to surround them. Then they proceeded to clear the forest of fugitives, delivering three hundred and fifty captives to Ivan. He sent one into Kazan with an announcement that if the inhabitants surrendered to the tsar he would pardon them. If they refused, he would put all his captives to death. The Kazan Tatars gave him no answer and the captives were all put to death in front of the city.[46]

On the following day, August 31, the tsar summoned "the meditator," a German sapper skilled in the demolition of cities. He was ordered to prepare a tunnel underneath Kazan. Then the tsar summoned Kamay and the Russians who escaped from captivity in Kazan. He asked them where the people in Kazan were getting their water, since the Russians long ago had cut them off from the Kazanka river. They told him about a secret vault under the bank of the Kazanka near the Muraley gate that contained a spring. It was reached through an underground shaft. The tsar then ordered the commanders of the rearguard regiment, Prince Vasily Obolensky-Serebriany (brother of Peter)[47] and the boyar Prince Simeon Sheremetev,[48] to destroy the secret vault. The commanders answered that this was impossible by direct assault, but that it might be possible to tunnel underneath the vault from the stone Dairov baths, which Russian cossacks had captured long ago. The tsar assigned Adashev to this task, with the help of the meditator, but then ordered the latter to send his apprentices to mine the tunnel under the vault while he remained to supervise mining the main tunnel under the city.

Day and night they worked on the tunnel under the vault, until finally they were underneath the shaft through which the people of the town went for water. Vasily Serebriany himself went into the tunnel with his assistants and heard over their heads the voices of those fetching water. He notified the tsar, who ordered eleven barrels of gunpowder positioned under the vault. On September 4 the vault was blasted into the air, along with those carrying water at the time. Part of the wall also was blown up, and many in Kazan were killed by stones and logs falling from a great height. The Russians used the breach to storm the city, where they killed or captured many Tatars before withdrawing.

Only after this setback did Kazan's defenders begin to despair. There was dissension. Some wanted to surrender to the tsar, but others disagreed and went to look for another source of water. They found one putrid stream. They had to make do with it throughout the remainder of the siege, although many became sick and bloated, dying from the foul water.

On September 6 at the cost of much bloodshed the Russians captured an important position. They took a fort which the Tatars had built some fifteen versts from the city on a hill in the middle of a swamp on the Arsk plain. Following this capture the Russian commanders moved on the town of Arsk, attacking and burning villages as they went. From Arsk they returned to Kazan by a different route. They mastered the entire Arsk countryside, killing many men, taking women and children captive, and freeing many Christians from servitude. They subdued an area one hundred fifty versts wide as far as the Kama river. They burned villages and drove much livestock back to the army at Kazan.

Meanwhile siege operations continued. Vyrodkov constructed a forty-foot tower opposite Kazan's Royal gate.[49] A large detachment was stationed inside the tower and supplied with muskets and ammunition. The musketeers opened fire from the top of the tower into the city, scoring many hits. Kazan's defenders took refuge in trenches. They dug them under the city gates and walls. They even dug burrows into the terraces, for every gate had a large earth-filled terrace behind the moat. Darting out of these burrows like snakes, they attacked their assailants unremittingly day and night. They fought so fiercely that for a long time they kept the Russians from moving their gabions forward to the moat. Finally Vorotynsky's men managed to move some gabions up to the moat's edge opposite the Arsk tower and the Royal gate.

Only the moat, measuring some twenty feet across and some fifty feet deep, now lay between the Russian gabions and the city walls. The Russians halted operations and withdrew to have their midday meal, leaving a few soldiers to guard their siege engines. The Kazan Tatars, seeing their chance, crawled out of all their holes under the terrace and fell of a sudden on the gabions. The guards wavered and fled. The commanders quickly re-formed their regiments and struck back at the enemy. They pushed some into the moat and shot at them there, but many were able to escape back into the city through their holes. Altogether it was a bloody affair and, although the gabions were safe, their rescue cost the besiegers many casualties in killed and wounded. Vorotynsky himself received several wounds and was saved only by the temper of his armor.

At the height of the struggle at the Arsk tower some Kazan Tatars and some Nogay made a sally from the Zboili gate against the gabions of the Ertoul Regiment[50] and the vanguard, but here the commanders were ready. They allowed the enemy to come right up to the gabions, then struck at them from all sides. They routed them without suffering a single casualty.

Ivan ordered his sappers to undermine the terraces, realizing that as long as the enemy could hide behind them the Russians' fire would cause little damage. He ordered his men to move their gabions right up to the Arsk and Royal gates the moment those terraces were exploded.

On September 30 the terraces flew into the air, along with those within. Falling logs struck many in the city. The rest were so terror-stricken they were unable to move for some time afterward. Arrows stopped flying from Kazan. The Russian commanders made good use of this time to position and reinforce their gabions by the Royal, Arsk and Atalyk gates. When Kazan's dazed defenders finally came to their senses they sprang out of all the gates at once and attacked the Russians in a vicious fury. The appearance of Ivan himself near the walls instilled the Russian attackers with renewed fervor. They closed with the enemy at the gates, on the bridges, at the walls. They fought with spears and swords in hand-to-hand combat. Smoke from the bombardment by cannon and muskets covered the city and the fighters.

At last the besiegers won the day. They scaled the walls, took the Arsk tower, and worked their way into the city itself. Vorotynsky sent a message to Ivan suggesting that they take advantage of the situation and launch a general assault, but the other regiments were not fully prepared. On the tsar's orders the warriors were pulled back from the city. The walls, gates, and bridges were set afire, and the Russian soldiers in the Arsk tower were reinforced. The bridges and walls burned the whole night, and the earth spilled out of the walls. The Russian commanders ordered their soldiers to build strong shelters at the seized positions and refill their gabions with earth. The Tatars likewise were busy, placing timbers in the walls' breaches and filling them with earth.

FALL OF KAZAN

On the following day, October 1, the tsar gave orders to fill in the moat with timbers and earth, to build bridges, and to maintain an uninterrupted cannonade. The bombardment lasted all day and in places knocked the city walls down to their foundations. A general assault was set for the next day, Sunday, October 2. The soldiers of all regiments were ordered to attend confession and take communion, but before the final assault the tsar made one last attempt at negotiating a peaceful settlement.

He sent Kamay to the city with a proposal for the people of Kazan to surrender to the tsar. If they threw themselves on his mercy and handed over their ringleaders, the tsar would forgive them. "We refuse to surrender!" the Tatars answered with one voice. "You Russians can be on the walls, in the tower—no matter. We will build other walls. We will withstand the siege or we will all die." So the tsar commanded his men to prepare for the final assault. He also ordered soldiers to position themselves along the roads so as to cut down anyone who might try to flee the city.

Between Saturday night and Sunday morning, October 1–2, Ivan spent some time alone with his confessor. Then he started to dress for battle. Prince Vorotynsky sent in a report that although the meditator had placed the powder in position under the city walls, the Tatars had found out about it, and there was no time for delay. The tsar sent word to all regiments to prepare for battle immediately. He himself entered the church and gave instructions to recite the office. At daybreak, sending his regiment to the city with orders to await him at an appointed spot, he attended mass. Just as the deacon finished reading the Gospel with "and may there be but one flock and one shepherd," the ground shook and there was a tremendous thunderclap. The tsar stepped outside the church doorway. He saw the city wall blown up, timbers and bodies flying through the air. Shortly afterwards the deacon continued the service with the prayer for the tsar which went "Humble underfoot his every enemy and foe." There followed a second explosion more powerful than the first. Numerous bodies could be seen thrown high into the air above Kazan, some ripped in half, others without arms or legs. At this the Russian army with cries of "God is with us!" launched the assault. The defenders of Kazan met them with their own cry "Mohammed! We shall all die for our faith!" A terrible battle commenced at the gates and on the walls.[51]

One of the tsar's attendants entered the church saying "Tsar! It is time for you to go. The regiments await you." "Let us hear the service through to the end," Ivan replied, "for then we shall receive Christ's perfect blessing." A second messenger arrived, saying "The tsar must come right away, the army needs his support." Ivan gave a deep sigh, tears streamed from his eyes, and be began to pray. "Do not desert me, O Lord my God! Do not leave me, hear me in my need!" The mass was concluded. Ivan kissed the icon of St. Sergius, drank some holy water and ate a piece of the Host. He received the blessing of his confessor. "Forgive me my sins," said he to the clergy, "bless those who suffer for Orthodoxy, and help us with your prayers." He left the church, mounted his horse, and galloped off to join his regiment.

Russian banners were flying from the walls as the tsar reached the city. His presence gave the men new strength. Vorotynsky sent word that the Russians were inside the city and needed the help of the tsar's regiment. Ivan ordered his regiment to dismount and go to their aid. The narrowness of the city's streets made fighting on horseback impossible.

The Kazan Tatars put up a desperate resistance. For several hours the Russians could not take a step forward. Finally they succeeded in climbing onto the roofs of the houses, whence they could strike at the enemy from above, but at this decisive moment the temptation of rich spoils intervened. Many soldiers stopped fighting and began looting. The Tatars threatened to overpower those who remained fighting. The commanders notified the tsar, who sent reinforcements which soon restored the balance. The Russians fought their way through to the mosque, whereupon the most bitter fighting broke out in which the chief mullah perished.

Beyond the mosque Khan Ediger shut himself in his palace and defended himself valiantly. Finally, realizing the impossibility of further resistance, he fled to the gates in the lower part of the city, but a small Russian detachment, previously under Kurbsky's command, barred his way while the main army pressed in from behind. Tatars clambered up to the tower over their dead piled high against the walls, and shouted out that they wished to negotiate.

The Russians ceased fighting and the Tatars began to speak. "While our temple and the court of our khan's throne stood, we protected them with our lives. Now we hand our khan over to you alive and well. Take him to your own tsar! We are coming out to the open fields to drain our last cup with you."

Turning the khan with three of his closest attendants over to the Russians, the Tatars proceeded to jump down from the walls onto the bank of the Kazanka. They tried to force their way straight ahead to the river but were met by a salvo from Russian cannon. They turned left and gained the river downstream where they discarded their boots and armor before plunging in. Altogether some six thousand got across the river. The Kurbsky brothers, Andrei and Roman, galloped round the enemy and cut into their ranks but were repulsed. Three other commanders—Mikulinsky, Glinsky, and Ivan Sheremetev—succeeded in delivering a final blow against the Tatars. Only a few wounded managed to reach the forest. In Kazan not a single defender remained alive, because Ivan gave orders to slay anyone armed, taking as captives only women and children.

When the tsar realized that Kazan was his, he ordered a prayer service held beneath his banner. With his own hands, with the help of his confessor, he raised a cross and commanded that a church to honor the icon "not made with human hands" be built on the very spot where the tsar's banner flew during the assault against the city. After the service Prince Vladimir and all the boyars and commanders congratulated the tsar. "Rejoice, O Orthodox tsar!" said Prince Vladimir. "By the Grace of God our adversaries are conquered! Long may you rule over the Kazan realm which God has given you! Through God you are our defender from the godless sons of Hagar. Thanks to you, poor Christians now are freed forever and a profane place has been illuminated with grace. Henceforth we pray God grant you many years of life, humble all adversaries under your feet, and give you a son to inherit your realm so we may live forever in quiet and peace." "God has allowed it thanks to your diligence, Prince

Vladimir Andreevich," the tsar replied, "and thanks to the efforts of all our warriors. He has answered the prayers of all our people. God's will be done!" Shah Ali too came up with his felicitations. When this Tatar khan congratulated the tsar on the destruction of the Tatar realm, Ivan felt moved to answer him with a justification for that destruction. "Khan my lord! You, our brother, must know this: many times did I send to them seeking peace. You have seen for yourself their stubbornness and the evil cunning with which they lied for so many years. Now a merciful God has shown His just sentence, taking revenge on them for the spilling of Christian blood."

Ivan gave orders to clear away the bodies from the street leading from the Muraley gate to the khan's palace. He entered the town, his commanders and service gentry to the fore, Prince Vladimir and Shah Ali behind. They were met by the Russian captives, now freed from servitude. When they saw the tsar they fell to the ground with tears in their eyes. "Our savior!" they cried. "You have delivered us from Hell. For the sake of us, your orphans, you risked your own life!" The tsar ordered them to be taken to his camp and fed, and arrangements made for them to be returned.

Entering the city, Ivan ordered his commanders to extinguish the fires. All treasures found in Kazan, as well as the women and children captives, he gave to his army. For himself he wanted only the khan, Ediger Mahmed, the khan's banners and the city's cannon. He remained for a short time in the khan's palace, then returned to camp. He went straight to the church of St. Sergius to offer a prayer of thanksgiving to the miracle worker. After cheering his army with words of thanks and promising them rewards, he returned to his pavilion.

Kazan was taken. It remained only to deal with the wild and warlike peoples living in the area. Ivan sent edicts out to all yasak-paying subjects in every settlement. He announced that they might come to him without fear, that he would grant them his favor; they need only render him the same tribute they formerly paid to the khans of Kazan. Shortly the people of Arsk and the Cheremiss plainsmen arrived to do him obeisance.

By October 4 the whole of Kazan was cleared of corpses. The tsar entered the city a second time and chose a central spot where he set up a cross, again with his own hands, to mark the foundation of a church to commemorate the Annunciation. They held a service, sprinkled holy water, and walked around the city walls with crosses. By the third day, October 6, the newly-founded Annunciation church was finished and consecrated. On the same day the tsar appointed as his viceroys in Kazan two boyars, Princes Gorbaty and Vasily Obolensky-Serebriany. He left with them his best service gentry, junior boyars, musketeers and cossacks.

VICTORIOUS TSAR RETURNS TO MOSCOW

On October 11 Ivan set off for home. The tsar himself travelled by boat up the Volga. The cavalry under Vorotynsky's command travelled along the banks as far as Vasilsursk. When he reached Nizhny Novgorod the tsar met envoys bearing congratulations from his wife the tsaritsa, his brother Prince Yury, and the metropolitan. Here he disembarked and travelled overland through Balakhna to Vladimir where a great joy awaited him— the boyar Yury Trakhaniot rushed in with the news of the birth of Ivan's first son Dmitry.[52]

From Vladimir the tsar travelled through Suzdal and Yuriev-Polsky until finally he reached the Trinity-St. Sergius monastery where the former metropolitan Joseph, the abbot and the monks greeted him with crosses. In the village of Taininskoe he met his brother Prince Yury. Near Moscow he was greeted by an enormous crowd of people, shouting "Long live our pious tsar, conqueror of barbarians, savior of Christians!" At the Presentation monastery he was greeted by Metropolitan Makary with crosses. After receiving his blessing Ivan made a speech which ended "and to you, our father and spiritual adviser, and to the entire consecrated assembly for your efforts and your prayers we are all, including Prince Vladimir and the whole army, most humbly grateful. Because of your prayers the Lord brought great miracles to pass."

Then the tsar, Prince Vladimir and the entire army bowed low to the ground. "Now I beg you to intercede with your prayers to God for our sins," Ivan continued, "and for the reconstruction of the land. Through your devout prayers may the gracious Lord send us His mercy and preserve in true faith and purity the flock of Orthodox Christians entrusted to our keeping. May He keep us on the path of salvation and protect us from our hidden enemies. May He preserve in His holy name the newly-christianized city of Kazan, granted to us through His blessed will. May He strengthen within it righteousness and the true Christian law. May the unfaithful turn to Him, so that they may praise with us the wonderful names of the Holy Trinity, of Father, Son and Holy Ghost, now and eternally, for ever and ever. Amen."

The metropolitan replied with a speech praising the mercy of God and the exploits of the tsar. He compared Ivan to Constantine the Great, to St.

Vladimir, Dmitry Donskoy and Alexander Nevsky.[53] At the end of his speech the metropolitan and all the clergy fell prostrate on the ground before the tsar, thanking him for his good works.

Ivan changed his attire at the Presentation monastery. He took off his armor and donned his regalia—crown of Monomakh on his head, mantle over his shoulders, cross on his chest. He proceeded on foot behind the cross-bearers to the Dormition cathedral in the Kremlin and from there into the palace. On November 8, 9 and 10 the tsar held banquets for the high clergy and magnates. During those three days presents were distributed to the metropolitan and higher clergy, and rewards to the commanders and warriors, from Prince Vladimir down to the lowest junior boyar. Not counting the award of patrimonies, estates and tax-farming privileges, rewards in the form of money, clothes, vessels, armor and horses amounted to forty-eight thousand rubles.

LIFTING THE TATAR YOKE

The rewards matched the feat. They corresponded to the impact of the victory on the minds of contemporaries. The Russians managed to defeat a Tatar force once before. It happened at the end of the fourteenth century when the Tatars arrived to reassert the old hegemony of Batu Khan. The Russians took a stand against the Tatars [at Kulikovo on the Don] and repulsed the attack, but for long afterward they could not make up their minds to take up the offensive. Later, as a result of power struggles within Kazan, Ivan III succeeded in strengthening his influence there. He placed a puppet khan on the throne, but by the time of Ivan III's death in 1505 the khan threw off his dependence on Muscovy. In the reign of Vasily III a series of campaigns were undertaken against Kazan in an attempt to restore the previous relationship. Again, during the minority of Ivan IV, Kazan not only threw off its dependence on Muscovy but went on the offensive and the neighboring districts suffered severe devastation. Now finally, thanks to the resolute efforts of the young sovereign, Kazan was taken, joined at last to the Muscovite state, *a Tatar realm was conquered.*

We must put ourselves back in the sixteenth century in order to understand the powerful impact those words had on contemporaries. A Tatar realm conquered! Only a few years previously the young grand prince decided to assume the fearful title of tsar, until now a title used primarily for the Tatar khans,[54] those supreme sovereigns before whom our princes bowed low. We need only remember that Ivan III, although he demanded equality with the German emperor and the Turkish sultan, did

Central "Tent-Roof" Tower, Intercession ("Basil the Blessed") Cathedral,
Red Square, Moscow. View from inside kremlin.
Commemorates Ivan's victory over Kazan.

Photograph by L.H. Rhinelander, 1976.

not dream of equality with the Crimean khan but paid him obeisance. Now, here at last—a conquered Tatar kingdom, conquered with exceptional efforts, as great as those required of Northeastern Russia for the defeat of Mamay Khan on the Don in 1380. Yet the results of the two actions were entirely different. The outcome of the struggle on the Don was merely the repulse of a fearsome khan. The outcome of Ivan's battle was the conquest of a tsardom.

The first Russian princes appeared in the mists of ancient antiquity, heroes who conquered foreign lands. Those felicitous times had long since passed, replaced by times of domestic strife and pagan attacks tearing the Russian land apart. Recently the Russian land began to gather itself together again, but without any notion of acquiring foreign territory. The annexation of Lithuanian districts was regarded merely as restitution of old Russian territory. The conquest of Kazan was, therefore, the first real conquest. More important, it was the conquest of a Tatar tsardom.

After centuries of suffering and humiliation Russia finally had its own tsar. He restored the auspicious times of its first conqueror-princes. Little wonder that Ivan IV thenceforward towered above his predecessors. For the Russian people of the seventeenth century he remained the greatest figure in Russian history. He eclipsed all other figures, just as the figure of Peter the Great would do for the Russian people of the following two centuries. Indeed, at least for the great mass of the Russian population, the impression produced by Ivan's exploits was far stronger than that produced by those of Peter, whose reforming activity related primarily to the highest stratum of society. The outstanding achievements of the Great Northern War, such as the victory at Poltava, hardly could have aroused within the whole mass of the population an enthusiasm as overwhelming as that which the conquest of a Tatar tsardom aroused among sixteenth-century Russians.

The conquest furthermore was not primarily the result a young ruler's vainglory, nor was it the result of aspirations whose importance was not immediately apparent as, for example, the attempts to conquer the Baltic territories. The conquest of Kazan was a necessary, sacred undertaking in the eyes of every Russian, a campaign to defend Christianity from Islam, to protect Russian territories ravaged by barbarians, to free Christian captives. Finally, the impression of the extraordinary obstacles overcome during the campaign gained strength with the telling. No previous campaign against cities—the Novgorod, even the Smolensk campaign—could compare with this final campaign against Kazan.

WIDER SIGNIFICANCE

In the history of Eastern Europe the taking of Kazan and the raising of the cross on the banks of its rivers had great significance. The sway of the Asiatic hordes there was shaken. Their decline in the fourteenth century was marked by the new European, Christian government taking shape in the region of the upper Volga. In the second half of the fifteenth century the Golden Horde collapsed, but the beast's sundered members still moved. Three Tatar realms appeared. Of these the Astrakhan khanate, which took shape at the Volga delta, constituted the least threat to the Christian states of Eastern Europe. The Crimean khanate soon showed its marauding face in its relations with Russia and Poland, but the wide steppe separated the Muscovite state from the Crimea. Nothing separated it from the third Tatar realm, the Kazan khanate, founded on the middle Volga and the lower Kama.

It was an important nexus. It was just there that the new Russia of the Northeast, following its natural course down the Volga, necessarily must collide with Asia. Here Asia—Islamic Asia—long maintained a refuge, not for the nomadic hordes, but for its own civilization. The Bulgars,[55] a trading and enterprising people, were long established here. Long before the Russian Slavs began to construct Christian churches on the Oka, before they occupied these places in the name of European civilization, Bulgars listened to the Koran on the banks of the Volga and the Kama.

It was here in Northeastern Europe that Christianity first collided with Islam. The collision was unavoidable the moment young Russia was established in the region of the upper Volga, and Slavic settlements discovered the way downriver. The first princes of the new, Northeastern Russia—Yury Dolgoruky, Andrei Bogoliubsky, Vsevolod III, Yury II— waged wars with the Bulgars and extended the boundaries of their realms to the confluence of the Oka and the Volga, which they fortified with the town of Nizhny Novgorod.[56] The Bulgars found it difficult to defend Asia and Islam in that direction from Russian pressure.

Just then Asia launched its Tatars. Russia's eastward movement down the Volga was halted for a long time, but with the weakening of Tatar dominion the movement began again. Asia—that is, the Tatars—mustered its last resources and staked out a position in a vulnerable spot, at Kazan. So long as Kazan existed, further Russian colonizing movement eastward along the Volga—Europe's aggression against Asia—was impossible. The Tatars, nomadic inhabitants of the steppeland, excelled in offensive but were ill-equipped for defensive warfare. The grim determination with which they defended Kazan therefore deserves the historian's close attention.

Central Asia with its banner of Islam was assailed at its last bulwark against Europe. The Muscovite tsar attacked under the banner of Christianity. Kazan fell, and the entire Volga became a Muscovite river. The conquest of Astrakhan was quick, a foregone conclusion following conquest of Kazan. Up to this point Russian colonization assumed a northeasterly direction, denied access to the great southeastern plain by the sovereign nomadic hordes. The fall of Kazan—that is, the extension of Muscovite authority over the whole Volga—enabled the Russian population to spread southeastward. It even spread toward the southwest, to the rich lands watered by the western tributaries of the Volga and the eastern tributaries of the Don.

PACIFICATION

Concentrated around Kazan were certain primitive peoples, used as auxiliaries—Cheremiss, Mordvinians, Chuvash, Votiaks and Bashkirs. They inhabited both sides of the Volga, west and east, highland side and plains side, in places that offered free and easy life for primitive peoples. We have observed how the population of the highland side—the highlanders—were forced after some wavering to submit to Moscow as a result of the founding of Sviiazhsk. We also have seen how Ivan's first step towards taking Kazan was to extend to these peoples an invitation to accept Muscovy's suzerainty voluntarily, to enter into the same relationship with Muscovy they previously had with Kazan. They agreed and the matter appeared to be settled.

Appearances were deceptive. Kurbsky described in his account how a council was convened to determine the organization of the newly conquered territory. Some boyars advised the tsar to remain with the entire army in Kazan until springtime in order to root out Muslim resistance completely. They drew his attention to these five diverse, non-Tatar peoples who inhabited the Kazan territory; but the tsar did not heed their advice, accepting instead that of his wife's brothers and certain other dignitaries, including the clergy, to return to Moscow. We do not know precisely what arguments the two sides advanced to support their opinions. Probably those who advised returning home argued that it would be ridiculous to keep an entire army at Kazan against the remote possibility of an uprising of either the plainsmen or the highlanders; that a force left with viceroys in Kazan would suffice to defend the city; that in emergency

other regiments could be sent; that it would be unwise to display such
inimical intentions and thus set against Muscovy those very people who
did obeisance and were prepared to pay tribute. Most important, we must
not forget the composition and the condition of the army at that point, nor
that some servicemen already declared themselves exhausted at Kolomna
and were excused from accompanying the expedition any further.

Kurbsky also recorded that some remaining but unnamed Kazan
princes joined the Cheremiss and other natives and stirred up war against
the Russians. One chronicler placed the blame on those boyars to whom
the tsar entrusted the management of Kazan's affairs. In his words, they
were concerned merely with their own tax-farming privileges[57] and
neglected the administration of Kazan.[58]

However that may have been, on December 20, barely two months after
the tsar's return to Moscow, his commanders at Vasilsursk sent him
disquieting news. Plainsmen and highlanders had attacked some couriers,
merchants and boyars returning to Kazan along the Volga with supplies
gathered from the territory. The tsar ordered his vicegerent at Sviiazhsk,
Prince Peter Shuisky, to discover the ringleaders among the highlanders.
Shuisky sent the commander Boris Saltykov to investigate. Seventy-four
offenders were rounded up. Some were hanged on the spot, and others at
Sviiazhsk, their possessions turned over to their victims. The viceroy of
Kazan, Prince Alexander Gorbaty, similarly reported that he hanged
thirty-eight men in Kazan, including some Votiaks, for seditious activity.
Tribute, he reported, once again was being collected without incident.

As a consequence of these reprisals Kazan caused Moscow no trouble
throughout the rest of 1552 or during the first two months of 1553, but on
March 10 bad news arrived. Gorbaty wrote that plainsmen broke their
promises, refused to render tribute, and killed the tribute collectors. A
number broke through to the Arsk plain and took a united stand. They
gained a foothold on a high hill by the fort. The commanders sent cossacks
and musketeers after them, but they became separated and were cut down.
Altogether three hundred and fifty musketeers and four hundred and fifty
cossacks were lost. After that the rebels built a town on the Mesha some
seventy versts from Kazan. They were building a wall around it and were
preparing to withstand a Russian siege.

Two weeks later even worse news arrived from Sviiazhsk. Rebel
Cheremiss and Votiaks brought war to the highland side. Shuisky sent
Saltykov again with junior boyars and some loyal highlanders to confront
them, but Saltykov suffered defeat and was taken prisoner. Altogether the

Russians lost two hundred and fifty killed and two hundred taken captive. Moscow's response to this news was to dispatch Daniel Adashev, Alexis's brother, to Viatka with more junior boyars. He was ordered to seek out the rebels along the Kama and the Viatka. Cossacks from all along the upper Volga were sent to help him. Adashev spent all summer working along the three rivers—the Kama, the Viatka and the Volga. In many places he attacked Tatars and Nogay at the ferries. Altogether he turned two hundred and forty captives over to the authorities in Kazan.

In September 1553 the commanders Simeon Mikulinsky, Peter Morozov, Ivan Sheremetev and Andrei Kurbsky were dispatched from Moscow. They commenced offensive action the following winter. They burned down the town the rebels built on the Mesha. They defeated them at every encounter. For four weeks they fought on, laying waste the countryside for two hundred fifty versts up the Kama. They took some six thousand men and fifteen thousand women and children captive. As a result the inhabitants of Arsk and the Kama valley promised obedience to Kazan and gave a peace-offering to the tsar.

The following summer more unrest broke out among the plainsmen. The commanders tried sending against them two Kazan Tatar princes with Tatar recruits from Arsk and the Kama valley, together with some highlanders, in order to test their loyalty. The experiment failed. Some Tatars refused to fight the rebels, joining forces with them instead and turning on those of the Arsk Tatars and the highlanders who remained loyal. They attacked some fishermen on the Kama and started to march on Kazan itself at haymaking time. Prince Ivan Mstislavsky set out to meet them and in two weeks laid waste twenty-two village districts. He routed the rebels when they retaliated with an attack on his rearguard. Later, bands of plainsmen appeared near Arsk. The inhabitants fought them off with the help of a hastily-built stockade and some Muscovite musketeers, whose volleys inflicted considerable damage on the attackers. The highlanders also remained loyal. They launched a surprise attack on the plains side of the Volga and harried it. The commanders dispatched the two Kazan Tatar princes with musketeers and some recently baptized natives. They defeated a host of rebels and brought captive to Kazan many princes and nobles, all of whom were executed.

The inhabitants of Arsk and the Kama valley distinguished themselves for their loyalty. In the autumn of 1554 alone they helped fetch 1,560 rebels of all ranks. The tsar sent rewards of gold for the commanders and for the loyal natives, but where the Arsk and valley peoples were loyal and paid their tribute faithfully, the plainsmen were not. Their leaders—Mamich Berdey and his comrades—refused to come into Kazan. They continued as before to pillage along the Volga and wreck vessels. Mstislavsky and the boyar Daniel Romanovich were sent out against them. We do not know precisely what action they took, but we do know that by the spring of 1556, according to Shuisky's report from Kazan, the Arsk and Kama valley inhabitants once again rose in rebellion. They killed the musketeers stationed among them and joined forces with the rebel chief Mamich Berdey, who had with him a candidate khan from the Nogay.

Fortunately the highlanders remained loyal and performed valuable service for the Muscovites, ridding them of Mamich Berdey who, after laying waste the surrounding countryside, drew up his force of two thousand against the highlanders in their fortified position. The highlanders pretended to agree to negotiate, swearing to act together with him against the tsar's army. To seal the pact they invited him to a feast. Mamich Berdey arrived with two hundred of his men, but his entire guard was slaughtered at the banquet. Mamich Berdey himself was taken alive and escorted to Moscow. The tsar granted the highlanders a huge reward and reduced their tribute.

In Moscow Mamich Berdey confessed that the Nogay candidate proved unsuitable and had been executed. The Cheremiss impaled his head on a high pole and said to it, "We chose you to rule over us so that you and your court would defend us, but you and your men gave us no help at all. You only ate our oxen and our cows. Now let your head rule us from the top of a high pole."

The rebels, deprived of their leader Mamich Berdey and the support of the Nogay, were attacked by the boyar Peter Morozov, who in the spring of 1556 reached the plains village of Chalymsk with some junior boyars, cossacks, musketeers and baptized natives. Completely routing a rebel band on the Mesha, he burned Chalymsk with great slaughter. He fought on for another ten days, devastating all the Arsk positions, killing many and taking countless captives. That took place in May. In June Morozov and the commander Fedor Saltykov together undertook a new expedition to within fifty versts of the Viatka. His soldiers took only women and children captive. All males they put to death. Shuisky launched yet more contingents from Kazan, as a result of which the Arsk and Kama areas were devastated totally. Those who managed to escape sword or capture came to Kazan to beg for mercy.

In the spring of the following year Shuisky ordered the inhabitants of Arsk and the Kama valley to build a fortified town, Laishev, on the Kama.

With a garrison of baptized natives and some musketeers under the command of junior boyars, nominally the town was to protect them from the Nogay. Shuisky ordered the baptized natives to till the soil, just as he ordered everyone, Russians as well as baptized natives, to till the fields belonging to the deserted villages around Kazan.

Meanwhile the plains tribes continued to be restive. Under the leadership of a new hero, Akhmetek, they attacked the highland side of the Volga, but they were defeated by Prince Kovrov, and Akhmetev was captured. Other plainsmen who arrived around Arsk also were routed, and meanwhile from Kazan, Sviiazhsk and Cheboksary, Russian detachments sallied to ravage the plains side. Finally in May 1557 the tsar received word that all tribes on the plains side had surrendered and begged to be forgiven their transgressions. Ivan sent a crown agent named Yartsev to Kazan and to the Sviiaga to administer the oath of allegiance to the plainsmen. Yartsev returned to report that the entire Kazan land was pacified.

MUSCOVY AND THE NOGAY NOMADS

It took five years of devastating warfare following the conquest of Kazan to pacify all its former subjects. In their struggle against Muscovy, just as in the recent battle for Kazan itself, the Nogay took an active part. Previously they did not appear in openly hostile conflict with Muscovy. Nogay envoys and merchants often visited Moscow, bringing with them large herds of horses for sale. The camps of these nomads sprawled along the river banks by the Simonov monastery and other places outside the city.

In their favored situation the Nogay merchants could hardly have refrained from mischievous ways. Brigands emerged from among the traders. The Muscovite government complained to the Nogay khans about their erstwhile guests wandering about the Russian countryside causing considerable trouble by robbing and burning villages, abducting people and selling them into slavery. Nevertheless friendly relations with the Nogay khans had to be maintained by sending gifts so that they would not meddle in Kazan affairs or ally themselves with the Crimeans. We need not trace the relations of the Muscovite government with the Nogay khans in tiresome detail. The descendants of Yedigey [the fifteenth-century khan of the Crimean Tatars] often wrote thus to the *White* [meaning Western] khan of Muscovy. "You should send us the money that you promised. Prove to us your word, and we shall not aid Kazan and shall keep away from the Crimea, for the Crimean khan is not friendly to us. You have money but you do not send it to us—may justice lie on your head. You sent my elder ambassador away empty handed. To my junior ambassador you gave scarce a remembrance. If you were really our friend would you act thus? Every year you lie to us. If you really considered us your friends, you would send us some of the furs you promised us, for every day now the khan of Kazan begs us to join him in war against Muscovy."

"In your communication to us," Ivan replied, "you wrote many unbecoming words, and such words are incompatible with friendship. If you now wish to demonstrate your friendship, send us an elder ambassador, and we shall send to you one of our own boyars. We shall send to you whatever we can manage."

Even though such unbecoming words indeed did not indicate friendship, open hostility would have been dangerous. Gifts were sent as promised when the elder Nogay ambassador arrived. In return for the gifts the Nogay khan was pleased to write to Ivan, "I am your cossack and the guardian of your gates. The sign of my friendship shall be that if my younger brothers or children wish to make war against you, I shall dissuade them if at all possible, and if I cannot prevail, at least I shall send you warning."

We have seen what great significance Kazan held for the whole of Central Asia, for the entire Muslim world. Thanks to Turkish arms, that world was now every bit as powerful as in the days of the first caliphs. Even during the rule of Ivan's father the Crimean khans brought to the sultan's attention the humiliation to the Islamic world, were Kazan left in a state of dependency on the Christian rulers of Muscovy. Even then the Turkish ambassador declared in Moscow that Kazan lay within the guardianship of the sultan. In Ivan's minority the Crimean khan laid down as a necessary condition of peace that Muscovy renounce its claims to Kazan. When the mature Ivan demonstrated clearly that he was not about to consider abandoning these claims, Bakhchisarai [the Crimean capital] and Istanbul could not remain indifferent. The Crimean khan by reason of distance and difficulty of communication could not help Kazan directly in defence against the Russians. He could only distract the tsar's attention from Kazan by attacking the Muscovite borderlands, and this he attempted to do.

The sultan instructed the Nogay khans to join forces with the Crimean khan to protect Kazan. According to reports of Russian ambassadors, the sultan wrote as follows to the Nogay khans. "In our Islamic books it is written that the Russian tsar Ivan has come of age and has raised his hand high over the Muslims. That is already a great insult to me. All my fields and rivers he has taken away. He has taken the Don river from me, he has removed all freedom from the Azov, his cossacks prey upon the Azov, they no longer allow us to drink the Don's waters. They also have caused great harm to the Crimean khan. They have contested Perekop.[59] The Russian cossacks have taken Astrakhan and both banks of the Volga. They despoil your villages. How can your bear this? Right now they are fighting for Kazan—but our own Islamic faith resides in Kazan! So we say to all Muslims, 'Unite to fight off the Russian tsar!'"

The Nogay fulfilled the sultan's wishes. They installed the Astrakhan crown prince Ediger as khan of Kazan. They defended Kazan as best they could, fighting against the Russians even after it fell, but the chief reason for their weakness during this struggle—indeed, the chief reason for the success of the Russians in Kazan from the very start, and later in Astrakhan, and in dealings with the Nogay—was the continual squabbling among the Nogay rulers. If one of them grew strong and adopted a hostile stance, Muscovy invariably could count on finding collaborators and even willing subjects among the other khans and crown princes, jealous of their kin.

At the very moment the Astrakhan crown prince Ediger was locked in mortal combat with the Russians over Kazan his relative Shah Ali, likewise an Astrakhan crown prince, could be seen within the Russian camp. Another crown prince, Kaibula, was in command of the city of Yuriev, and Derbysh Ali, a khan banished from Astrakhan, was living in the city of Zvenigorod. Recently Derbysh Ali's successor, the Astrakhan khan Yamgurchey, rode to Moscow to beg the tsar to accept him and his clients into his service. When Ivan's campaign against Kazan sparked a movement among the Muslims to rally to its defence, Yamgurchey no longer could remain an overt Muscovite supporter in Astrakhan. He demonstrated his hostility by seizing Ivan's ambassador.

One Nogay khan, Yusuf, father-in-law of Safa-Girey, did not get on with Moscow. He welcomed the sultan's advice and, in 1551, seized a Muscovite envoy. He showered him with demands and abuse, uttered many threatening and boastful words, but another crown prince, Izmail, continued to support Moscow and told Yusuf, "Your men are going to bargain in Bukhara, but we are heading for Moscow. Even if I must fight for Moscow alone and naked I shall do so, for I have no wish to have a shroud sewn for my corpse." This same Izmail to the very moment of the fall of Kazan urged the tsar to take Astrakhan, expel Yamgurchey and enthrone Derbysh Ali in his place.

After the fall of Kazan he repeated his suggestion. In October 1553 envoys journeyed to Ivan from the Nogay—from Izmail and other leaders—to petition the tsar and grand prince to grant them his protection against the Astrakhan khan Yamgurchey. Should Ivan send his soldiers there and place Derbysh Ali on the throne of Astrakhan in place of Khan Yamgurchey, Izmail and the other Nogay leaders would be forever loyal to the tsar. Ivan instructed Alexis Adashev to question the Nogay envoys closely about their proposals and to make arrangements for taking concerted action against Astrakhan.

It was agreed that the tsar send a commander with cannon down the Volga to Astrakhan by boat. Izmail was to help them by proceeding overland or sending his sons and relatives to Astrakhan. If the commanders took Astrakhan, they would name Derbysh Ali as khan. Izmail then must wage war on his brother Yusuf, who defied the tsar and grand prince and disgraced his envoys.

Izmail's proposal could not have been more timely for Muscovite purposes. It offered the possibility of strengthening Muscovite authority over Astrakhan, always of great importance to Russian trade. Furthermore it promised to weaken the hostile Nogay who now represented a considerable threat to Moscow in alliance with the rebels in Kazan. It is nevertheless interesting to read the justifications which the chronicles presented as having forced Ivan to take up arms against Astrakhan. He went to war because of the insult he sustained. Khan Yamgurchey originally sent envoys to do him obeisance, then turned traitor and seized the tsar's envoy. Further, the tsar was conscious of his ancient ancestry. When the sainted [Kievan grand prince] Vladimir distributed patrimonies to his children, he gave Astrakhan—then called Tmutorokan—to his son Mstislav.[60] A temple was built there in honor of the Virgin, and many Christian princes ruled there, the descendants of Vladimir and thus the kin of Tsar Ivan,[61] but internecine struggles among the Russian rulers caused Astrakhan to pass into the hands of the rulers of the impious hordes. For all these reasons, relate the chronicles, the tsar and grand prince decided to send his warriors against Astrakhan.

ASTRAKHAN CAMPAIGN

In the spring of 1554, when the ice broke up, a Russian army of thirty thousand under the leadership of Prince Yury Ivanovich Pronsky-Shemiakin[62] floated down the Volga to Astrakhan. Servicemen from Viatka also were sent there, commanded by Prince Alexander Viazemsky. On August 29, when the tsar was celebrating his name-day[63] with the clergy and boyars in the village of Kolomenskoe as was his custom, a courier galloped up with news from Pronsky-Shemiakin that Astrakhan was taken.

On June 29, wrote Pronsky-Shemiakin, they arrived at Perevolok, the portage between the Volga and the Don. He sent Viazemsky and the commander Daniel Chulkov on ahead with junior boyars and cossacks to find informants from Astrakhan. Viazemsky met a band from Astrakhan above Cherny island. He attacked and overpowered them, and not one escaped. The captives informed the commanders that Khan Yamgurchey sent them to gather information about the Muscovite army, and that Yamgurchey himself was stationed five versts below Astrakhan in a town with few men, a place where everyone lived on islands. Pronsky-Shemiakin left the larger barges behind and hastened to Astrakhan, sending Viazemsky on to Yamgurchey's camp.

He reached the city on July 2. Disembarking in two different places, the Russian troops moved against the fortress and took it without encountering the slightest resistance, because its defenders fled at first sight of the enemy. The same happened with Viazemsky, who reached the khan's camp to find it empty. Yamgurchey skipped off to Azov after sending the women and children down to the sea in boats. Eventually the Russians captured the khan's wives and children but searched in vain for the khan in every corner and along every road. On July 7 they caught up with a crowd fleeing from Astrakhan. They killed some, took others captive, and freed many Russian slaves. The remaining inhabitants of Astrakhan sent a petition to the commanders, pleading for the tsar's mercy, begging the tsar not to kill them or to have them taken away, but to allow them to serve him under Khan Derbysh Ali. The commanders agreed to this request on condition that they free all Russian slaves, no matter how or where acquired.

The new khan Derbysh Ali agreed. In the villages altogether there were five hundred khans and nobles, and seven thousand peasants. Although commoners were allowed to remain, he ordered the elite to take up residence with him in the city. Afterwards more refugees, some three thousand altogether, were apprehended along the roads and taken into Astrakhan.

Before giving the city and its subjects over to Derbysh Ali, Pronsky-Shemiakin extracted certain promises. The khan must pay a yearly tribute to the Muscovite tsar of forty thousand altyns and three thousand fish. The tsar's Russian fishermen were allowed to fish the Volga from Kazan to Astrakhan and down to the sea itself without payment and without prior arrangement, although Astrakhan fishermen might fish with them if they caused no trouble. Should Khan Derbysh Ali die, the inhabitants of

Astrakhan must not seek another khan themselves but must request one from the tsar or his descendants, and they must honor the ruler the tsar was pleased to assign to Astrakhan. The commanders then set out for Moscow to have these conditions ratified. They released all captives taken at Astrakhan save the khan's wives and children, whom they took to Moscow together with the freed Russian slaves.

STEPPE POLITICS

In February 1555 news arrived that Moscow's Nogay henchman Khan Izmail killed his brother Yusuf and many Nogay leaders. He drove away Yusuf's sons and relatives. Izmail wrote Ivan that now the whole Nogay horde was obedient to himself and his followers. The Nogay would be loyal to the tsar and grand prince until death. He requested the tsar to grant them the right to trade freely in Moscow, Kazan, and Astrakhan.

A Tatar in Ivan's service, originally sent to Yusuf as an envoy from Moscow, was enslaved by him. Freed again by Izmail, he was sent back to Moscow and explained what happened. The two brothers Izmail and Yusuf had fought each other for several days before Izmail finally overcame Yusuf. Nogay natives fell in great numbers on both sides. The Nogay horde in all its history never knew such a disaster.

Thus did the nomads slash away at one another in the Volga steppes, preparing a final triumph for the Muscovite realm. Izmail requested the tsar to dispatch musketeers and cossacks to the Volga river crossings to guard against attack by Yusuf's sons. The request immediately was granted. The chief musketeer Kaftyrev and the cossack ataman Pavlov set out for the Volga. In this steppe warfare Izmail, though victorious, had to beg for Russian protection. He could not afford to rest a single day so long as even one of the sons of the murdered Yusuf remained alive.

Derbysh Ali's position was similarly precarious. He lived in constant expectation of an attack by Yamgurchey. His sworn enemies included the Crimean khan and, more important, the head of Islam, the Turkish sultan. The tribute demanded by Moscow, a tribute imposed on the khanate against the wishes of the inhabitants, had burdensome implications. It explains why Derbysh Ali threw himself into the camp of the Crimeans and the Yusuf clan as soon as they promised to protect him from Yamgurchey.

In April 1555 Derbysh Ali informed Moscow of Yamgurchey's arrival at Astrakhan. Yamgurchey, together with the Yusuf clan, the Crimeans and some Turkish janissaries attacked the city, but Derbysh Ali, with the people of Astrakhan and the Russian cossacks left behind by Pronsky-Shemiakin, warded off the enemy.

In May a certain Turgenev, chief of the Russian detachment stationed in Astrakhan, sent a conflicting report of the arrival of Yamgurchey and the Yusuf clan. It appears that the khan omitted one important detail. According to Turgenev, Derbysh Ali made a deal with Yusuf's sons. They proceeded to kill Yamgurchey and his brother, in return for which Derbysh Ali escorted them across the Volga, thus giving them a chance to seize Izmail, which was all they really wanted. They caught their uncle unawares and forced him to flee.

Turgenev later met Kaftyrev on the Volga and told him that Derbysh Ali had forced him out of Astrakhan. The khan did not send envoys to the tsar but instead joined forces with the Crimean khan. Kaftyrev ordered Turgenev to turn around, and together they floated down to Astrakhan with their musketeers and cossacks. Kaftyrev found the city deserted. Its inhabitants had fled, frightened by rumors that the Muscovite tsar was sending his army against them and had given orders to have them all killed. Meanwhile three crown princes from the Crimea, with cannon and guns, joined the exiles.

Kaftyrev sent word to Derbysh Ali and the people of Astrakhan that the tsar and grand prince held absolutely no desire to wage war against them. On the contrary, he was sending them his ambassador Mansurov[64] to grant them certain favors. He would return some of the khan's captive wives, as Derbysh Ali requested. He would release their envoys, both those taken recently by Derbysh Ali and those taken earlier by Yamgurchey, and he would give them an annual allowance. On hearing this announcement, Derbysh Ali and the citizens returned to Astrakhan.

Then came the news that Izmail, gathering some supporters, drove his nephews away and again established himself as ruler of all the Nogay. In the autumn Izmail himself sent envoys to Moscow with a complaint against Derbysh Ali, who was not being true to the tsar and grand prince and was causing the Nogay much distress. He sought the tsar's protection against Derbysh Ali, even if it meant putting Astrakhan like Kazan under the tsar's direct rule. Behold, members of the horde themselves demanding that the tsar destroy another Tatar khanate!

For their part, Izmail and all his chieftains signed a pact. They promised they would march wherever the tsar and grand prince ordered them and fight as one against his enemies. Izmail even took it into his head to describe himself as a father to the Muscovite tsar and demanded that he be paid two thousand rubles yearly from Kazan. "We have given orders," Ivan answered, "for our affairs in Astrakhan to be handled firmly, for your sake; if affairs in Astrakhan go well and it becomes necessary for you or your wives and children to live there, we have given orders for a small number of men to be assigned to you, as many as are needed to maintain you, and we have instructed them to protect you from your enemies. Should affairs in Astrakhan not go well, you may come freely to Kazan, also with a few men, fifty or sixty, as many as you need for your maintenance in Kazan.

"Yet the many impolite words you have written to us in your missives have made us angry indeed. You are familiar with our realm and the manner in which former Nogay khans and chieftains wrote to our father and to ourselves. May you henceforth never again use such idle words. This time we shall set aside our anger, for you have suffered many sorrows from your enemies and we would like to help you for the sake of your previous friendship."

Izmail never again wrote as a father to Ivan, but instead "to the sovereign of all Christendom, the white tsar, many many salaams." His requests nonetheless were unchanged. "Send me three birds—a gerfalcon, a falcon, and a hawk, also much tin, much saffron, many dyes, much paper, and also five hundred thousand nails."

In March 1556 Izmail notified Moscow that Derbysh Ali had broken finally with Moscow, joined the Crimean khan and the Yusuf clan, and chased the Russian ambassador Mansurov from Astrakhan. He, Izmail, was prepared to proceed to Astrakhan should the tsar send him soldiers. At the same time news arrived from Kazan about Mamich Berdey's uprising and of his being joined by a crown prince from the Nogay. This gave cause to believe that the movement in Kazan was connected to that in Astrakhan, and that both doubtless were being provoked by the Crimeans.

Several days later a report arrived from Mansurov himself. The ambassador explained that Derbysh Ali had broken his oath and killed the khans remaining loyal to the tsar and grand prince. He and his men attacked him, Mansurov and his men, for three days. Mansurov's troops finally repulsed the Astrakhan warriors in an area known as Little Town on the Volga and went upriver on boats, but found no cossacks at Perevolok. Of his five hundred men, only three hundred and eight remained; some were killed, others drowned, still others starved to death along the way. The tsar immediately sent fifty cossacks armed with muskets to Izmail, ordering him to send his army down the Volga against Astrakhan. The tsar wrote that he would send overland another five hundred cossacks under Ataman Liapun Filimonov to aid Izmail in the campaign.

The Russian forces gathered outside Astrakhan after their voyage down the Volga. There were musketeers under their captains Cheremisinov and Teterin, cossacks under Ataman Kolupaev, and some Viatka soldiers under their leader Pisemsky. Ataman Filimonov preceded them. He attacked Derbysh Ali, killed many of his men, took numerous prisoners, and stood waiting for Cheremisinov and his comrades. Informants told how the Crimean khan was sending seven hundred Tatars and three hundred janissaries with guns and cannon to Astrakhan.

ASTRAKHAN OCCUPIED

On September 25, 1556, when the tsar was at Trinity monastery for the feast of St. Sergius as was his custom, he received a report from Cheremisinov, who arrived at Astrakhan and found the city empty. The khan and his people had fled, defeated by Ataman Liapun. The leaders settled their men in Astrakhan. They fortified the city and proceeded to the Caspian Sea, where they discovered all the Astrakhan boats abandoned. They broke up the boats and burned them. The men were hiding far down the shore. Pisemsky and Teterin went out a second time and found the khan some twenty versts distant from the river. They attacked him at night and killed many of his men. In the morning Derbysh Ali regrouped his Nogay and Crimean chieftains and all the troops from Astrakhan. The Russians retreated. Derbysh Ali pursued them and harried them all day, all the way back to the Volga.

Then Derbysh Ali offered to negotiate with Cheremisinov. He begged to be pardoned. He had broken his oath to the tsar under duress. He implored the tsar to be merciful. He swore to return to the city with all the men of Astrakhan and to serve the tsar. The Russian leaders, expecting an attack by the Astrakhan force, nevertheless remained in their fortified position in the city so as to be safe. They stationed cossacks and musketeers along the Volga, detained all Nogay and sequestered all of Astrakhan's fishing nets and ferry boats.

Derbysh Ali broke his word again, not returning to the city as he promised. He was enticed away from the tsar by the Yusuf clan and the Crimean commander sent by Devlet-Girey, the Crimean khan, but the Yusuf clan did not remain on the Crimean side for long. Once again slaughter broke out among the Nogay. For three days two families fought against each other, the Yusuf clan against the Shah Mamay clan. In the end Yusuf's sons made peace with their uncle Izmail, their father's murderer. They offered to surrender to the Russian captains, saying they wished to serve the tsar just as their uncle Izmail served him. They would set up their camp around Astrakhan and never cause trouble again. The Russian captains accepted the surrender, then gave them boats so they might join Izmail and make their living on the Volga.

These developments marked a turnabout in steppe politics. The fate of Astrakhan was decided without the Muscovite musketeers in the Astra-khan fortress ever having to fire a shot. The Yusuf clan attacked their old comrade Derbysh Ali and forced him to flee. They captured his Crimean cannon and delivered them to Cheremisinov in Astrakhan. Derbysh Ali fled to Azov and never returned.

Now the common folk of Astrakhan approached the Russian leaders, begging to be allowed to swear allegiance to the tsar and to return to live in Astrakhan. They agreed to pay tribute, if only the tsar would not punish them, for they were simple people and had been forced to follow the khan and his chieftains against their will. Indeed the Nogay rounded up many of the inhabitants of Astrakhan when they fled the Russian army.

Thus the Volga delta finally was secured for Muscovy. The captain of the Moscow musketeers easily could supervise the Nogay from the Astrakhan fortress. The nomads asked only to camp freely near Astrakhan, to catch fish in the Volga and to trade without hindrance. The tsar ordered Filimonov to take up a fortified position on the Volga near the portage to the Don, and the cossack sergeant Kobelev to do the same on the Irgyz, to protect the Nogay both from Russian cossacks and from Crimean horse-men, and to ease the passage of envoys.

The security of these Russian possessions beyond the steppe was ensured in another way, for the nomadic inhabitants continued their internecine fighting. Yusuf's sons did not remain long at peace with their uncle Izmail. In the autumn of 1557 they deposed him as ruler, but the event occasioned not the slightest change in Nogay relations with the Russian authorities. The eldest of Yusuf's sons, having become khan, vowed eternal obedience to the tsar. He promised that if he remained khan he would serve the tsar and grand prince. Even if driven out he would still remain the tsar's slave, for he had not a single desire to serve anyone else. The tsar must not be angry at him for having fallen out with Izmail, for blood flowed between them when Izmail killed his father.

We know why the Nogay so feared Muscovy. "If the sovereign tsar gives Izmail musketeers," was the word in the camp of the Yusuf clan, "all the Nogay will perish. The tsar has taken the whole Volga right to the sea. Quickly he will take Saraichik too, the whole Yaik river, the cities of

Shemakha and Derbent, and we all will be taken. Our books say that all Muslim rulers must obey the Russian tsar."

"The Nogay are perishing," Russian emissaries reported, "few are able bodied, they are hungry, they go on foot. Even born brothers do not trust one another. Their land has disappeared, and they pillage one another." Izmail, who previously thought to describe himself as a father to Ivan, now had to agree to address Ivan as sovereign. A Muscovite envoy, as well as some of his own men who were in Moscow as envoys and knew of the tsar's power, convinced him. "Do not be ashamed, Khan Izmail!" they said. "Write to the white tsar as your sovereign. The Germans are much stronger than you, but still the tsar managed to take all their cities."

Izmail again overpowered his nephews but then Yunus, the eldest, enlisted in Muscovite service. "The Nogay have all but disappeared," the Russian envoy related, "only a few remain with Izmail and even those few disagree with him. Izmail is very much afraid of Yunus, for all the tribesmen love him greatly and wish to see him return to rule them, for no one but Yunus can rule the tribe. Izmail is not the right man for the tribe, and besides he is now old. His followers are upset, they threaten him and wish to run off to the Crimea."

"Previously you were friendly and brotherly toward us," wrote Izmail to Ivan in 1562. "Previously you told us that if you took Kazan you would grant it to us. You took Kazan, but you did not turn it over to us. Then you took Astrakhan and promised that to us too, but you did not give it. The Volga empties into the sea through sixty-six estuaries, and you rule them all. I beg you, give me one, the Buzan river! I am told that I may not request from my friend, the white tsar, a single river! Would that be in either your best interests or mine? With your favor I can keep my servants. We are hungry and in great need, for we receive no money from anywhere. Might you please send us four hundred rubles?"

"There was never a word uttered about our intention to give Astrakhan to you," replied the tsar, "and as for the Buzan we have investigated and discovered that from earliest times the Buzan has been the boundary of Astrakhan. You can always allow your people to camp on your side of the Buzan, but not to cross it."

Izmail requested that the tsar expel from Astrakhan those khans who were his enemies. "We cannot just expel those khans," Ivan answered, "for when we took Astrakhan we gave them our solemn word they need not fear banishment or execution at our hand. Thus people in other lands cannot say that one faith is inimical to another and that therefore the Christian tsar

is persecuting Muslims. For in our Christian books it is written that force
may not be used to bring a man into our faith. God will decide on the day
of judgment who has believed truly and who falsely, but that is not given
to mortals to decide."

CAUCASIAN POLITICS

Control of the Volga delta opened up a whole world of diminutive North
Caucasian rulerships before the Muscovite state. Their rulers quarreled
among themselves and were victimized by the Crimeans. The moment
they realized that they had a powerful Russian state for a neighbor they
threw themselves at it. They asked for treaties, for free trading rights in Astrakhan, even to be accepted as subjects. Slowly but surely they dragged
the Muscovite realm further and further, to Caucasia and beyond.

In November 1552, immediately after the fall of Kazan, two Cherkess
chieftains arrived in Moscow. They petitioned the tsar's protection and
acceptance into his service. In August 1555 three Cherkess chieftains from
Zhazhen[65]—Sibok, his brother Atsymguk, and Tutaryk—arrived in Moscow with an escort of one hundred and fifty. They begged the tsar on behalf
of all the Cherkess land to help them against the Turkish and Crimean
rulers. In return they, their wives, and their children would be the slaves of
the tsar and grand prince for ever. The tsar granted them a large reward.
Concerning the Turkish ruler he must deny their request, for the tsar and
grand prince was at peace with the Turkish sultan, but he would do his best
to protect them from the Crimean khan. Prince Sibok asked the tsar to have
his son baptized. Tutaryk himself asked to be baptized.

In the summer of 1557 other Cherkess chieftains arrived in Moscow.
Then two Cherkess chieftains from Kabarda, Temriuk and Tizriut, sent an
envoy to the tsar begging to be allowed to serve him. They asked him to
order his commanders in Astrakhan to send them aid against the ruler of
Tarki, the shamkhal.[66] The envoy said that the tsar should favor them as he
favored the Zhazhen chieftains. Were he to help them against their enemies, the king of Georgia and all the Georgian land also would come
begging to enter the tsar's service, since the Georgian king had a treaty
with the Kabarda chieftains.

On the other hand, envoys also arrived from the shamkhal of Tarki and
from the chief of Tiumen, situated on the Terek. They too begged the tsar
to accept them into his realm, to order his Astrakhan commanders to
protect them on either side, and to grant free entry to their traders. They
would send every year whatever the tsar deemed necessary.

Thus Cherkess chieftains were asking for help against the shamkhal. The shamkhal was asking for help against the Cherkess. One aspirant in Tiumen asked for assistance against his uncle, the chieftain of Tiumen. If the tsar made him chieftain in Tiumen he would be the tsar's slave. The shamkhal's subjects asked the tsar to grant them another ruler, whereupon they and their whole land would be enslaved to the tsar. Even the khans of Khiva and Bukhara sent an urgent request for the tsar to give their merchants free passage to Astrakhan.

STRUGGLE WITH CRIMEA

It is easy to imagine how this all looked to the Crimeans. The attempt to deflect Ivan from Kazan by an attack on the Muscovite borderlands had failed. The idea of sending strong regiments to give effective aid to Kazan and Astrakhan by waging a defensive war devoid of spoils was not to the liking of brigands. They managed only to instigate uprisings along the Volga but not support them, so Kazan and Astrakhan became Muscovite cities.

After Ivan's return from Kazan, Devlet-Girey again entered into correspondence with Moscow. In the autumn of 1553 he even sent a charter of truce written exactly as the tsar demanded—except that it omitted the title tsar. It was stipulated that should the Muscovite ambassador suffer any indignity in the Crimea the Muscovite tsar had the right to subject the Crimean ambassador in Moscow to the same indignity, as he did before. The khan complained as earlier that Ivan sent him too few presents. Were the tsar to send him more, he would remain more steadfastly at peace with Muscovy. Ivan deigned to answer that friendship cannot be bought with gifts. To ensure a firmer peace with the khan he ordered the construction of a new town, Dedilov, in the steppes beyond Tula.

In the summer of 1555 Devlet-Girey decided once again on a sudden attack on the Muscovite borderlands. He incited Derbysh Ali in Astrakhan against the Russians. As was his custom, *aiming his bow to one side but shooting to the other,*[67] the khan let it be known that he was marching against the Cherkess. Living up to his promise to protect these new subjects, Ivan became the first Muscovite ruler to take the offensive against the Crimea. He sent his boyar Prince Ivan Sheremetev[68] with thirteen thousand soldiers to round up the Crimean herds in the Mamay meadows on the Perekop and deflect the khan from the Cherkess.

Sheremetev set out. On the road he received word that the khan with sixty thousand soldiers was moving in the direction of the Riazan or Tula borderlands instead of against the Cherkess. Sheremetev notified Moscow, and the tsar immediately sent his commanders, Prince Mstislavsky and his comrades, on campaign. He himself set out after them three days later with Prince Vladimir Andreevich. At Kolomna he learned that the khan was heading for Tula. Ivan also headed there.

The khan, when he learned that the tsar himself was coming to meet him, turned back. Sheremetev meanwhile was chasing after him, intending to attack the Tatar detachments as they split off into small numbers to raid for booty in the borderland areas. He dispatched a third of his army against the Crimean horse camp. The Tatars usually left their remounts in such camps about five or six days' journey to the rear of the main army so that the horses and camels could forage more easily. The Russians captured the entire camp, comprising sixty thousand draft horses, two hundred argamak thoroughbreds and eighty camels. They also sent on to Sheremetev twenty captives, who told him that the khan was heading for Tula. Sheremetev continued to chase after him, but by that time the khan learned about the tsar's expedition and turned back.

About a hundred and fifty versts from Tula, at the village of Sudbishchi, the khan came upon Sheremetev's approaching force. Sheremetev stood his ground despite the fact that his numbers were depleted by one third, for the soldiers who attacked the Crimean rear were not yet returned. The fighting began at noon and continued until nightfall. The Russians crushed the advance regiment, then the right and the left wings, and captured the standard of the Shirin princes, but the Tatars did not leave, determined to continue battle the following day.

Sheremetev sent couriers to the detachment that captured the Crimeans' rear. He instructed them to hurry to his aid, but towards morning only a few riders galloped in. The rest of the detachment was sent with their prize to the nearest Russian cities, Riazan and Mtsensk. Meanwhile during the night the khan tortured two Russian captives in an attempt to determine the size of the force that fought him so bravely during the day. One of the prisoners gave in to the torture. He admitted that Sheremetev had but few men, since a third of his force were dispatched against the Crimean horse camp. Heartened by this news, the khan recommenced the battle at daybreak.

They fought until noon. At first the Russians managed to break up the Crimeans so that the khan was left with just his janissaries around him, but then Sheremetev was seriously wounded and fell with his wounded horse. Without their commander the Russians fell into confusion and suffered a serious setback. The two commanders Basmanov and Sidorov gathered five or six thousand soldiers and positioned themselves in a wooded ravine. Thrice the khan attacked them with his entire army but without success. Evening came on. The khan, fearing the approach of the Russian army, left Basmanov and Sidorov in peace and hurried across the Sosna river. The Russians lost altogether three hundred and twenty junior boyars and thirty-four musketeers in the battle at Sudbishchi.

The tsar crossed the Oka and was approaching Tula when he was told that Sheremetev was defeated and that the khan was heading for Tula. Opinion was divided among the commanders. Some said they should fall back across the Oka and return to Moscow. Others said they must not turn tail before the enemy. It would tarnish their previous victories. Although the khan managed a victory over Sheremetev, they argued, his army was exhausted, for the stubborn two-day battle cost him many casualties in killed and wounded. The tsar adopted the latter counsel and pressed on to Tula. Arriving there, Ivan learned that the khan was hastening back to the Crimea, covering some seventy versts a day. To catch him would be impossible since four days' march lay between them. Ivan remained in Tula for two days to regroup his soldiers and then returned to Moscow.

RZHEVSKY'S BOLD OFFENSIVE

In March of the following year, 1556, Ivan learned that the khan again was gathering his army. He intended to invade the Muscovite borders by early spring. The tsar sent the crown secretary and commander Matvey Ivanovich Rzhevsky[69] to the Dnieper with some cossacks from Putivl. He was to proceed down the Dnieper as far as the Crimean encampments, find informants, and learn about the khan's plans. When Rzhevsky reached the Psel river he constructed boats. He ferried his men down the Dnieper and proceeded as instructed. At the same time another reconnaissance detachment set off down the Don.

In May an escaped Russian captive brought news from the Crimea. The khan had departed with enough supplies to last all summer. The tsar decided to proceed to Serpukhov with his boyars, there to gather men and march to Tula. From Tula they would go out on the steppe and await the khan. God willing, they would do business with him face to face.

In Serpukhov the tsar received a courier from Chulkov, leader of the amphibious detachment sent down the Don to reconnoiter. Chulkov wrote that he met two hundred Crimeans near Azov and defeated them completely. He learned from his captives that the khan indeed was preparing to march on Muscovy's borderlands when he received news that the tsar was preparing to oppose him. The khan marched instead against the Cherkess, but at the Mius river received news from the Crimea that many Russians appeared near Islam-Kermen[70] on the Dnieper, whereupon the khan hurriedly returned.

Those Russians were Rzhevsky's soldiers. He was joined at the Dnieper by three hundred Zaporozhian Cossacks from Kanev. Thus reinforced he proceeded to Islam-Kermen. The inhabitants ran off when they heard of the approach of these unwelcome visitors, so the Russians could only drive off their horses and cattle. From Islam-Kermen, Rzhevsky led his fleet further, to Ochakov,[71] where he captured the fort, killed some Turks and Tatars, then sailed back upriver, the Turks following him. He ambushed them from the reeds along the Dnieper, killed many of the enemy with musket volleys and got safely away.

Rzhevsky reached Islam-Kermen where he encountered the eldest of the khan's crown princes with the rest of the Crimeans, including khans and nobles. He held them off from an island, firing his guns across at them for six days. One night they rounded up the Tatars' horses and brought them across to their island. They crossed over to the western, Polish-Lithuanian bank of the Dnieper and so escaped safely from the Crimeans. Rzhevsky sent word to the tsar that the khan no longer would invade the Muscovite borderlands for he feared the tsar's army too much and, furthermore, plague had broken out in the Crimea.

COSSACKS

Rzhevsky's campaign gave rise to a powerful movement among the Zaporozhian Cossacks in the Polish-Lithuanian borderland. Something unprecedented had happened. Muscovites appeared on the Dnieper and went downriver, actually hunting Tatars and Turks on the cossacks' home territory! We have seen how three hundred Zaporozhian Cossacks did not hesitate to accompany the Muscovite commander on his foray against the Muslims. The acknowledged chief of all the borderland was the Kanev elder, Prince Dmitry Vishnevetsky,[72] a true cossack by nature and a worthy successor to Evstafy Dashkovich.[73] When Rzhevsky's expedition succeeded, Vishnevetsky could not restrain himself. In September 1556 one of the cossack atamans who accompanied Rzhevsky to Ochakov appeared in Moscow. He presented the tsar with a petition from Vishnevetsky asking the tsar's permission to enter his service. If granted, he, Prince Dmitry, would abandon the king of Poland-Lithuania. He would construct a settlement on Khortitsa island in the Dnieper,[74] across from the mouth of the Konskie Vody [Horse Waters] river and not far from the Crimean encampments.

The tsar sent two junior boyars to him with a safe conduct and a salary. Vishnevetsky told them that he, the tsar's slave, would come to Moscow when it was time to take his oath of allegiance. He promised first to raid the Crimean settlements and Islam-Kermen in order to prove his devotion to the tsar and grand prince. The tsar learned about this service in December directly from the Crimea. A courier arrived from Devlet-Girey with news that the khan was releasing for ransom all captives taken in his battle with Sheremetev. In the document the khan wrote that he was abandoning all hostilities and sought a lasting peace. In order to ratify such a peace, plenipotentiaries needed to be exchanged.

Dmitry Davydovich Zagriazhsky,[75] the Muscovite resident ambassador in the Crimea, also wrote that the khan spent the summer in great alarm, awaiting the tsar's attack on the Crimea. He sent to the sultan asking to be rescued from his plight. Then on October 1 Vishnevetsky captured Islam-Kermen, killed its inhabitants, and took its artillery away to his village on Khortitsa island in the Dnieper. From the khan's other side the two Cherkess princes from Piatigorsk in Muscovite service captured two more cities, Temriuk and Taman. That was why the khan wanted to send his plenipotentiaries to Moscow to make peace.

The tsar answered that if the khan wished to establish a lasting friendship, first let him swear before Zagriazhsky and then send his plenipotentiaries to Moscow. The khan preferred first to dislodge Vishnevetsky from Khortitsa. In the spring of 1557 he marched there with all his men, attacked the place for twenty-four days, but was forced to abandon the attack with great shame and many casualties. Vishnevetsky, communicating with the tsar, wrote that so long as he was on Khortitsa the Crimeans never would be able to go to war anywhere.

Yet if such was the significance of Khortitsa, Vishnevetsky must also have realized that the Crimeans and Turks would never leave him in peace. In the autumn of the same year he had different news for Moscow. He wrote that an army of Crimeans, Turks and Wallachians marched on his settlement. For want of food supplies he had to disperse his cossacks and abandon the island. He was now in his former towns of Cherkessy and Kanev, awaiting the tsar's further instructions. Ivan instructed him to turn Cherkasy and Kanev over to the king of Poland-Lithuania, with whom he was at peace. Vishnevetsky was invited to Moscow where he received as his patrimony the town of Belev with all its districts and villages, as well as some villages in other districts.

The khan was cheered by Vishnevetsky's departure from Khortitsa. He wrote to the tsar that were he to send him some nice gifts and the same tribute the Polish-Lithuanian king gave him, then fair would be fair and they would be friends indeed. If this not please the tsar, at least they could exchange ambassadors. Ivan responded that the khan's demands were not conducive to friendship. At the beginning of 1558 he sent Vishnevetsky down the Dnieper with an army of five thousand and orders for reinforcements from the Zaporozhian Cossacks on the other side. The khan was frightened and wanted to make peace, but he also wanted to profit by it. Realizing now there would be no free gifts from Moscow, he decided to raid Lithuania. He would find supplies for his horde and collect a reward from Moscow into the bargain. Ambassador Zagriazhsky returned to Moscow with the news that Devlet-Girey swore friendship and brotherhood to the Muscovite tsar and sent his son against Lithuania. Having given his oath, the khan attempted to persuade the tsar to send him a gift in the amount that was sent to Mehmet-Girey.[76] Then there would be friendship indeed and, if not, an oath was not an oath. Later, when the khan defeated the king, the tsar might send to the Crimea the same tribute the king submitted.

This proposal likewise found little acceptance in Moscow. The tsar pointed out that the khan accepted gifts and made oaths but always broke them, and he would not send a new ambassador to the Crimea. He did send a courier with a note in which he wrote that if the khan really meant well he would forego all hostilities and large requests.

In May Vishnevetsky sent word that he reached Perekop but did not meet a single Tatar on the Dnieper, nor did he find any encampments, the king having informed the khan about the Russian approach. The khan resettled all Tatar encampments beyond the Perekop and himself prepared for a siege. Vishnevetsky proposed spending the summer in Islam-Kermen, but the tsar ordered him back to Moscow, leaving behind on the Dnieper small detachments of junior boyars, musketeers and cossacks. The Crimeans tried to force their way through to the Volga in small parties of one hundred to three hundred men. They attacked some fishermen but nowhere had any real success. Some were routed by Caucasian highlanders, others by the Russians. Summer passed, and autumn, but the khan did not appear. He was waiting for an opportune moment.

TATAR ATTACK

At the end of 1558 some Tatars in Moscow sent the khan word that the city was undefended, for the tsar had set out with his army for Livonia. Devlet-Girey was anxious to avenge the damage done by Rzhevsky and Vishnevetsky, and particularly the lack of gifts from Moscow, so he decided on a winter raid. He would take advantage of the opportunity and strike unexpectedly at Muscovy's defenseless borderlands.

Gathering together a force of some one hundred thousand men, the khan sent it in three separate divisions against Riazan, Tula and Kashira. At the Mecha river Crown Prince Mehmet-Girey, leading the largest division, discovered that Ivan was still in Moscow. He inquired as to the whereabouts of Prince Vishnevetsky and Boyar Ivan Sheremetev, two men particularly well known to the Crimeans and particularly fearsome. On learning that Vishnevetsky was in Belev and Sheremetev in Riazan, he turned back.[77] Campaigning in the winter thoroughly exhausted his horses and his men. Yet the attack demonstrated one thing. The khan was ready and determined to take whatever measures he could to injure Muscovy. The tsar decided to take measures of his own.

At the beginning of 1559 he sent Vishnevetsky with five thousand men to the Don. At the same time he sent Daniel Adashev with eight thousand men to a town on the Psel, whence he could float down to the Dnieper and thence on to the Crimea. In the spring, near Azov, Vishnevetsky defeated two hundred fifty Crimeans who penetrated Kazan territory. Adashev did even better. Emerging in boats at the mouth of the Dnieper, his men captured two Turkish warships. They landed on the Crimea, devastated some encampments, and freed some Muscovite and Lithuanian prisoners. The Tatars, caught unawares, were terror-stricken. They failed to gather their wits and rally around the khan, and so could not counterattack Adashev in the Crimea. They followed him up the Dnieper as far as Monastyrka, a promontory near the Insatiable falls.[78] There the khan decided not to attack and returned home. In Moscow they prepared a fitting reception for the khan and waited all summer for him. The tsar deployed his regiments, intending himself to take the field at the first report. One or two small detachments of Crimeans came to raid the borderlands, but the khan never arrived.

Worse befell the Crimeans. Zaporozhian and Don Cossacks threatened their encampments on one side. The Nogay and auxiliaries from Astrakhan were moving against them on the other. Within the Crimea itself a savage famine raged. The khan made peace overtures, complaining about being attacked on all sides. The tsar told him to abandon all hostilities. As soon as there were honest dealings between them, no one would attack the Crimea. The tsar gave him a choice. Did he prefer war or peace with Muscovy? He warned that the Russians now knew the way to the Crimea, both by land and by sea.

IVAN FORGOES CRIMEAN WAR

The offensive against the Crimea revealed the weakness of its inhabitants. They were brave only when pillaging defenseless villagers. Yet they remained a constant danger to the Muscovite government with their lightning raids, requiring regiments always to be kept at the ready. Under the existing conditions of Muscovite military organization such a requirement was extremely taxing. It convinced Ivan's closest advisors to urge him to finish off the Crimea, just as he finished off Kazan and Astrakhan.

Ivan rejected the advice. In this he was, of course, justified.[79] The campaigns against Kazan were relatively easy because its settled territories adjoined the settled territories of the Muscovite realm. Even in the deserted or sparsely populated stretches the forests and rivers abounded with food for a sizeable army. Furthermore the Moskva, Oka and Volga represented an excellent transportation and communications network. The Volga served as the link binding Astrakhan to the Muscovite state after its conquest, but the Crimea was separated from the Muscovite borders by a wide prairie, the steppe, which began just beyond Tula and Pronsk. It was easy enough for the destructive missions of Rzhevsky, Vishnevetsky and Adashev, in the old Viking or the new cossack style, to descend the Dnieper in light boats, but that route would be impossible for the huge army that a campaign to conquer the Crimea would entail.

Ivan's decision was also completely justified in terms of later events. Witness Golitsyn's disastrous campaigns at the end of the seventeenth century, after Ukraine was united with Muscovy;[80] or the brilliant campaigns of Field Marshal Münnich in the eighteenth century, which were no less disastrous in terms of loss of men.[81] They demonstrate in evident fashion the impossibility of grand campaigns against the Crimea for sixteenth-century Muscovy. Even were it possible to conquer the Crimea in the mid-sixteenth century, would it have been possible to defend it? How many forces were required finally to subdue all the tribes that lived around Kazan? How much destruction did that warfare entail? Every time everything seemed peaceful, uprisings flared up again. It drove some magnates

to despair. They even advised abandoning this luckless territory altogether. We can understand their despair when we remember that a standing
army was non-existent, or at best barely nascent. The peoples of Kazan
were left all alone in their struggle against Moscow. The Nogay could not
render them any effective aid, the Crimeans even less, but the Crimean
khan in his campaigns against the Muscovite borders employed Turkish
janissaries. The Turkish army would have had to come to the khan's
defence in the Crimea, for the khan was a Muslim ruler and a vassal of the
sultan.

An offensive war against the Crimea necessarily would have resulted
in a war with Turkey, which was at the height of its power. All Europe
trembled before it. Could the Muscovite government in its existing condition have fought with Turkey, torn the Crimea from its grasp, and then
defended its conquest beyond the steppes?

Ivan saw the impossibility. Adashev, who captured several Turks in his
raid on the Crimea, was ordered to turn them over to the Turkish governor
at Ochakov. He was instructed to say that the tsar was fighting his enemy
Devlet-Girey, and not the sultan, with whom the tsar hoped to remain in
eternal friendship.

II

LIVONIA

Only after the passage of two hundred years could Muscovy sustain
successfully a conclusive war with the Muslim East, with Turkey. By then
it was the Russian empire and commanded all the resources of a European
state. Muscovy's primary task in the sixteenth century was to acquire those
resources, and therefore it must turn to where they might be found.

WAR AND PEACE WITH SWEDEN

Thus did Ivan turn his attention to the West as soon as he stabilized his
eastern boundaries upon taking Kazan. In the West it was war with Sweden
that occupied him from the start. It began in 1554 as a result of border
disputes. But for the Swedish king, the conflict might have been settled
peacefully. He grew annoyed with the custom that the Muscovite court,
unwilling to treat with him directly, entrusted communications to its
vicegerents in Novgorod. This was beneath the king's dignity.

The Swedes laid siege in vain to Oreshek. The Russians had the same luck with Vyborg, although the city's outlying districts were devastated. The Russians put their captives up for sale: one grivna for a man, five altyns for a girl. King Gustav Vasa[1] opened hostilities expecting Polish and Livonian aid which never arrived, so the aging king was obliged to sue for peace in Moscow and conclude a treaty advantageous to the tsar. His suit to Ivan began,"We, Gustav by the grace of God king of the Swedes, Goths, and Wends, *bow down* before your majesty, prince and sovereign Ivan Vasilievich, to beg your mercy, grand prince and tsar of all the Russian land!"

"For the sake of the king's humble petition," Ivan answered, "we order an end to the spilling of Christian blood. If the king means to abandon his arrogant thoughts and atone for his perfidy and for all his wrongdoings, by appearing before us represented by his high ambassadors humbly to bow down before us, we accept his petition, and order our Novgorod vicegerent to confirm with him the truce as it is stated in the old documents. We also order the borders to be established according to the old peace treaties. We have no wish to take his lands anywhere beyond the old border, for as befits our sovereign justice we are content with our own lands which God gave to us in ages past. If the king is still so arrogant as to suppose he cannot communicate with our Novgorod vicegerents, he should not have sent his ambassadors, for the old customs may not be broken. If the king himself does not know, let him ask his own merchants, for they have an idea how much bigger even the Novgorod bytowns[2] of Pskov and Ustiug are than Stockholm."

The high ambassadors arrived and again requested direct relations between the sovereigns. "The Novgorod vicegerents are great men," they said, "but a slave is not a brother to the tsar." "The Novgorod vicegerents are men of importance," was the answer. "Prince Fedor Dairovich is the grandson of Khan Ibrahim of Kazan. Prince Michael Kislo and Prince Boris Gorbaty are princes from Suzdal of the same stock as the Russian rulers. Prince Bulgakov is third cousin to the Lithuanian king. Prince Michael Vasilievich Glinsky has a grandfather, Prince Michael Lvovich Glinsky, who is known to many people in the German lands. Pleshcheev comes from a well-known boyar family of thirty generations and more. Consider now your king! We will tell you, though not in reproach, about his ancestors, how they traded in cattle and came to the Swedish land, all of which happened not long ago, as everyone knows." "Please do not be angry," the ambassadors replied, "we uttered those words in conversation, not in argument. We were instructed to do so by our own sovereign at the request of yours."

The terms of the treaty were spelled out. The Swedes would buy back the Russians' captives but return their own captives without cost. The king would communicate only through the Novgorod vicegerents, and the borders would remain as of old. The ambassadors begged the tsar not to insist on stating in the treaty that the peace was broken by the king's perfidy, and Ivan agreed. The ambassadors thanked him for such a high favor, saying "We never expected to receive such a supreme favor." Nevertheless similar expressions did remain in the document, for example "and the righteous tsar and grand prince visited his wrath on King Gustav and all the Swedish land for breaking the peace."

The final document included a statement about reciprocal free trade, and free passage to other countries. "Swedish merchants may travel freely to the patrimony of the grand prince, to Novgorod the Great, Moscow, Kazan and Astrakhan, and they and the Swedish ambassadors may travel beyond to all countries, to India and China." The tsar allowed this condition to be included because, for his part "the tsar's leading merchants[3] and the other merchants in many cities of the patrimony of the grand prince say that, in order to be free in trading affairs, whosoever wished to trade in the Swedish land should be free to do so, and whosoever wished to travel from the Swedish land beyond to Lübeck and Antwerp, to the Spanish Netherlands, England or France, should be free to do so and be protected, and ships be made available for them."

RELATIONS WITH LIVONIA

The Russians thereby expressed their intentions to institute active commercial ties with Western Europe. Such ties necessarily depended on the sanction of neighboring states situated on the Baltic since Muscovy had no port of its own. Yet those neighbors were usually hostile. This constriction was all the more unbearable because Russians were beginning to feel a strong desire to assimilate the fruits of European civilization. The scientists and artists who might have brought those fruits to Muscovy were barred by unfriendly neighbors. Those neighbors feared with some justification that the Muscovite state, already frightening in its material might, would be unbeatable if it also gained spiritual might, that is to say knowledge.

Livonia had the most to fear from the might of Muscovy, for it was the weakest of those neighbors. In his great need to have direct communications

with Western Europe, to have a port on the Baltic, the Muscovite tsar was
bound to turn his gaze on Livonia. It was an easy prey, judging by its weak
internal structure, undermined further by the current shift from the Catholic to the Protestant faith. At the same time it was a prey to which many
states held old claims. Even in the reign of Ivan's father the Polish government frightened the Livonians with such claims. The Livonians were
quite naturally more anxious than anyone else to keep knowledge from
penetrating to Muscovy, but their behavior merely served to strengthen
the Muscovite government's desire to acquire some of the Baltic shore,
thereby hastening the fall of their own state.

In 1539 a certain Peter Friazin[4] fled from Moscow to Livonia. He
presented himself to the bishop of Dorpat,[5] who asked him if he knew a
German named Alexander in Moscow. "I know him," said Peter, "we lived
on the same street. He used to tell the boyars in Moscow that he had a friend
in Dorpat who knew how to cast cannon as well as shoot them, and who
was thinking of coming to Moscow to serve the grand prince." When he
heard this, the bishop found out who the German friend was and exiled him
to parts unknown.

In 1547 the seventeen-year-old Ivan sent to Germany the Saxon adven-
turer Hans Schlitte, whose assignment was to engage as many scientists
and craftsmen as he could find. Schlitte requested permission for this from
Emperor Charles V, assembled one hundred twenty-three men and took
them to Lübeck, but the Livonian government pointed out to the emperor
the danger that might arise for Livonia and other neighboring countries.
Charles was convinced and gave the master of the knightly order full
authority to prevent any scientist or artist from going to Moscow. As a
result Schlitte was arrested in Lübeck and put in prison, and the men he
gathered were dispersed. One of these, the master craftsman Hans, tried to
make his way to Moscow anyway. He was arrested and put in prison. When
he was released he again set out for Moscow. Two miles from the Russian
border he was arrested a second time and executed.[6]

The earliest extant treaty negotiated between the Russians and the
bishop of Dorpat mentioned a tribute that the bishop was obliged to render
the grand prince. It also mentioned the antiquity of the obligation. In a
treaty concluded in 1503 with Plettenberg[7] the obligation of tribute from
Dorpat was affirmed, but it was ignored for the next fifty years. Vasily III,
occupied with Lithuania and even more so with Kazan and the Crimea,
had no thought of breaking off relations with his ally the grand master
over the Dorpat tribute, nor could it have been considered during Ivan's

minority. Conditions changed when in 1554 a Livonian legation appeared in Moscow with a request to extend the treaty.[8]

The lord-in-waiting Alexis Adashev was sent to treat with them. He announced that the Germans' tribute due from the Dorpat district was long in arrears. They also obstructed Russian merchants and took over for their own use Russian churches and way stations. This transgression aroused the tsar's wrath against the master of the Order, the bishop and the whole of Livonia. He ordered his vicegerents not to grant a truce.

The legates answered that they did not know of the tribute to which the lord-in-waiting referred. They could not find in their old documents any mention of their country having to render a tribute to the grand prince. Adashev said to them regarding this point, "It is astonishing how you choose to overlook the fact that your ancestors came to Livonia from across the sea, invading the patrimony of the Russian grand princes and causing much blood to flow. The tsar's ancestors were unwilling to countenance the spilling of Christian blood, and they allowed the Germans to live in the land they seized on condition that they pay a tribute to the grand princes, but they broke their promises, did not pay the tribute, and must now make payment for all the arrears."

The legates agreed to sign a new treaty. According to its conditions the bishop of Dorpat was obliged to pay a tribute to Moscow from his diocese at the rate of one German grivna a head, excluding clergy. He would pay the arrears of the past fifty years within three years. The Russian churches and way stations would be restored, and Russian residents were to obtain justice without delay. Russian factors and merchants were permitted to trade freely with Lithuanian and foreign merchants in all goods except coats of mail. All foreigners arriving from abroad and intending to enter the tsar's service were allowed to pass through to Moscow. No aid would be given the Polish king or the Lithuanian grand prince against Muscovy. The ambassadors argued that they agreed to tribute without the knowledge of the master or the bishop, who reserved the right to refuse the treaty's conditions.

The Livonian chronicler himself testifies to the fate of the Russian churches. In Dorpat, Reval, Riga and many other places they indeed were plundered by Protestant fanatics. The chronicler even brings in as evidence to the case a letter from the Muscovite tsar to the Order's leaders. "Unruly Livonians, you have transgressed against God and your rightful government! You have altered your faith and defied the authority of the emperor and the pope. Those two might be able to endure your contempt and quietly watch while our temples are plundered, but I cannot and will not countenance the indignity brought against me and my God. The Lord has appointed me His avenger and charged me to bring you into obedience." The chronicler adds that the tsar sent a lash along with his letter as a symbol of reprimand to the Livonian rulers. The information is interesting, for it demonstrates the viewpoint of those Livonians who lamented the decline of the earlier regime and saw the fall of Livonia in the Muscovite war as a consequence of the new regime. The tsar sent an envoy, a cellarer named Terpigorev, to Dorpat to conclude the treaty. He demanded that the bishop without delay follow the customary procedures, namely, upon ratification of the treaty to cut off the ambassadors' seals and replace them with his and the master's personal seals.

The bishop sought advice. How was he to answer the envoy? It was a difficult matter, and Terpigorev would not wait. The bishop's councillor Jacob Krabbe advised him, "If we ratify this treaty, in all likelihood it will mean that we and our wives and our children will become the subjects of the grand prince. We must either pay the tribute, or see the devastation of our country. I know for certain that the grand prince will gather all his forces to use against us." They all sat in deep despair. Then the bishop's chancellor Goltschur arose. "It is a difficult matter," he said, "and we must endeavor at least to stall for time. Let us call in the tsar's envoy and tell him that for our part we have agreed to ratify the treaty and we shall ratify it, but that it will have not authority without the concurrence of the emperor, the supreme sovereign of the country." Goltschur's advice was adopted and a courier was dispatched to the emperor, requesting him to send a delegation to Moscow to petition the tsar to remove the tribute.

Terpigorev was invited into the council. In the presence of two notaries the treaty was ratified with new seals and the old ambassadors' seals cut off. Terpigorev asked Krabbe, "What is it they are still writing?" When Krabbe explained the matter he replied abruptly, "What business does my sovereign have with the Holy Roman emperor? Just give me the document, not the tribute for the tsar, since he himself will collect that." On the way home he was entertaining some of his junker escorts with vodka when he pulled the treaty out of his shirt. He instructed his servant to wrap it up in a silk kerchief, saying, "You watch—we shall protect and feed this little calf and it will grow up and get fat."[9]

The bishop was obliged to pay all the arrears within three years. Three years passed. In February 1557 Livonian envoys appeared in Moscow without money, but with a request that the tribute be rescinded. Adashev replied that since the master, the archbishop of Riga, and the bishop of Dorpat all broke the treaty, the tsar must collect his debt in person from the master and from all the Livonian land. Ivan refused to see the envoys, and they left in March empty-handed.

In April the tsar ordered Prince Shestunov to start construction of a town and a harbor with landing stages at the mouth of the Narva river below Ivangorod.[10] He also ordered barriers set up in Novgorod, Pskov and Ivangorod so that no one travelled to Livonia with goods for sale, although German merchants visiting the tsar's territory might trade without any interference.

In November a Russian army of forty thousand set out on campaign to the Livonian borders. It was led by Prince Michael Vasilievich Glinsky, the tsaritsa's brother Daniel Romanovich, and other commanders. Tatars, Cheremiss, Mordvinians and Piatigorsk Cherkess[11] all marched alongside the Russian regiments.

The Livonians requested safe conduct for their ambassadors who appeared in December. They begged the tsar to drop the poll tax of one grivna a head and accept instead a lump sum payment of forty-five thousand efimoks (eighteen thousand rubles in Muscovite money) in payment for the previous arrears as well as for present military expenses. Thereafter Dorpat would pay a yearly sum of one thousand gold Hungarian florins.

When the negotiations were concluded the tsar demanded the money, but the legates had none. Ivan lost his patience. He felt that the Livonians were deceiving him just to play for time. He ordered the legates to return and his army to invade Livonia. According to the Livonian chroniclers, the legates set out for Moscow without any money because they relied on the promises of Muscovite merchants then trading with Livonia. The merchants said that if peace were concluded, they would lend the legates money in return for a promissory note. The tsar forbade the merchants on pain of death to loan the money. The legates even suggested that they themselves remain in Moscow as hostages until the money arrived from Livonia, but the tsar did not agree to this either. One Livonian chronicler tells the story that before their departure the legates were invited to the tsar's table and served empty plates.

LIVONIA INVADED

In January 1558 the Russian army invaded Livonia from Pskov. They devastated the countryside for a distance of two hundred versts. They routed Livonian detachments whenever they came out to meet them. The

Theatre of the Livonian War, 1558-1583

Source: G.V. Vernadsky, *The Tsardom of Moscow, 1547-1682*

(A History of Russia, Vol. 5; New Haven: Yale, 1969), p. 97

army lived off the country for a month and then returned with an enormous amount of booty.

Prince Andrei Kurbsky, one of the commanders, later wrote, "The land was rich and its inhabitants proud, but they spurned their Christian faith and abandoned the customs and affairs of their honest forefathers. They descended the wide and easy path to drunkenness and intemperance, to slumber and laziness, to falsehoods and blood-feuds." Even according to the Livonian chroniclers the debauchery in their country at this time reached such a level that the rulers were no longer ashamed but actually proud to set such examples for their subjects.

Khan Shah Ali, the Tatar princes, the boyars and commanders sent a note to the master when they fully withdrew from Livonia. "The tsar has visited a war upon you for your unruliness and perfidy. Your blood has flowed. If you wish to redeem yourselves before the tsar and stop the bloodshed, surrender to the tsar and we shall intercede for you." The master requested safe conduct for his ambassadors, which was granted. The tsar ordered a cease-fire, but the inhabitants of Narva refused to stop fighting. They continued to fire at neighboring Ivangorod, separated from it only by the width of the Narva river. The commanders at Novgorod notified the tsar and sent a message to the inhabitants of Narva, telling them they were breaking the truce. "It is our governor who is firing," they answered, "we cannot stop him."

The commanders received instructions from the tsar to resume hostilities. They opened massive fire from Ivangorod. Narva could not hold out for more than a week and on April 9, the Saturday before Easter, the city officials emerged from Narva and surrendered to the Russian commanders. They begged the tsar to be merciful and accept them as his subjects. They were abandoning the master and the entire Livonian land and no longer supported their governor, who was entirely responsible for the crime. They gave the commanders two of their leading citizens as hostages, and sent deputies to Moscow.

When they appeared at court Adashev asked them the subject of their petition, what favor they were seeking from the tsar. The deputies answered that they decided to ask permission not to forsake the master, but for the rest whatever pleased the tsar. "Despite your truce," Adashev retorted, "you fired at one of the tsar's towns and its population. Then, sensing disaster, you petitioned to leave the master. Now you wish to subject yourselves completely to the tsar's will. The tsar's will is as follows. Turn over the governor who commands your fortress and hand the fortress over to our commanders. The tsar then will allow you to remain in your houses and will not disturb your customs or your trade. The tsar's commanders will rule both the citadel and the city of Narva itself, just as the master and his governor used to rule it. The matter can be settled in no other way."

The deputies agreed and swore allegiance on behalf of the entire district of Narva.When the commanders at Ivangorod sent notice to this effect to Narva, the inhabitants answered that they had not sent deputies to Moscow in order to abandon their master, from whom they received aid. Their master, it turned out, had just sent them reinforcements which, however, did not save Narva. On May 11 the Russians took advantage of a conflagration that broke out in the city. Despite fierce resistance on the part of the inhabitants, the Russians took over the lower town and moved towards the citadel until evening, firing from the cannons in Ivangorod as well as from those captured in the lower town and in Narva proper. Finally the citadel offered to surrender. The commanders could take possession of the fortress with all its artillery if they allowed the governor and his recent reinforcements to leave freely. The commanders agreed. The soldiers and the leading citizens left, though without their possessions. The commoners swore to be subjects of the tsar and his descendants for ever.

The capture of this strategic spot greatly heartened Ivan. He immediately sent an archimandrite and an archpriest from Novgorod with orders to build churches in Narva and cleanse it of the Latin and Lutheran faiths. He rewarded the commanders and the junior boyars. He even granted a special charter to the inhabitants and gave instructions to search out all natives of Narva earlier taken as captives, and send them home.

Even before the capture of Narva some Livonian high ambassadors arrived in Moscow, headed by Theodor Fürstenberg, brother of the master of the Livonian Order. They brought sixty-six thousand thalers as payment of their arrears and for military expenditures. Regarding the tribute from the Dorpat district, they asked the tsar not to insist on it just now since that district was utterly ruined and would not recover for several years. They also pointed out that the tsar's army already had captured in the war far more than the stipulated sum. At the start Ivan was not inclined to consider these conditions, but the Muscovite merchants were unsparing in their gifts to the boyars since they wanted peace with Livonia. Negotiations were just proceeding when news about the capture of Narva arrived.

Adashev explained the situation to the ambassadors. The Livonians had accepted a truce, yet continued to fire for two weeks at Ivangorod with some fatalities. The tsar therefore gave orders to his commanders to take action against Narva and other cities. The Livonians were not to be trusted, since they did not keep their promises. If they seriously wanted peace the master, the archbishop of Riga and the bishop of Dorpat must do as Shah Ali and the khans of Kazan and Astrakhan. They must appear in person before the tsar with tribute from the entire Livonian land. They must bow down before him and henceforth fulfill his every command. The conquered cities must remain with Muscovy.[12]

The ambassadors departed and the war continued. Several towns surrendered without opposition. The commanders constructed Orthodox churches and administered to the inhabitants, both Letts and Germans, an oath of allegiance to the Muscovite tsar. Neuhausen was taken only with great difficulty. The master, Fürstenberg, was not able to help. He dared not face the Russian army in pitched battle since he had at most only eight thousand soldiers. At the capture of Neuhausen he only barely escaped from the Russians to Walk where, pleading old age, he relinquished the office of master. The knight commander of Fellin,[13] Gotthard von Kettler,[14] was chosen to take his place.

The young master was just as powerless as the old to help the order. Popular morale was destroyed. In vain did the noble voice of Thiele, burgomaster of Dorpat, ring out. He said that since they could expect no help from anywhere, they must sacrifice all their wealth to save their native country, stand as one and with their united strength throw the enemy back, not waiting for each place to fall in turn. No one listened, none wanted to sacrifice his own possessions for the common good. Those who earlier cried that they sooner would sacrifice one hundred reichsthalers on a war with Muscovy than one thaler for tribute to the tsar to buy peace, now, when the crucial moment arrived, were unwilling to sacrifice anything, either for peace or for war.

In July 1558 the Russian army under the command of Prince Peter Shuisky laid siege to Dorpat. It was defended by its citizens, including Bishop Hermann Weiland and two thousand[15] German mercenaries from overseas. Most of the nobles[16] abandoned the town during the night when they heard of the enemy's approach. From the start the defenders fought bravely, returning the besiegers' fire, making frequent sorties, as befitted knights, to use Kurbsky's expression, but the besiegers moved closer and closer. The walls began to crumble from the pounding. Many perished. The rest were utterly exhausted by their efforts to defend the city. They sent a plea for help to the master. The messenger returned with the answer that the master censured the behavior of the nobility, praised the courage of the city's bishop and citizens, and hoped they could defend the city. He himself was in no position to oppose such a strong enemy, but he was making every effort to augment his army. The Muscovite commander declared that the tsar would be merciful if the defenders surrendered; if not, he threatened to kill even the tiniest infant.

DORPAT CAPITULATES

The defenders requested a two-day truce to think things over, then they asked for a third day. On the fourth day they declared that they would surrender under the following conditions. (1) The bishop was to receive as his personal residence the Falkenau monastery, two miles from Dorpat, together with all its lands, peasants and revenues. The Latin clergy and churches with all their property were to be left under his jurisdiction. (2) The nobles who wished to remain and accept the authority of the tsar were to be allowed to keep all their lands and peasants, remain under the bishop's jurisdiction, and not be deported to Russia. (3) In matters of religion, the citizens of Dorpat were to be allowed to keep their Augsburg creed[17] without any changes whatever, and not be forced to abjure it. Their churches with all their belongings were to be left intact, and their schools also. (4) The municipal government was to be left as before. (5) Marriages with overseas Germans were to be allowed. (6) All citizens and inhabitants were allowed to leave the city any time within eight days following the city's surrender, with all their belongings. Whatever they could not take with them, they might leave with their friends or in their houses, to be fetched later at a convenient time. (7) If they themselves or their children wished later to move back to Dorpat and live under the authority of the tsar, they were permitted to do so. (8) Soldiers were allowed to leave the city with their possessions and their weapons. (9) Foreign merchants, German and Russian, could not trade directly with one another but only with the citizens of Dorpat. (10) Russian soldiers were not to be billeted in citizens' homes. (11) The tsar promised not to transfer forcibly the citizens or inhabitants from Dorpat to Russia or anywhere else. (12) All crimes, even those against the tsar, were to be judged by the municipal court. (13) The status of burgher could be granted, as before, only by the municipal government, and new citizens would have to swear allegiance to both the tsar and the municipal government. (14) The city government requested that in its judicial proceedings it be allowed to make appeals to the municipal government of Riga.

On July 18 the city's plenipotentiaries set forth, representing the bishop, the aristocracy, the chapter of the Order, the city council and the commune. They presented their conditions for Shuisky to ratify. Shuisky did so, trusting that the tsar would confirm them. The plenipotentiaries requested him not to allow Russian soldiers to invade citizens' homes nor terrorize their wives and children. This was promised, and the promise was observed strictly. The bishop, the soldiers and all those citizens who wished to leave the city with their families did so. They were escorted by a Russian detachment to protect them from any harm. Then Shuisky made his entrance into the city. He gave notice that, on pain of severe punishment, the soldiers were not to offend the inhabitants. He also warned the inhabitants not to sell any strong drink to the soldiers.

According to the testimony of a contemporary German witness, order was preserved. Offenders were subjected to severe punishment. Junior boyars undertook daily tours of inspection in the city to gather up the drunk and disorderly. The inhabitants did not suffer any violence, which helped to alleviate their misfortune. Shuisky declared that his ears and his house were open to anyone who might have a complaint against Russian soldiers. The council and the commune sent him presents of wine, beer and various supplies of food. After a few days Shuisky entertained all the councillors and leading citizens at a great banquet in the castle.

On September 6 the tsar granted the inhabitants of Dorpat a charter. Some of their original conditions were left unchanged while others were changed. For example, a Russian official, termed the *drost,* must be seated on the municipal court in order to look after the interests of Russians. Appeals to the municipal court of Riga were not allowed but could be made instead to the Russian commander of Dorpat. Those matters which the commander was unable to settle would be referred to the tsar. On coins the arms of the city might appear on one side but those of the tsar had to appear on the other. The tsar's arms also had to appear on the town seal. In cases of necessity soldiers could stay in the houses of commoners. Citizens of Dorpat could trade duty-free in Novgorod, Pskov, Ivangorod and Narva, but if they took goods to Kazan, Astrakhan or any other Muscovite city they must pay the same duties as Russian merchants. They could, however, travel freely overseas and trade in all goods. If they did not choose to live in Dorpat, they were free to emigrate; they could even take their possessions if they first paid a tenth of their value to the tsar's treasury.

There were more conditions. Should any inhabitant of Dorpat be judged guilty of a capital crime, his property went to the treasury, which then settled all his debts. Should a criminal go overseas, his property likewise must be turned over to the treasury, to pay off his creditors. Should he escape with all of his movable property, his real estate was confiscated; in that case the treasury paid nothing to creditors, who ought to have been wary of such men. The inhabitants of Dorpat might buy houses and gardens freely in Novgorod, Pskov, Ivangorod, Narva, and in all other Russian districts, and make their residence there. Similarly, residents of Novgorod, Pskov, Ivangorod, Narva and all other Russian districts might buy houses and gardens anywhere in Dorpat.

Such privileges, granted to a subjugated city, demonstrated clearly the tsar's intentions. He was determined to conquer Livonia and keep it for himself forever. He granted lands in the subjugated districts to junior boyars. Prince Shuisky sent a demand to Reval[18] to follow Dorpat's example. If it submitted, the tsar would grant it even more privileges than it exercised before; if not, it would be subjected to the tsar's fury.

Reval did not submit, but several other towns did. By autumn the number of subjugated towns reached twenty. As was customary after the completion of such a brilliant campaign, the commanders stationed garrisons in the subjugated towns and in September returned to Moscow. Master Kettler took advantage of their absence. He gathered together a force of more than ten thousand and lay siege to Ringen, which he captured in an attack that cost him, according to rumors, two thousand casualties.[19] The Russian commanders remaining in Livonia could not gather more than two thousand and were therefore unable to withstand the Livonians' onslaught. They were put to flight when they encountered the master. They were barely able to defeat some isolated detachments of Livonians sent to gather supplies.

The Livonians forced their way through into purely Russian territory. They burned down the trading quarter at Krasny, a Pskov bytown. They even got as far as Sebezh and burned down the St. Nicholas monastery. Yet the master had to be satisfied with the capture of Ringen. He could not lay siege to the more important cities with the small force at his disposal and returned home at the end of October.

During the siege of Ringen the Russians evacuated the male population of Dorpat to Pskov, where they were kept until the master returned to Riga, then allowed to return to their families. According to the witness of a Livonian chronicler, their families did not suffer the slightest harm in their absence. The evacuation is explained by information in the Russian chronicles that the Livonians in Dorpat sent word to the master summoning him to their city, informing him that the Russians left only a few soldiers there. Kettler soon brought down revenge upon himself by his expedition. In January 1559 a large Muscovite force (a hundred and thirty thousand men, according to Livonian sources) invaded Livonia and defeated the Livonians at Tirzen. For a whole month they met no opposition and ravaged the entire land, all the way from the sea on the one side to the Prussian and Lithuanian borders on the other. They did not even spare babes in their mothers' wombs, as the chroniclers put it.

APPEAL TO SWEDEN

The Livonian government turned to Duke John, governor of Finland and son of the Swedish king Gustav.[20] They asked him for a loan of two hundred thousand reichsthalers and an army, and offered him some land in Livonia as security. The young prince was not opposed to negotiation, since he liked the idea of extending his own domain at Livonia's expense, but his old father advised him not to have any part in the matter. It would, he said, necessarily embroil him not only with Muscovy but also with the Holy Roman emperor and the Polish and Danish kings, who all had claims to Livonia.

Furthermore, when ships from Reval descended upon Russian ships in Swedish waters near Björkö and Nyland and killed the crews, King Gustav gave orders to seize all Livonians from Reval living in Vyborg. He dispatched armed ships into the Gulf of Finland in order to protect other Russian merchants. He notified Moscow. "You wrote to us," Ivan replied, "about the transgressions of the citizens of Kolyvan (Reval) and about the remonstrance which you sent them. Your missive was read to us and we learned of your reprimands. You do well to make reprimands in our interests. Your actions have pleased us and we compliment your years of discretion. May you continue to do us good service by being unfriendly to those who would do us harm."

The Livonian Order then sent envoys directly to Gustav in Stockholm with a request for aid. They informed the elderly king that they were expecting strong reinforcements from the emperor, the German princes, and the Polish king. Therefore, they argued, with such collaborators he would have nothing to fear from Moscow. King Gustav answered that they should put no faith in German or Polish aid. The emperor and the German princes at the moment were fighting off the Turks. The Polish king previously promised him help in a war against Muscovy and let him down.

The same thing would happen to the Order. Nevertheless, he bore no malice against them and would intercede with the tsar on Livonia's behalf.

His intercession was not very strong. "We hereby make a presentation to you on behalf of the Livonians," Gustav wrote to Ivan. "It is not done to please them (since they have not treated us very well) but to please the emperor, who wrote to ask us about the matter. Let it be known to you, therefore, that we intend immediately to send an emissary to the Livonians to ask whether it is their intention to fall at your feet and fulfill all your demands. We will let you know what answer we receive from them." "His highness my sovereign," added the Swedish ambassador to Moscow, "stands now well armed, with many ships, and is barring passage to Danes or Germans going to the aid of the Livonians." "Previously we understood," Ivan answered Gustav, "that you were concerned for the Livonians because you yourself thought it was important, but now you write that you do it only for the emperor. We think that you would not have sent to the Livonians suggesting they surrender to us, unless you considered it important."

APPEAL TO DENMARK

The citizens of Reval, not expecting to find disinterested help anywhere, turned directly to the Danish king Christian III,[21] asking him to accept them as subjects, since in times past Reval and Estonia were under Danish rule. Christian III, like Gustav I, was an old man nearing the grave. He declared to Reval's envoys that he could not accept their country into his kingdom since he had not the strength to defend it at such a distance and against such a powerful enemy. He promised only to make representation to Moscow on their behalf. He appointed envoys, but died before he could send them. When the envoys finally arrived in Moscow they appeared on behalf of Christian's successor Frederik II,[22] who requested the tsar in very polite terms not to send his army into Estonia since it belonged to Denmark.

"We shall not deny the king our friendship," Ivan replied. "Just as he desires to preserve a friendly alliance with us, so would we remain in amity and a friendly alliance with him. Six hundred years ago the Russian grand prince Georgy Vladimirovich, called Yaroslav, conquered the Livonian land and founded the city of Yuriev in his own name.[23] He built Russian churches and palaces in Riga and Kolyvan and imposed a tribute on all the Livonians. Afterwards, as a result of certain misfortunes and unbeknownst to our ancestors, the Livonians took two crown princes from the Danish kingdom. Our ancestors visited their wrath upon the Livonians, committed many to fire and sword, and banished the Danish princes from our Livonian land. For this reason King Frederick may not be admitted into our city of Kolyvan."

To the request not to oppress the Livonians, the tsar gave this answer to the envoys. "Because of the actions of our ancestors all Livonians are of old our tributaries. When we succeeded our father to the throne at the age of three, our foreign enemies, taking advantage of our tender years, attacked our lands. The Livonians, realizing our adversity, stopped paying tribute. In Riga they turned over our church of St. Nicholas the Miracle Worker, our barracks and our palace to the Livonian priests and merchants. In Kolyvan the local inhabitants seized the Russian barracks and the palace for themselves. In Yuriev the townsmen demolished the church of St. Nicholas the Miracle Worker and built stables on the site. They took over the Russian streets, palace and warehouses."

Evidently at this time the tsar needed his entire army on his southern borders for action against the Crimeans. Thus he issued a truce to the Danish envoys, addressed to the Livonian rulers. The document stated that, for the sake of King Frederik, the tsar was granting an armistice to the Order from May to November 1559 during which the master either might surrender in Moscow or send his highest dignitaries to the tsar to conclude a lasting peace.

Kettler understood that surrender never achieves an advantageous peace. Seeing no help forthcoming from either Sweden or Denmark, he turned to his third neighbor, which had the strongest motive for coming to his aid in order to prevent Muscovy from gaining strength at Livonia's expense, the king of Poland-Lithuania.

APPEAL TO POLAND-LITHUANIA

In 1545 the elderly Sigismund[24] entrusted the government of Lithuania to his son Sigismund Augustus,[25] who notified Ivan about the change. In 1548 Sigismund the Old died. A period of armistice ensued but without any formal declaration from Lithuania. It was not that the new king was contemplating a war. Indeed, war was the last thing to be feared from Sigismund Augustus, the Lithuanian Sardanapalus.[26]

In 1548 he was already involved in a war: a fight over his wife, Barbara, née Radziwill, whom he married secretly without the knowledge of his father, his mother or the Polish magnates who now were demanding their divorce. Yet where matters concerned his beloved lady, Sigismund Augustus showed great firmness and stood up for Barbara.

At the moment a sovereign of such character ascended the Polish-Lithuanian throne, the young Muscovite grand prince adopted the imperial title of tsar. When he donned the crown of Monomakh[27] he thought of how he might regain Monomakh's patrimony, the Kiev of ancient Rus; but first the Muscovite descendant must accomplish the same deeds for which the Kievan ancestor became famous; namely, he had to protect Russia from the *heathen.*

For this reason Ivan decided to undertake the final subjugation of Kazan, although he knew that war with Kazan meant war with the Crimea. He could not at that moment have wished for a renewal of hostilities with Lithuania. His boyars wrote to the bishop and to the commandant of Wilno, telling them and the other lords of the Lithuanian council to keep the king at peace. As a result of this *peremptory demand,* in January 1549 the high ranking Lithuanian envoys Stanislaw Kiszka, the governor of Vitebsk, and Jan Kamajewski, a Polish marshal, arrived in Moscow.

There was no possibility of a permanent peace. Poland-Lithuania did not want a peace without Smolensk. The envoys were explicit. "Without the return of Smolensk there can be no peace," they said. The boyars answered that "not one shingle from Smolensk will our sovereign give up." If Sigismund Augustus did not want a permanent peace without Smolensk, Ivan did not want one even with Smolensk. "The king has our age-old inheritance," he told the boyars, "Kiev, Volhynia, Polotsk, Vitebsk, and many other Russian cities. His father took the city of Gomel[28] from us during our own minority. Would it be advantageous, then, to conclude a peace with the king? If we conclude a permanent peace now, we should have to swear on the cross never again to seek to regain our patrimonies, and I refuse ever in any way to break an oath on the cross."

The tsar and the boyars resolved not to conclude a permanent peace with the king, for the tsar still wanted to recover his ancient patrimonies. Rather, they should work out an armistice to last long enough to allow the population to recover and to allow themselves to deal with other enemies. Thus if the envoys tried to find out from the boyars whether or not the tsar wanted a permanent peace, they should demand the concession of Gomel, Polotsk and Vitebsk. They should demand Polotsk and Vitebsk as the only way to establish a permanent peace, since if the Russians had to concede Gomel, Smolensk, Sebezh and Zavolochie, it would be impossible even to talk to them of a lasting peace.

THE IMPORTANCE OF BEING CALLED TSAR

They concluded an armistice for five years, but a new difficulty arose in the wording of the document. Ivan wanted to use his new title, the imperial title of tsar.[29] The ambassadors would not agree at all, saying that it was unprecedented. The boyars answered that it was never used before because Ivan was not yet crowned tsar, but recently, following the example of Vladimir Monomakh, he was crowned. This argument failed to convince the envoys, and they insisted on the title's removal.

Ivan discussed the question at length with his boyars. Would it be possible to give in to the envoys and write the document without using the title of tsar? The boyars said that, in view of Muscovy's two present enemies Kazan and Astrakhan, it would be inadvisable just then to insist on the imperial title. The tsar settled the matter as follows. "We shall write the full title in composing our document, which the king will keep under his seal, but in the other document which the king will compose, to be kept by the tsar in Moscow, let them write the title as of old, without the imperial name. We must do it that way because now the Crimean khan is becoming most unfriendly and the Kazan khan likewise. If we are going to quarrel with the king over one word in a title, we shall exhaust ourselves by having to face three enemies. It would be a sin before God were Christian blood to flow for the sake of a name rather than for territory. If by the grace of God things go favorably against the Crimeans and the tsar prevails over Kazan, thereafter we can insist upon the title of tsar, and never again correspond with the king without it."

Meanwhile, regarding the envoys, it was decided to proceed as follows. If they refused to agree to the title, they were to be dismissed but instructed to convey greetings to the king. They were not to be offered handshakes, however, since the envoys' reaction to these words was likely to be hostile. If, after being dismissed, they gave up trying to pursue the matter and asked for leave to return to Lithuania, their Russian escort was to *provoke* them into seeing the boyars again. When they arrived at court the boyars once again were to speak to them firmly about the title, but if they still did not agree it was to be settled as prearranged; that is, the title of tsar would be written only in the one document.

After their dismissal Kiszka and Kamajewski themselves demanded new negotiations. Again they refused to accept the title. They requested a written document stating everything about the establishment of the tsardom, how the ruler was crowned and where he found precedents for the imperial name. The tsar conferred with his boyars and decided not to give them such a document. The envoys merely would try to refute it, but it would be difficult to discuss it verbally. The ambassadors bade their farewells. They were seated in their sleighs when they were called back yet again. Permission was given to write the document to be signed by the king without using the imperial title.

The boyar and lord-in-waiting Mikhail Yakovlevich Morozov[30] later was sent to Lithuania to obtain the king's promise not to break the armistice. He was also to demand the imperial title for Ivan, saying he received that title from his ancestors, namely from Prince Vladimir Monomakh of Kiev. The king ordered that Morozov be told that neither Ivan, nor his father, nor even his grandfather ever used this title. As regards Grand Prince Vladimir Monomakh of Kiev, first, this was in the dim and distant past; second, the Kievan throne was, and would forever remain, in the king's hand. If anyone had the right to call himself tsar of Kiev it was he, the king of Poland, but since this title could not bring him any fame or advantage he did not care to use it. Furthermore all Christian sovereigns were accustomed to call only the Roman-German ruler emperor. Although the king and the Muscovite grand prince were accustomed to calling the Crimean khan and other pagan rulers tsars, this custom stemmed from antiquity. In any event, they were called so only in the Slavic language, not in their own.

We have watched how Ivan declared his intention never to break an oath taken on the cross. In this regard it lay on his conscience that in the armistice documents there was inserted a clause to exchange fugitives. This clause, along with the others, was confirmed by oath, but meanwhile nothing was being done about it. "Lest failure to fulfill this clause weigh upon our souls," the tsar wrote to Sigismund Augustus, "you, our brother, must make a decision. Shall we cut the clause out of our agreement or fulfill it by turning over all fugitives?" The king refused to eliminate the clause, but regarding its fulfillment his answer was vague. He was doing nothing contrary to the armistice agreement.

The king rejected Ivan's new demands on the grounds of antiquity and convention. Morozov reminded the king of another threatening precedent. "If blood is spilt, it shall be on the heads of those who did not wish a Christian peace. There are examples. King Alexander[31] refused to address Ivan III, grandfather of our tsar, as ruler of all Russia, but what did God ordain? King Alexander paid dearly, and still we have the same God."

The king also rejected Ivan's third demand. Morozov requested him to free two captive Muscovite dignitaries, Prince Mikhail Bulgakov-Golitsa[32] and Fedor Obolensky-Ovchina[33] for two thousand rubles. In place of money for their return, the king demanded some towns and districts, namely Chernigov, Mglin, Drokov, Popova Gora, Sebezh, and Zavolochie. Naturally Ivan could not agree.

UNEASY ARMISTICE

The two courts wrangled over various issues during the course of the armistice. In 1550 a Polish envoy by the name of Stanislaw Jedrowski arrived in Moscow. The king instructed him to give Ivan this message. "Our subjects the Jewish merchants of our state have been complaining to us. It seems that from early times under your ancestors, until recently, all our merchants, Christians and Jews, were free to travel with their goods to Moscow and anywhere in the whole country for purposes of trade, but now you forbid the Jews to enter your realm with goods."

"More than once," Ivan answered, "have we written to you about the vile doings of the Jews. They lead our subjects away from Christianity, they bring in poisonous potions, and they do much evil to our subjects. It would be indecent to describe to you, our brother, these things in much detail, such evil doings of theirs have we heard." During Sigismund I's lifetime the Jews from Brest were expelled from Moscow and their goods burned for having brought *mummies* in to sell.

More important for both realms was the following request that Ivan made to the king. "I have sent orders to all the vicegerents along my borders to allow your guards into our lands to keep a watch for Tatar incursions. I have ordered them to protect your guards so that our men cause them no harm. Similarly you should instruct your vicegerents in Kanev and Cherkasy categorically to grant our guards access to your lands. Whenever your vicegerents have news about the Tatars they should not keep ours uninformed."

At one point the king showed Ivan a great courtesy. He freed the old commander Prince Mikhail Bulgakov-Golitsa without ransom and sent him to Moscow. The tsar welcomed the old man affectionately. He hugged him, asked about his health, asked him to sit with him, presented him with a fur robe, and invited him to dinner. Bulgakov-Golitsa excused himself, saying he was exhausted, so the tsar allowed him to go home and sent him dinner from his own table.

Even this gesture did not lead to great goodwill between the two sovereigns. The king's refusal to use the title of tsar continued to irritate Ivan. In the instructions to the envoy Astafiev whom he sent to Lithuania we read, "If they question you as to the reason your sovereign has for calling himself a tsar now when always previously the Muscovite rulers were content to describe themselves as grand princes, answer, 'Our sovereign acceded to the tsardom according to the same ancient custom whereby his ancestor, Grand Prince Vladimir Monomakh, was crowned Russian tsar when he fought with his army against the Greek tsar Constantine Monomachus, who did him obeisance and sent Metropolitan Neophytos of Ephesus to him with gifts of an imperial crown and diadem, and to crown him tsar. Thenceforth he was called Tsar and Grand Prince Vladimir Monomakh. Our present sovereign was crowned tsar of Russia by his spiritual father Metropolitan Makary with that very same crown, since now he is sole ruler of the entire Russian land.'" These explanations did not help. The king did not call Ivan tsar in his documents, and in return Ivan refused to address Sigismund Augustus as king in his answers. The couriers preferred to go empty-handed rather than accept such documents.

Such was the state of affairs before the Kazan expedition. After the conquest of Kazan, in November 1552, an envoy by the name of Jan Gajko arrived in Moscow. He was sent by the bishop of Wilno and two Radziwills—Nicholas the Black and Nicholas the Red,[34] the two most powerful lords in Poland-Lithuania—to talk with Metropolitan Makary and Boyars Prince Ivan Shuisky[35] and Daniel Romanov, the tsaritsa's brother.[36] Gajko was received by Makary and the two boyars in the metropolitan's residence. Three bishops and a number of archimandrites and abbots attended the meeting.

The metropolitan, who remained sitting, asked after the health of those who sent Gajko. The boyars remained standing. When the metropolitan greeted him, the envoy kissed his hand, but when the boyars greeted him he stepped back and made them a low bow. After his reception the envoy dined with the metropolitan. In the document Gajko brought with him, the bishop and the Radziwills wrote to ask the metropolitan and boyars to persuade the tsar to agree to a permanent peace and to send Muscovite envoys to Poland-Lithuania to conclude it. The metropolitan, on the tsar's instructions, told Gajko that his document concerned state and not church affairs. Secular affairs did not concern the metropolitan, so he would leave it to the boyars to answer the bishop and lords. With God's help the metropolitan would continue to counsel and guide the sovereign, Tsar and Grand Prince Ivan and his son, to prevent Christian blood from being spilt.

The boyars gave their answer to the lords. They claimed that all the unfriendliness and lack of communication between the rulers derived from the fact that the king did not acknowledge Ivan's imperial title. The tsar, consequently, did not call Sigismund Augustus king. The boyars composed this message. "We believe that even the oldest members of the council of lords of the Lithuanian grand principality cannot recall our sovereigns ever having sent envoys to deal with them directly. Grand Prince Vasily III never sent his envoys even as far as the border to negotiate with Lithuanian envoys, despite the pleas of the emperor and the Pope. The father of King Sigismund Augustus never secured this even during Ivan's minority. Now that the tsar is of age, and he has conquered his enemies and taken Kazan, we would not dare show him your document, not even his uncles and brothers."

In 1553 the king sent two envoys named Dowojna and Wolowicz. The tsar did not welcome them or invite them to dine. He ordered the credentials they brought returned to them because the imperial title was omitted. The envoys said that before discussing the title they must conclude a permanent peace. To achieve this Ivan must to surrender to the king all lands previously taken from Lithuania. Only after this could discussions commence concerning the title, to which the king anyway could not agree without the concurrence of the emperor and the Pope. The boyars answered that the emperor and the Pope long called the Muscovite rulers tsars, and that until a decision about the title was made there could be no discussions about anything. The envoys departed.

The tsar summoned the boyars and declared, "It behooves us to remain firm about our title. Nonetheless, Kazan is not yet entirely subjugated. It seems to me that, for the sake of our Kazan affairs, we ought to conclude a truce with the king for one or two years, to give us time to secure Kazan, after which we can insist upon our proper title." The boyars answered that the matter of Kazan did indeed require an armistice with Poland-Lithuania. The envoys were brought back and a two-year armistice was concluded.

Up to this point Ivan referred only to Vladimir Monomakh for justification of his adopted imperial title. Now other justifications were unearthed. The Muscovite envoys sent to Poland-Lithuania to ratify the two-year armistice were given the following instructions. "When they ask why the grand prince calls himself tsar, answer that his ancestor Grand Prince Vladimir Sviatoslavich, as soon as he accepted Christianity and baptized the Russian land, was crowned tsar of Russia by the Greek tsar and patriarch. He was addressed as tsar; for proof, he was depicted as a tsar on icons. Then talk about Monomakh. Finally, say that Ivan's conquest of the tsardom of Kazan confirms him as tsar."

Muscovy soon conquered another tsardom, Astrakhan. Ivan sent a declaration about it to the king. The emissary was given, among other things, the following instructions. "When they ask why the Cherkess are your sovereign's servants, answer thus: the Cherkess are ancient servants of our sovereigns because they ran away from Riazan." The king sent one of his aristocrats, a lord named Tishkevich[37] to congratulate Ivan on his conquest of Astrakhan. Tishkevich was a Russian, of the Orthodox faith, and requested permission to receive the metropolitan's blessing. The tsar appointed a day for Tishkevich to visit Makary. Meanwhile he instructed the metropolitan to see that the dining hall was made ready for the envoy's reception. He ordered that everything be put in readiness in Makary's court, that all the higher clergy and archimandrites in Moscow attend the reception, and that everything be done in proper stateliness.

The metropolitan received Tishkevich in regal fashion, just as the tsar customarily received ambassadors. He asked the envoy which rites he followed. When Tishkevich answered that he followed the Greek Orthodox rites, Makary delivered an exhortation of the faith to him and gave him his blessing. Tishkevich told the metropolitan in private that all Christians living along the Lithuanian border who followed the Orthodox rites were distressed by the unfriendliness between the two rulers, for they foresaw bloodshed.

Tishkevich requested the metropolitan to persuade Ivan to send envoys to the king to conclude a permanent peace. He added that he spoke only for himself, for he was told by Lithuanian lords that the Polish lords and the entire Polish council relentlessly urged the king to start a war with the Muscovite ruler, having little concern for Christianity and insisting that the king not send his envoys to Moscow. The Lithuanian lords were dismayed that such a storm had arisen between rulers and bemoaned the fate of Christendom. The metropolitan answered that since Tishkevich was speaking on his own without instructions or letters to this effect it would be impossible to petition the tsar. The hostility between the rulers arose solely over the question of the sovereign's title.

As the truce expired Paul, bishop of Wilno, and the commander Nicholas the Black dispatched a merchant named Dementy from Wilno with a message for the metropolitan and Prince Ivan Shuisky, requesting them to try to extend the truce. Dementy, like Tishkevich, declared that this communication was secret, because the Polish council wanted war. The metropolitan replied that although it was out of his jurisdiction, he nevertheless understood the concern of Wilno's bishop and commander. As a good pastor he would undertake to incline the boyars and tsar towards peace. Ivan was occupied with the Swedish war, so he granted a safe conduct to the Lithuanian envoys. He also provided them with excerpts from documents written by Emperor Maximilian and Sultan Suleiman in which the Muscovite ruler was referred to as tsar.

IVAN BUYS MORE TIME

In 1556 another envoy named Prince Janusz Zbarazski arrived and concluded a truce for a further six years. Nothing was said about the title. Boyar Ivan Vorontsov and Treasurer Fedor Sukin were sent to Poland-Lithuania to ratify the truce. They were ordered to repeat to the king Ivan's claim to the imperial title, with a new twist. Riurik, it was now proven, was a descendant of Caesar Augustus. In conclusion, it was reiterated that "God not only vouchsafed us this title for the Russian realm, but now He also bestows upon us the title of Tsar of the Kazan and Astrakhan realms."

Ivan had no intention of concluding a permanent peace with Poland-Lithuania. He was absolutely determined to retrieve his patrimony of Kiev and other Russian cities. The king's refusal to recognize the imperial title of the Muscovite ruler could only precipitate the rift. Nevertheless the truce was extended, first for the Kazan undertaking, then for the Swedish war. Finally Ivan turned all his attention to Livonia. The Baltic coast became more important for him than the lands around the Dnieper, so war with Poland-Lithuania again was put off indefinitely. Meanwhile action had to be taken against the Crimean khan in order to foil his attacks on the Muscovite borderlands. Successful action against the Crimea could be had only by acting in concert with Poland-Lithuania, which ruled the lower reaches of the Dnieper.

In February 1558 news reached Moscow that a Crimean crown prince had attacked Polish-Lithuanian territory. He attacked many places in Podolia and posed a considerable threat to Polish-Lithuanian land. The tsar summoned his boyars and spoke to them as follows. "We have abandoned all hope of friendship with the Crimean. He used to be the king's ally, but now he has provoked the king seriously too. This is the moment, when they are not at peace, to *goad* the king into a defensive alliance with us against the Crimean." They decided to send Roman Alferiev to the king with a proposal for alliance with Poland-Lithuania against the Crimea.

Alferiev returned from Poland-Lithuania to report that the tsar's message to the king was well received by the entire council of lords. Everyone appeared pleased by his visit and gave him a grand welcome. Some lords nonetheless voiced fears that if the Turkish sultan came to the aid of the Crimean khan, the tsar might not live up to his promises and might instead, once fighting commenced between the Polish-Lithuanians and the Turks, seize some Polish-Lithuanian towns.

Alexis Adashev was sent to negotiate with Tishkevich, the king's ambassador, who asked him the conditions under which Ivan would conclude a permanent peace. Adashev answered frankly that Ivan, with his customary passion, had become involved in Livonian affairs and had a change of heart about Poland-Lithuania. "All previous matters must be set aside," said Adashev, "and an honest arrangement made between the rulers for the deliverance of Christians. If we are going to start out speaking as before, we are going to demand from you Cracow, Kiev, the territory of Volhynia, Podolia, Polotsk, Vitebsk, and all the other Russian cities that we are going to name as necessary parts of the patrimony of our tsar. You for your part are going to demand Smolensk, the principality of Seversk, and Novgorod the Great. Can such a matter be discussed with such unseemly words?" Adashev called for a permanent peace, drawn up along the lines of a truce.

Tishkevich answered that it would be impossible to establish peace in such a manner. Muscovy first must return to Poland-Lithuania all the conquests of Ivan's father and grandfather. "St. John Chrysostom[38] writes in *The Golden Spring,*" said Tishkevich, "how a certain man had in his house a serpent that ate up his wife and children, yet the man still wanted to keep it. The peace that you want resembles that; having eaten the man's wife and children, the serpent will eat the man himself. Your present sovereign, of course, is not like that. We see that he does everything before God. He fulfills the tenets of Christianity and strengthens Christianity throughout his entire realm. Christian churches blossom there as in ancient Jerusalem during the reign of Emperor Constantine, who was equal to the apostles, but our sovereign cannot be at peace without recovering his lost patrimonies. What kind of peace is that—not to return what has been taken?"

"Lords, be reasonable!" Adashev answered. "How can you talk about something that even in your dreams you could not imagine? What do you get if you plant a rotten seed? Futility indeed!"

Tishkevich reiterated the previous position. Without the return of Smolensk there could be no permanent peace. He openly stated the apprehensions of the Polish-Lithuanian lords. "One of the stipulations of a permanent peace would be that we unite against the Crimean. The Crimean is a vassal of the Turk, so the Turk will attack our ruler on behalf of the Crimean. It is feared that your ruler would not help ours, and in the end we would destroy our own homeland." Adashev refuted this fear. He insisted that the tsar would stand united with the king against all enemies, but Tishkevich could not shake off his doubts. "Even if these icons of your sovereign's father and grandfather were not icons but live saints," he said, "what would they have to do with Poland-Lithuania? If you were rid of the Crimean, we would be the first you would attack. A permanent peace is now impossible, but is an honest truce not a peace?" Tishkevich requested that the six-year truce negotiated by Zbarazski be extended for several years, but the tsar refused.

At the conclusion of negotiations the envoys asked Ivan, in the name of the king, to make peace with the Livonians. "The Livonians, our ancient tributaries," Ivan replied, "have destroyed God's churches, defamed the holy icons, and refuse to pay their due. For these actions we have punished them. If they correct themselves before God and assuage our anger with their obeisance, we will forgive them."

The Polish-Lithuanian government admitted openly why it did not want an alliance with Muscovy against the Tatars. Muscovy represented a greater danger to it than the Crimea. Indeed, Muscovite soldiers had sailed down the Dnieper, which never had happened before. Sometimes, in fighting with the Crimeans, they crossed over to the west bank. Muscovite guards were stationed along the Dnieper.

Moscow tried to forestall complaints. The following instructions were issued to an envoy named Ivov, who was sent to the king with a list of offenses committed by Polish-Lithuanians against Muscovite merchants and border dwellers. "If they ask, 'Is it just that your sovereign interferes with the patrimony of our sovereign on the Dnieper and stations his troops on the Dnieper, especially when his men devastate the cossack homelands and rob fishermen?' you are to answer, 'In no way has our sovereign interfered with the king's lands and waters anywhere. Our people do not rob fishermen or devastate the cossack homelands. Our men are stationed on the Dnieper to protect Christians from the Tatars. Furthermore this stationing of troops on the Dnieper defends not only our own, but also all the king's territory. Has even one Tatar appeared across the Dnieper since our men guarded it? You should praise us for such a Christian-spirited defense, but instead the king's cossacks are forever stealing our horses. We are not aware of any official actions between the rulers concerning the Dnieper, such as are described. Besides, since there is nothing written between the rulers about the Dnieper, it has never been established whose side is whose, so it belongs to God! Whoever wishes to live by it may do so. Hitherto we have not heard that the Dnieper lands facing the Crimea belong to the king. It seems to us that the Dnieper is ours since it flows out of our sovereign's land.'"

POLAND-LITHUANIA TO THE RESCUE

It was not the Dnieper that became the primary issue for Poland-Lithuania. Livonian affairs forced Ivan to consider a permanent peace and an alliance with Poland-Lithuania, but his actions there could not lead to a permanent peace. They could only make the disagreement worse.

On September 16, 1559, a treaty was concluded in Wilno between the Livonian government and Sigismund Augustus, according to which the king promised to protect the Order's possessions from Muscovy. In return the archbishop and the master granted him nine districts as security on condition that were the Livonians to redeem them later, they must pay seven hundred thousand Polish guilders. Sigismund Augustus promised above all to send an envoy to Moscow to demand that the tsar not interfere in Livonia since it now enjoyed the protection of the king.

Martin Wolodkow arrived in Moscow in January 1560 bearing the demand. After delivering the king's document, he requested an audience with Adashev. The king's envoy had this to say. "Poles throughout the land want our sovereign to start a war with your sovereign, but the commander of Wilno, Nicholas Radziwill, and the Lithuanian high notary Wolowicz, stand firm in their belief that the king and your ruler should be friendly. The Poles are very critical of Radziwill, accusing him of helping the Russian ruler for the sake of gifts. They are saying that Poland must not give away Livonian land, and that if the king does not support Livonia the Poles will not support the king. They argue strongly against the king's sending an emissary to your ruler. You should explain all this to your ruler so that he might send an emissary to our ruler to reach an understanding about Livonia. If so, Radziwill immediately will take charge of the affair and guide it to a peaceful settlement." Adashev answered that for the tsar to send such an envoy to the king was out of the question since the king invaded a *tributary* Livonian land. If the envoy Wolodkow had his doubts as to whether or not Livonia really was required to pay tribute to the Muscovite tsar, they would show him the signed document containing the promise of the bishop of Dorpat to pay one grivna for each inhabitant.

To the king's order forbidding him to invade Livonia, Ivan sent this answer. "You are perfectly aware that the Livonian land from the time of our ancestors up to the present never belonged to any other government but ours. It rendered us tribute and chose masters and clergymen for its own creed from the government of the Holy Roman empire only according to charters of approval obtained from our ancestors. You write that when you previously chose to invade Livonian territory I did not intervene on its behalf, thus proving that it is not my territory. Know you, that by the will of Almighty God we have ruled the Russian realm, starting from the great Russian ruler Riurik, up to the present day.

"We view the conduct of our ancestors as in a mirror, and we do not wish to write or speak about useless matters. You went and you stood on your own territory, you did not attack the territory that pays us tribute, and you did not cause it any harm, so why should we have written to you about territories which were your own? You did as you wished and occupied them, and if you caused them any injury, that is your affair; but if the master and the entire Livonian land, in contradiction of their oath on the cross and their ratified written agreements, have come to you and destroyed our Russian churches, they cannot prevent fire, sword and destruction from falling upon them until they repent and expiate their misdeeds."

The king sent back his answer. "You call Livonia your own, yet how was it that in your grandfather's time near Moscow there was fierce fighting against Livonians, only ended by a truce? What ruler concludes a truce with his subjects?" All this sarcasm, each striving to prove to the other his right to Livonia, could lead nowhere. The matter could be settled only by force of arms.

ENGLAND AND THE RUSSIA COMPANY

At this time Muscovy considered it necessary to establish communications with Western Europe. To this end the Muscovites were making tremendous efforts to get control of the Baltic shore. At the same time the states of Western Europe were feeling just as strong a desire to move in the opposite direction, to the rich East. This desire resulted in the establishment of commercial relations between Russia and England on the barren shores of the White Sea, which for a long time to come was to serve the Muscovite realm as a substitute for the coveted Baltic shores.

In the mid-sixteenth century English merchants experienced falling demand for their goods in neighboring as well as distant countries. Prices were falling despite the fact that English merchants themselves were taking their goods to foreign ports. At the same time the demand for foreign goods in England was increasing and those prices rising inordinately. The situation forced the leading citizens of London to give it some serious thought. They started to look for ways to remedy their affliction. They settled on the same solution which enriched the Portuguese and the Spanish, namely the discovery of new countries and new trade routes.

They held lengthy consultations with the famous navigator Sebastian Cabot. As a result they decided to send three ships to explore the northern areas of the world and find new markets for the sale of English goods. They formed a company, requiring each member to put in £25. In this way they collected £6,000, purchased three ships, and dispatched them to the northern seas under the command of Hugh Willoughby and Richard Chancellor.[39]

The expedition set out on May 20, 1553. A storm scattered the fleet and only Chancellor on his ship the *Edward Bonaventure* reached Vardö in Norway, where he had arranged to meet Willoughby. After waiting fruitlessly for seven days he decided to proceed. Thanks to the continual daylight prevailing at this time of year in the northern countries, he soon (on August 24) reached a large bay in which he spotted several fishing boats.

The fishermen were frightened by the appearance of the biggest vessel they had ever seen. They tried to run off but were captured and brought before Chancellor, who reassured them with a kindly greeting. After the inhabitants of the district came to visit him, bringing presents of food, the Englishmen learned from them that the country was called Russia, or Muscovy, and was ruled by Tsar Ivan Vasilievich, whose authority extended over a vast territory. The Russians in turn asked the Englishmen where they came from and were told they were sent by King Edward VI. They had various articles from him for the tsar. They were seeking only the Russian tsar's friendship and permission to trade with his nation, from which could arise great advantages for both the Russians and the English.

The local authorities, the elected elders of Kholmogory, wrote to the tsar about the arrival of the foreigners and inquired as to what should be done with them. The tsar replied that they were to invite the Englishmen to come to Moscow to see him. If they did not consent to making such a long and arduous journey, the Englishmen might trade with the Russians there. Chancellor was not afraid of the long and arduous journey and set out for Moscow even before receiving the tsar's answering letter. In vain the elected elders delayed his trip from one day to the next under various pretexts, while waiting for news from Moscow. Chancellor finally declared that if they did not let him go to Moscow he would sail immediately back to his own country.

Chancellor spent thirteen days in Moscow before finally being summoned to appear before the tsar. He observed him seated on his throne with a gold crown on his head, wearing a gold cloak and holding a costly scepter.

The Englishman found a greatness in Ivan's appearance that suited his high position. For his part Chancellor was accorded the ceremonious reception and entertainment reserved for ambassadors. He received a letter from Ivan that constituted a favorable response to that of King Edward, who requested protection from all rulers for Captain Willoughby.

Chancellor set out for England, where he found Edward no longer alive and Queen Mary ruling in his place. In the name of the new queen and her husband Philip of Spain, Chancellor reappeared in Moscow as an ambassador in 1555. He was accompanied by two agents of the company set up to trade with Russia.[40] The tsar received Chancellor and his companions graciously. Following that, they were allowed to begin negotiations with the crown secretary Ivan Viskovaty and the leading merchants of Moscow concerning the future activity of the company.

Negotiations ended with the English receiving the following charter of privileges. (1) The members, agents, and servants of the Company were to have free access everywhere and the right to engage in trade anywhere without hindrance or duties; also the right to leave the country for any other lands. (2) Neither persons nor goods could be detained anywhere, not for any debt or guarantee, unless the English themselves were the chief debtors or guarantors, nor for any crime which the English themselves did not commit. In the event of a crime being committed by an Englishman, the tsar would judge the case himself. (3) The English were to have complete freedom to hire directly workers of any sort and take oaths from them for the exact fulfillment of obligations. In the event that such workers broke those oaths the English had the right to punish and dismiss them and to hire others to replace them. (4) The chief factor in Russia appointed by the Company would rule all resident Englishmen, administering justice and meting out punishments among them. (5) If any of the Englishmen disobeyed the factor the Russians, both officials and private individuals, were obliged to help him bring the offender to justice. (6) Strict and swift settlements were promised to English merchants in their complaints against Russians. (7) If any Englishman were wounded or killed in Russia a swift and thorough investigation was promised, as well as fitting and immediate punishment for the offender as an example to others. Should servants of the English merchants be found guilty of capital or other crimes, the property and goods of their employers could not be expropriated by the treasury. (8) If an Englishman were arrested for debt the police could not put him in prison without first determining whether or not the factor or his deputies would post bond for him; if so, he must be released.

Chancellor set out for England with the Russian envoy, Osip Nepeia.[41] A terrible storm caught them off the Scottish coast. Chancellor was drowned, but Nepeia was saved and eventually reached London where he was received with much honor by the king and queen and by the Russia Company.

Philip and Mary, in gratitude for the privileges granted to the English by the Muscovite state, granted Russian merchants the right to trade freely and without duties, both wholesale and retail, in all parts of their realm. They promised to place them and their property under their own special protection and to assign them suitable warehouses in London and any other English cities they deemed appropriate. If their ships were destroyed by storm, the recovered goods would be kept intact for their owners. Russian merchants would answer in law only to the lord chancellor. Finally, the king and queen consented to the free departure from England to Russia of artists and craftsmen, as a result of which Nepeia took back with him many master-craftsmen, physicians, mining experts and others.

III

THE OPRICHNINA

We shall return to an examination of the outcome of the struggle that began in Livonia. Meanwhile let us turn our attention to the domestic changes in the relations between the tsar and those closest to him at the Muscovite court.

IVAN AND SYLVESTER FALL OUT

Ivan was sensitive and passionate by nature. We have seen what a strong impression the disastrous fire of 1547 in Moscow made on him.[1] It was the strength of his religiosity, noticeable throughout his life, that made him so susceptible to the religious urging of a cleric, the priest Sylvester. Besides, his youth was so filled with hatred for the aristocrats that he was particularly open to anyone not belonging by origin or rank to the aristocracy. Ivan himself admitted that it was precisely that motivation which moved him to place his complete confidence in Alexis Adashev, a man of such humble origins.

Ivan grew accustomed to conferring with and listening to Sylvester on religious and moral issues. He demonstrated an unlimited confidence in the priest. As a result, the tsar could not help conferring with him on political matters too. It was precisely here, quite apart from all else, that they were bound to collide. Sylvester grew accustomed to demanding from Ivan, as from a private individual, the acceptance of his religious and moral counsels. It led him to demand acceptance of his political counsels too, but this occurred at a time when the tsar no longer was willing to sacrifice his political ideas just because he respected Sylvester's dignity. From this arose the resentment Ivan began to feel towards Sylvester's pretensions.

For example, Ivan firmly resolved to subjugate Livonia. This resolution became the constant, ruling aspiration of Ivan's successors, something for which Peter the Great revered Ivan. Yet the boyars, and especially Sylvester, opposed the idea. They advised the tsar to subjugate the Crimea instead of Livonia. We have examined the difficulties inherent in such a plan, the reasons why Ivan rejected it and continued the Livonian war. How did Sylvester act in this instance? He tried to suggest to Ivan that all the later troubles that befell him—his own illness and that of his wife and children—were God's punishment for not following his advice and instead continuing the Livonian war.

There can be no doubt of Sylvester's good intentions. The strictness of his piety in particular accounted for his influence over the devout Ivan. Undoubtedly in opposing the Livonian war he expressed plausible reasons. Instead of warring against weak and harmless Christians, better to fight the infidels who, moreover, continually devastated the borderlands, and so forth. At the same time we can see, as much from Sylvester's famous *Household Manager* [2] as from other sources, that sometimes he was preoccupied with trivialities. Having undertaken to direct the conscience and moral development of the young tsar, he entered into such unnecessary detail as must have exasperated Ivan, whose nature certainly demanded strong guidance, but guidance towards caution and moderation.

IVAN'S ILLNESS AND FRACTIOUS BOYARS

The clashes arising out of a difference of opinion over politics, though disagreeable, might not have mattered. Ivan's confidence in and affection for Sylvester and Adashev doubtless would have remained unshaken had he remained convinced of their utter devotion to himself and his family, but an unfortunate incident caused him to doubt that devotion.

In 1553, shortly after his return from the Kazan campaign, Ivan fell dangerously ill. He was persuaded (no doubt by the tsaritsa's brothers)[3] to draw up a will and to extract oaths of allegiance to his son, the infant Dmitry, from his cousin Prince Vladimir of Staritsa[4] and from the boyars. The appanage prince Vladimir hastened to advance his own claim to the succession ahead of his cousin's son Dmitry. This was contrary to the new pattern of succession by which the Muscovite princes set so much store. Unlike those loyal to Ivan and his family who ranged themselves with Dmitry in this matter, Sylvester took Vladimir's side. Then the lord-in-waiting Fedor Adashev, father of Ivan's other favorite, openly declared himself likewise opposed to Dmitry and for Vladimir.

In order to understand this turn of events we must keep in mind the previous positions of Sylvester and Adashev. They both enjoyed the tsar's unlimited confidence in the choosing of personnel. Even had they not intended to do so, they created at court and throughout the government a numerous and powerful party whose members owed their elevation, their very positions, to the two counsellors and therefore shared their aspirations. It is known, for example, that when Ivan considered the appointment of a particular clerical dignitary he sent the candidate to talk with Sylvester, who discerned his mind and morals. Alexis Adashev exercised the very same influence in filling military and civil positions.

Many dignitaries and princes realized the impossibility of independent action should Ivan turn against them. They too sided with Sylvester and Adashev, though the favorites may have sought them out, since they needed all the support they could muster among members of the highest society. Furthermore the two counsellors undoubtedly recruited supporters among their previous relationships and connections. The chronicler is explicit in describing the long-standing and close relationship between Sylvester and the appanage prince Vladimir Andreevich. Ivan in his personal letters to Andrei Kurbsky named as Sylvester's chief cohort Prince Dmitry Kurliatiev, or Shkurliatiev, whom we have observed previously as one of Prince Andrei Shuisky's accomplices.[5] From there the chronicles go on to list the aristocrats who opposed the boyar Fedor Vorontsov.[6] It is also worth noting that soon after the fires in Moscow, just when Sylvester's influence was particularly strong, Ivan married off his brother Yury to the daughter of Prince Dmitry Paletsky, formerly one of Shuisky's chief accomplices who fell into disfavor.[7]

The influence of Sylvester and his supporters encountered only one obstacle, namely the family closest to the tsar, the Romanovs. This accounts for the hatred Sylvester's party felt for Tsaritsa Anastasia and her

Ascension Church, Kolomenskoe (near Moscow). Built 1532.

Photograph by L.H. Rhinelander, 1976.

brothers. The hatred was mutual. Sylvester's cohorts compared Anastasia to Eudoxia, wife of the Byzantine emperor Arcadius and the tormentress of John Chrysostom,[8] whom they compared to Sylvester. Kurbsky termed the Romanovs slanderers and impious destroyers of the entire Russian tsardom. In the event of the tsar's death Anastasia would become regent for her son during his minority. Naturally she would give her brothers a large voice in government. Sylvester's adherents declared openly that they had no wish to obey the Romanovs, and therefore recognized Vladimir as the legitimate successor to the throne.

Prince Vladimir Vorotynsky and Crown Secretary Ivan Viskovaty tried to persuade the appanage prince not to persist, but to obey the tsar and swear allegiance to his cousin Dmitry. The Staritsa prince was incensed. "You had best not argue with me," he said to Vorotynsky, "or order me about or speak against me." "I pledged my word to my sovereign Tsar and Grand Prince Ivan Vasilievich," Vorotynsky replied, "and to his son Tsarevich Dmitry, to serve them in absolutely every way. My sovereigns ordered me to speak to you. I serve them, my sovereigns, and I do not wish to serve you. I speak to you on their behalf and am prepared to fight with you if need be." Great turmoil, shouting and noise broke out among all the boyars. "If you do not kiss the cross in allegiance to my son Dmitry," said the ailing tsar, "that means that you have another ruler. Since you have kissed the cross repeatedly before me, you may not look for other sovereigns besides us. I hold you to your oaths on the cross and order you to serve my son Dmitry, not the Romanovs. I cannot talk much with you. You are unmindful of your souls. You do not wish to serve us and our children although you seem to have forgotten that you swore on the cross to do so. Whoever does not serve the infant tsar does not serve the adult tsar. If you find us unnecessary, may that lie upon your souls."

Prince Ivan Shuisky objected on this pretext. "We are not allowed to kiss the cross except before the sovereign, but to whom are we to take the oath when the sovereign is no longer here?" Fedor Adashev, lord-in-waiting and father of the tsar's favorite, spoke out more directly. Perhaps he felt it on his conscience more than the others. He was vehement. "We are prepared to take our oaths to you, O tsar, and to your son the tsarevich, Prince Dmitry, but we refuse to serve the Romanovs, Daniel and his brothers. Your son is still in swaddling clothes and therefore the Romanovs, Daniel and his brothers, will rule over us. Yet during your youth we experienced many misfortunes at the hands of the boyars."

Violent discord, noise, and many speeches broke out among the boyars. They entertained no desire to serve an infant but towards evening the

boyars Prince Ivan Fedorovich Mstislavsky, Prince Vladimir Ivanovich
Vorotynsky, Ivan Vasilievich Sheremetev, Mikhail Yakovlevich Morozov, Prince Dmitry Paletsky and Crown Secretary Ivan Mikhailovich
Viskovaty kissed the cross for Dmitry. Three of the Romanovs also kissed
the cross, including Daniel and his cousin Vasily Mikhailovich Zakharin,
but three princes, Peter Shcheniatiev-Patrikeev, Simeon Rostovsky, and
Ivan Turuntay-Pronsky (who originally was a partisan of the Shuiskys and
supported them against Vorontsov but later broke away to join Prince Mikhail Glinsky),[9] went on to say, "Suppose we are ruled by the Romanovs.
Why should we serve the young tsar and let the Romanovs rule us, when
we would rather be subject to the older prince, Vladimir?" A lord-in-
waiting, Saltykov, added that Prince Dmitry Obolensky-Nemogo said to
him while they were walking about the square, "Lord only knows what is
to be done! The boyars tell us to swear allegiance, but they themselves
have not kissed the cross. Anyway, how can we serve a baby over an adult?
Is it for the Romanovs to rule over us?"

The tsar gave orders to prepare a written oath that would secure Vladimir's allegiance. The document is notable for the clause finally abolishing
the right of departure.[10] "I shall not accept serving princes with patrimonies nor your boyars, nor indeed any of your servitors without your
permission." When Vladimir came to see Ivan he was given the document.
The tsar told him to take the oath as it was written, but Vladimir flatly
refused to kiss the cross. "Do you realize," Ivan said to him, "the burden
you place on your soul if you do not kiss the cross? It is not just for my sake
that you must do this ."

Ivan turned to the boyars who kissed the cross and said, "Boyars! I am
sick. This is already beyond me. Since you have kissed the cross to me and
my son Dmitry, act accordingly." The boyars who kissed the cross tried to
convince the others, but they answered with sharp abuse, shouting "You
want to rule, but we would have to serve you, and we refuse!"

Meanwhile Vladimir and his mother gathered their junior boyars and
distributed rewards among them. The loyal boyars tried to tell Vladimir
that he and his mother were behaving indecently, distributing money to
their supporters when the tsar was ill. Vladimir grew extremely angry with
those boyars. They guarded him closely and repeatedly prevented him
from visiting the sick ruler. Sylvester, who had remained silent up to now,
spoke up. He said to the loyal boyars, "Why do you not allow Prince
Vladimir to see the tsar? He wishes the tsar well!" "We gave our oath to
the tsar and his son," the boyars answered, "and in accordance with our
oath we are doing what we can to make their realm stronger." These

incidents marked the start of an antagonism between the loyal boyars and Sylvester's supporters.

The following day Ivan called together all the boyars and told them to swear allegiance to his son, Tsarevich Dmitry. He wished the oath to be administered in the antechamber since he was very ill and administering the oath in his presence would be too tiring for him. He ordered the boyars Princes Mstislavsky, Vorotynsky and their companions to represent him at the oathtaking. "You have given me and my son your word that you will serve us," said he to the loyal boyars, "but the others do not wish to see my son on the throne. If it is God's will that I die, please do not forget you kissed the cross to me and my son. Do not let those boyars take my son away, but flee with him to a foreign land, wherever God shows you the way. As for you Romanovs, why are you so smug? Or are you thinking perhaps that the boyars will spare you? You will be their first victims. You must be willing to die for my son and for his mother. You must not turn my wife over to the disrespectful boyars."

These words sharply reveal that the Romanovs feared greatly the strength of their opposition. The tsar had to remind them that their own fate was bound firmly to that of the tsaritsa and tsarevich. If they gave in to the opposition party's demands and accepted Vladimir as tsar instead of Dmitry, they would be treated without mercy. Ivan's words about the fate of his family were Vladimir made tsar also frightened the boyars, who realized what thoughts were troubling the invalid and where those thoughts would lead should he recover. Frightened by these harsh words, according to the chronicles, the boyars proceeded to the antechamber to kiss the cross.

Turuntay-Pronsky went up to where the cross stood. When he saw Vorotynsky next to it, he could not control himself. To the man who was about to receive his oath he expressed his rancorous feelings. "Your father," he said to Vorotynsky, "and even you yourself were the first to turn traitor after Grand Prince Vasily III died,[11] yet now you are administering the oath to us!" "I may be a traitor," was his rejoinder, "yet I am giving you the cross to kiss so that you may serve our sovereign and his son Tsarevich Dmitry faithfully. You call yourself loyal, but in refusing to kiss the cross for the tsar and his son you refuse to serve him." Turuntay-Pronsky was confused. He could think of no reply but took the oath without saying another word. Prince Kurliatiev and the treasurer Nikita Funikov, pleading illness, took their oaths after everyone else, but rumors circulated that they were in collusion with Vladimir and his mother to put Vladimir on the throne.

Paletsky demonstrated how some of those who swore allegiance intended to fulfill their oaths. Paletsky, along with Mstislavsky and Vorotynsky, were among the first to swear allegiance to Tsarevich Dmitry. Nevertheless he let Vladimir and his mother know that, should they agree to give the appanage territory named in Vasily III's will to his son-in-law, Ivan's younger brother Yury (who because of mental disability was unfit to administer anything) and his wife (Paletsky's daughter) he would not be opposed to Prince Vladimir's elevation to the throne, and was prepared to serve him.

According to one chronicler the boyars forced Vladimir to take the oath, telling him that unless he did so he would not be allowed to leave the palace. Thrice they sent an ultimatum to his mother to convince her to put her seal to the written oath of allegiance. "Many were the abusive words she uttered, and out of those times arose enmity, strife among the boyars, and complete destitution for the tsardom," records the chronicler.

Ivan did recover. We have noted the sentiments he harbored for the boyars as a legacy of the days of his minority. He expressed those sentiments clearly and widely, at every opportunity, such as his speech to the assembly of the higher clerical order, or his speech to the people from the platform on Red Square in Moscow. Ivan himself realized that his dislike for the boyars forced him to rely on Adashev. Kurbsky tells how on the third day after the capture of Kazan Ivan said to Adashev, "Now, thanks to the Almighty, I have some protection from you."

We can understand why the feeling of hostility increased after his illness. A number of things must have struck Ivan with particular force. There was the inaction and unenthusiastic allegiance of Alexis Adashev, the overt opposition of Alexis's father Fedor, Sylvester's apparent championing of Vladimir when he said Vladimir only wished the tsar well, and the suspicious absence of Kurliatiev, the closest friend of Sylvester and Adashev.

Ivan drew Sylvester and Adashev close because of his hostility to and distrust of the aristocrats. They owed him everything and he, naturally, felt he could count on their gratitude. More important, these two did not win his confidence through flattery and complaisance. He not only loved them as willing servants but respected them as men of high moral character. He looked on them more as friends than as servants. One he treated as his own father.

Now these same two men, out of hatred for Ivan's wife and her brothers and anxiety lest they come to power, joined his enemies. Rather than see his son on the throne they turned to an appanage prince, his cousin. Ivan knew very well the fate that awaited his family should Vladimir become tsar. He naturally would regard young Dmitry, son of his older cousin, the son of a tsar, as his most dangerous rival. Everyone knew how the Muscovite princes, Ivan's ancestors, got rid of their dangerous rivals, their princely relatives. Before Vladimir's eyes was the fate of his father as well as of his uncle.[12] Little wonder, then, that Ivan entreated his loyal boyars to flee with his wife and infant to distant lands, or the Romanovs to protect his wife with their lives from the disrespectful boyars. We can understand how Ivan must have felt about the men who wished to lead his family straight to destruction, amongst whom he now saw Sylvester and Adashev!

The chronicler is justified in saying that enmity arose out of those times, but the chronicler does not speak about the direct expression of this enmity, about swift vengeance. Upon the tsar's recovery these dark feelings were concealed deep within the soul. The unexpected and miraculous deliverance from a terrible danger produced different feelings. Joy and thankfulness to God counteracted notions of vengeance. On the other hand the serious problem had to be tackled. What touched one touched all. To harm any of Sylvester or Adashev's supporters meant harming Sylvester and Adashev themselves, and this by reason of their previous standing was difficult, neither was the ground prepared. It was difficult to start a campaign against the leaders of the numerous party surrounding the throne, having none upon whom to rely. Finally, if explicit and decisive measures were to be taken against Sylvester and Adashev, what would the charges be? They themselves had not actually spoken out against Dmitry in favor of Vladimir.

FATEFUL PILGRIMAGE TO ST. CYRIL'S

Ivan made a vow during his illness. If he recovered, he would make a pilgrimage to the St. Cyril monastery near Beloozero. Thus early in the spring of 1553 he set out together with his wife and baby son, but the infant died on the way. One of the most important members of Sylvester's party, Kurbsky, has left us some interesting details about the journey to the St. Cyril monastery. Faces from the reign of Vasily III reappeared on the scene, among them Maxim the Greek and a former monk of the Joseph of Volokolamsk monastery [Vassian Toporkov]. They served to resurrect previous circumstances, the earlier struggle that began in the time of Ivan III and Sophia Paleologa.

Kurbsky's information came from the testimony of the records of the Patrikeev and Riapolovsky families. According to them, Sophia's grandson

[Ivan IV] needed to confer with a former pupil of Joseph of Volokolamsk[13] before commencing a last bloody struggle with the Patrikeevs. It was then that Vassian Patrikeev-Kosoy's friend Maxim the Greek,[14] the victim of Sophia's son [Vasily III], attempted to render one last service to the disciples of Vassian. He tried to dissuade Ivan from making his journey to the St. Cyril monastery in order to keep him from meeting with Joseph's pupil. We can make no judgment as to the veracity of Kurbsky's sources, but the information is valuable to us as an expression of the awareness of contemporaries about the continuing connection between situations and persons.

MAXIM THE GREEK

Maxim the Greek, as we have observed,[15] was transferred from the Volokolamsk monastery to the Otroch monastery in Tver. He received better treatment there but still, as a heretic, was not allowed to partake of the holy sacraments. Prince Peter Ivanovich Shuisky visited Maxim in his straits and conversed with him. It encouraged the outcast to apply to him with a written request. "I do not ask," wrote Maxim, "that I be allowed to go to the pure and holy Mount Athos, the desire of all the Orthodox. I know that such a request would be displeasing to you. I ask only to be allowed to partake in the holy sacraments." Later in this same letter Maxim asked that he be sent Greek books, adding that the request be granted for the peace of Grand Prince Vasily's soul.

The request went unheeded. Maxim addressed the same plea to Metropolitan Makary. Asking for holy communion, Maxim also petitioned to be allowed to return to Mount Athos. Makary granted him permission to attend church and receive communion. In response, Maxim wrote two letters of exculpation in which he tried to clear himself of the accusations of heresy. In the conclusion to the first letter he wrote, "If I am correct, show me mercy and deliver me from my suffering, which I have endured for so many years, so that I may be enabled to pray for the Orthodox autocrat and grand prince Ivan Vasilievich and for all of you. If I am not correct, let me go to Mount Athos." Maxim was not allowed to go to Mount Athos despite the requests of the patriarchs of both Constantinople and Alexandria.

Maxim yearned for Athos, his spiritual homeland. Complaints about his confinement and requests to return home appear practically everywhere in his writings of this period. He wrote this disquisition to the young Tsar Ivan. "The tsar is the living, visual image of the heavenly tsar; and the heavenly tsar is the essence of all that is blessed, all that is just, all that is merciful, the source of all things. The Greek tsars were humbled for their sins because they ravaged the possessions of their subjects.... Most Orthodox tsar! I beseech your most Orthodox and glorious majesty to forgive me for speaking openly how best to strengthen the godliness of your realm and of all your most illustrious dignitaries. I am compelled to do so, partly fearing the fate of the idle slave who hid the golden talent of his lord,[16] and partly in return for the many kindnesses and honors conferred upon me in the course of nine years by my sovereign, your memorable father, Grand Prince and Autocrat of All Russia Vasily Ivanovich. He would have vouchsafed me, sinner that I am, an even greater honor had not certain false brethren slandered my name to him.... Accept my word with your accustomed gentleness. Allow me, your slave and destitute pilgrim, to return to Mount Athos." In another instance he addressed Ivan as follows. "The true tsar and autocrat is he who with justice and righteousness tries to organize the worldly affairs of his subjects, he who tries to overcome the speechless passions and lusts of his soul such as rage and wrongful anger.... Reason does not permit the eyes lecherously to delight in strange beauties nor the ear to bend to indecent songs and envious calumnies...."

Maxim did not speak out against the clergy's practice of owning villages, but he did lash out at clerics who used the church's possessions not for taking care of the poor but for their own pleasure and the enrichment of their families and relatives. Maxim advised the tsar to put a stop to it. In the same disquisition he wrote, "We cannot mislead ourselves into thinking we shall receive help from above just by praying hard." He ended by alluding to his own fate. "A tsar should be hospitable to strangers and take pains to see that everything is well with the foreigners who come to visit him."

The disorders occurring in Ivan's minority induced Maxim to write the following about Vasily. "Travelling along a cruel road full of misfortune, I came upon a woman sitting by the road with her head bowed down to her knees, bitterly moaning and crying." The woman was named Vasilia, implying authority and the tsardom.[17] "Those who rule me," Vasilia told Maxim, "must be the fortress and support for those who live under their care, not their ruination and source of unending troubles." Also in this composition we find the author remarking on his own fate, Maxim praising Melchisidek for his hospitality to strangers.[18]

Such was Maxim's activity under Ivan. Persecution did not move him to change the nature of his activity or, in his own words, to hide the golden talent of his lord. He denounced and preached as much as ever. At the request of Artemy, abbot of the Trinity monastery, Maxim was transferred from Tver to the Trinity-St. Sergius monastery. It was there that Ivan, on his way to Beloozero, found him.

Maxim tried to convince Ivan not to undertake such a long journey, particularly not with his wife and newborn child. "Even though you made a promise to go to the St. Cyril monastery in order to obtain St. Cyril's intercession, such vows are contrary to reason, and here is why. At the time of the siege of Kazan many brave Christian warriors fell. Their widows, orphans, and mothers are left behind, consigned to tears and grief. Would it not be far better for you to reward them, supporting and comforting them in their misfortune by receiving them at your seat of majesty rather than attempt to fulfill your unwise promise. God is omnipresent and omnipotent. He gazes everywhere with an unblinking eye. Furthermore, the saints do not always hear our prayers made at appointed places no matter how praiseworthy our intentions or how much power we exercise. If you will listen to me, you and your wife and child will be healthy and long-lived."

Ivan would not be dissuaded from his purpose. Maxim then told four men close to Ivan—his confessor Andrei, Prince Ivan Mstislavsky, Alexis Adashev and Prince Kurbsky, the author of the story—to relay a message to the tsar. "If you do not heed me and the godly advice I give you, if you ignore the spilled blood of the martyrs slaughtered by the heathen in defence of Christianity, if you scorn the tears of orphans and widows and stubbornly continue on your way, you must know that your son will die on the way."

Did Maxim really say this to Ivan about his journey? The least we can say is that these words were perfectly consistent with the point of view expressed in his writings. However that may have been, they made no impression on Ivan. From the Trinity monastery he travelled to Dmitrov and from there to the Pesnosh monastery where he came upon yet another monastic prisoner.

VASSIAN TOPORKOV

Vassian Toporkov had been a monk in the monastery of Joseph of Volokolamsk. In 1525 Grand Prince Vasily, who was particularly fond of that monastery and Vassian personally, influenced his elevation to the see of

Kolomna. Vassian remained devoted to the tradition of his monastery[19] and an active supporter of Metropolitan Daniel, which earned him the hatred of those who sided with the Patrikeevs and the Kurbskys.[20] In 1542, immediately after the second triumph of the Shuiskys,[21] he was forced to give up his bishopric and retire to the Pesnosh monastery.

Ivan remembered that Vassian was one of his father's favorites. He went to him in his cell and asked, "How shall I rule so as to maintain the obedience of my dignitaries?" "If you wish to be an autocrat," whispered Vassian into the tsar's ear, "do not keep around you any adviser who might be wiser than you, because you must be the best of all. If you act thus you will remain firmly in control of your tsardom and keep everything in your own hands, but if you have about you those wiser than yourself, you must be obedient to them." The tsar kissed Vassian's hand. "Were my father alive," he said, "even he could not have given me more useful advice!" Kurbsky only guessed what Vassian said. In his and his friends' minds that is what a monk from the Volokolamsk monastery, a favorite of Grand Prince Vasily and a cohort of Metropolitan Daniel, ought to have said. Their guess may well have been accurate, but it was still only a guess. What is whispered in the ear is not for others to hear.

Kurbsky claims that everything that went wrong, meaning the changes in Ivan's behavior, sprang from Vassian's devilish syllogism. On the other hand, already we have noted how the chronicler, more dispassionately, perceived the onset of troubles in what occurred during Ivan's illness. Kurbsky saw fit to remain silent about those occurrences, yet the two testimonies can be reconciled. Ivan, alarmed by what took place during his illness, for this very reason might have wished to meet Vassian, his father's supporter and enemy of the magnates. Furthermore he might have listened with particular pleasure to his arguments which of course hardly favored Sylvester's counsellors. However that may have been, even Kurbsky does not imply that Vassian's advice had immediate results, in fact writing that following his meeting with Vassian, Ivan ruled well for yet a few years. On the other hand as early as 1554 we can detect a significant groundswell of discontent.

TREASON OF PRINCE ROSTOVSKY

Among those princes refusing to swear to Dmitry was Prince Simeon Rostovsky. In July 1554 his relative Prince Nikita Rostovsky tried to flee to Lithuania. He was arrested at Toropets and under questioning admitted that the boyar Prince Simeon Rostovsky sent him to Lithuania to tell the king that he, Prince Simeon, was coming over to the king with his brothers and relatives.

Prince Simeon was arrested. He declared that poverty and stupidity made him think of deserting. He ran short of good thoughts and deeds, and his government salary and his inheritance both were insufficient. His servants, when taken in for questioning, admitted that he made contact with the Lithuanian envoy Stanislaw Dowojna, with whom he met twice when he was in Moscow, and whom he told what was being said in the boyar council about peace with Lithuania. He abused the tsar, plotted with Dowojna, and sent one of his men to the king for a guarantee of safe conduct.

Prince Simeon admitted all these charges. He reiterated that he did it all out of stupidity and declared that his relatives, Princes Lobanov and Priimkov, wanted to flee with him. The tsar and the boyars sentenced Rostovsky to be executed for his words and deeds but the metropolitan, together with the archbishops, bishops and archimandrites, managed to have the death penalty commuted. He was exiled to Beloozero and imprisoned there. All his followers were dispersed.

The prince excused himself on the grounds of stupidity. The chroniclers also make no mention of his motives for attempting to leave, but the government itself made the reasons clear in the instructions issued to the envoy sent to Lithuania. "If there are questions about the Prince Simeon Rostovsky affair, say that the tsar made him a boyar to serve his country but he was physically unfit, simple in mind and unqualified for service. He himself wanted the tsar to reward him alongside the fittest, but the tsar refused. His stupidity made him so angry that he said unpleasant things about the tsar and about his country to all visiting foreigners, and it annoyed the tsar. The tsar found him guilty of causing quarrels between the tsar and many countries, and ordered him executed. Should there be questions as to whether many boyars and courtiers wanted to flee with Prince Simeon, ask how could any decent man associate with such a fool. Only his relatives, who were also fools, considered fleeing with him." Ivan complained about Rostovsky in a letter to Kurbsky. He claimed that following the affair Sylvester and all his followers came strongly to the defence of Prince Simeon. They rendered him every assistance, not only him but his whole clan.

WHY WERE SYLVESTER AND ADASHEV DISGRACED?

In 1560 we find Sylvester and Adashev removed from court. As for Sylvester, the sources give as little explanation for his banishment as for his initial appearance at Ivan's side. Kurbsky explained his appearance, although quite unsatisfactorily, but he did speak about the reasons for Sylvester's removal. Later Ivan himself did the same in one of his replies to Kurbsky. It behooves us to examine in detail both testimonies.

When the tsar, says Kurbsky, defended himself with brave commanders from the enemies surrounding him, he repaid these commanders with evil for good. How did it all begin? Like this, says Kurbsky. First of all Ivan banished from his presence the priest Sylvester and Adashev, guilty of no offense against him. The tsar's ears were bent by his scurrilous flatterers, his brothers-in-law and others, privately castigating these two saintly men. Why did they do this? Lest their own iniquities be exposed, lest they be deprived of unrestricted rule over us all, judging unjustly, taking bribes and fostering other wickedness, thereby increasing their ill-gotten gains.

What, continues Kurbsky, were the slanders whispered into his ear? When the tsar's wife died they blamed Sylvester and Adashev and the tsar believed them. Sylvester and Adashev, when they got word of this, according to Kurbsky entreated the tsar both in letters and through the metropolitan to grant them an open confrontation with the slanderers. "We do not shun death if we are guilty," they wrote, "but let there be open judgment before you and before all your council."[22]

What according to Kurbsky did the slanderers plot? They prevented letters from reaching the tsar, they obstructed and threatened the metropolitan. "If you admit these men to your presence," they told the tsar, "they will bewitch you and your children. Furthermore, all your army and your people, who love them more than they love you, will stone you and us. Even if this does not happen, they will bind you and subject you again in servitude to themselves. Thus did these evil men and worthless sorcerers hold you before, as it were in chains, you, the sovereign, so great and glorious and wise, the tsar crowned by God, ordering you what to eat and drink and how to live with your wife, not granting you your own will in anything great or small, allowing you neither to have mercy on your people nor to rule your tsardom! Had they not been with you ... and had they not held you as it were with a bridle, you would have ruled almost all the universe.... Now that you have driven them away, you have indeed seen reason; that is to say, you have come to your senses and opened your eyes, freely supervising all your tsardom.... You alone govern."[23]

The tsar, according to Kurbsky, took this advice to heart. He made favorites of his advisers and listened to their slanders. He armed himself, as though they were enemies, against all innocent decent men who wished him well and would lay down their lives for him. Then what did he do? He convoked an assembly of boyars and clergy and gathered together several of the most crafty monks, such as Misail Sukin,[24] long notorious for his scurrility, a certain Vassian, and others filled with hypocrisy and unscrupulousness. These he seated about him and listened gratefully to their slanders against saintly men. What did they do at this assembly? They read out the crimes of Sylvester and Adashev behind their backs. "The accused," said the metropolitan, "should be brought here so that we may hear how they will answer these charges."[25] All decent men agreed with him, but the flatterers together with the tsar cried out "Such must not be done, for they are notorious evildoers and great sorcerers. They will bewitch the tsar and destroy us if they come!"[26]

SYLVESTER AND ADASHEV SENTENCED

Thus, declares Kurbsky, they were sentenced by default. Sylvester was banished to an island in the Arctic Sea, to the Solovetsk monastery in the land of the Karelian tongue in wild Lapland.[27] Adashev was driven away without trial from the tsar's presence to a newly captured city in Livonia where he was appointed commander, although not for long. When his enemies learned that Providence still looked after him there, for many Livonian towns wished to subject themselves to him on account of his goodness, they piled slander upon slander and led the tsar to order his transfer to Dorpat. There he was placed under arrest, and after two months he fell ill of a fever and died. His calumniators rejoiced to the tsar, saying "Now your traitor has poisoned himself."

Before his banishment, relates Kurbsky, the priest Sylvester observed that the tsar was beginning to do all kinds of ungodly things. He visited him and strongly admonished him no longer to pay attention to flatterers or give them his ear. Then the priest, seeing the tsar already turning his face from him, left for a monastery a hundred miles distant from Moscow where he accepted the tonsure and led the chaste life of a monk. His slanderers, when they heard that the other monks there admired him, in envy and in fear that the tsar, if he heard about it, might call him back to his side, had him arrested and deported from there to the Solovetsk monastery, trumpeting that he was sentenced by an assembly.

So according to Kurbsky's version it would first appear that the matter began with the banishment, which occurred after the alleged poisoning of Tsaritsa Anastasia, but suddenly we learn that Sylvester already was tonsured at the St. Cyril monastery near Beloozero,[28] and that only then did his enemies in envy and fear manufacture the slander, sentenced him by default, and remove him to the Solovetsk monastery. Consequently the matter began not with rumors of poison but earlier.

Sylvester left, says Kurbsky, when he observed that the tsar was turning his face away from him. What made Ivan turn his face away from Sylvester, Kurbsky does not say. He confuses the sequence of events as if on purpose. He places later what must have occurred earlier in order to alter the story and deceive the reader. He tries to satisfy the reader with one explanation when in fact there must have been two. He loses credibility by indicating that either he did not know or he did not wish to mention the reasons for the tsar's displeasure leading to Sylvester's banishment. As for Adashev, Kurbsky says that he was banished from the tsar's presence without trial and was appointed commander of Fellin after Tsaritsa Anastasia's death [in August 1560]. Yet it is known that as early as May 1560 Adashev was sent on campaign in Livonia as third in command of the great regiment.

IVAN'S CHARGES

Let us examine Ivan's version to see if it is more reliable. We notice first of all that although the tsar attempts to justify his cruel behavior, he never denies it. Hence we have reason to rely on his words. Here is what he writes in his letter to Kurbsky, citing Sylvester and Adashev's misdeeds. "Seeing such treachery on the part of the magnates, we raised your chief Alexis Adashev from the dung-heap, making him the equal of the magnates and hoping for honorable service from him. What honors and riches did I not heap upon him and upon his family! .... Afterwards, for the sake of spiritual counsel and the salvation of my soul, I took into my service the priest Sylvester, thinking that he, because of his ministry at the altar of the Lord, would have care for his soul.... He began well and I submitted to his spiritual counsel, but then he became puffed up with power and gathered a group of friends (to form his own party) just like a man of the secular world.... He conspired with Alexis, and they began to hold counsel in secret without our knowledge, deeming us incapable of judgment. Little by little they began to bend to their will all you boyars, taking power from us.... In honor they made you equal to us, and the junior boyars equal to you.... They began to award you patrimonies, towns and villages which by the decree of our grandfather had been taken away from you.... They trampled upon that decree of our grandfather, by which they secured many followers. Then they admitted their confederate Prince Dmitry Kurliatiev into our council ... and thus did they begin to establish their evil counsel.

Not one position did they neglect in which they did not appoint their favorites.... The two of them with Kurlatiev began to decide even matters relating to precedence. They did not report to us about anything, as though we did not exist.... They rejected our good opinions and reasons ... but their own corrupt counsel was considered acceptable.

"Thus it was in foreign affairs. In domestic matters too I was not allowed to do anything my way, whether how long to sleep or what to wear—they determined everything and I was treated like a child. Now, is this 'contrary to reason' that I, having reached a man's estate, did not desire to be treated like a child? Later it also became a habit that I was not allowed to utter a word, even to one of his most insignificant counsellors ... but his advisers could say anything they pleased to me, treating me not as a master or even as a brother but as an inferior being.... Whosoever did listen to us or did as we wished, to him befell persecution and torment. Whosoever annoyed us, to him befell wealth, glory and honor. If I tried to object, how they cried out to me that my soul was being destroyed and the tsardom ruined.... Such afflictions increased, not day by day but hour by hour....

"When with Christ's banner we set out against the godless Kazan tribe ... and when we obtained victory over them and returned home ... what sort of well-wishing did those you call martyrs show us? Like a galley slave they conveyed me with a small number of followers through a godless and faithless land! ....

"Following my return to Moscow ... when I fell ill these 'well-wishers' rose up like drunkards with Sylvester and Adashev and, thinking we were no longer alive, forgot our good deeds and their own souls, for they forgot they had kissed the cross for our father and for us, vowing to seek no other sovereign but our children. Yet they desired to raise to the throne Prince Vladimir, who is far removed from us in the line of succession, and once having enthroned Vladimir, to destroy our own child. If while we were yet alive we enjoyed such well-wishing from our subjects, what would it have been like after us? .... When we recovered ... Sylvester and Adashev did not alter their conduct.... They thought up all sorts of persecutions against our true well-wishers and indulged every whim of Prince Vladimir. They stirred up great hatred against our tsaritsa Anastasia and likened her to all the impious empresses of old. As for our children, they found it difficult to pay them any heed.

"When Prince Rostovsky ... betrayed us and ... we dealt with him leniently ..., Sylvester and you his evil counsellors surrounded him with every protection and helped him with every possible favor—and not only

him, but all his kin. In this manner was it made good for our traitors while
we endured oppression, in which you also partook. You even wanted to
arbitrate between me and Kurliatiev over the Sitsky affair.

"Then began the war with the Livonians. Sylvester together with you
his counsellors attacked us fiercely on this score, claiming that my illness
and that of the tsaritsa and our children were all according to you God's
punishment for not listening to you. How am I to recall that hard journey
… back from Mozhaisk with the ailing tsaritsa Anastasia? Owing to one
single little word was she considered worthless. Prayers, journeys to her-
mitages, gifts and vows to the saints for salvation of the soul and for bodily
health … of this were we deprived by your cunning scheming. As for
human measures such as medicines during sickness, there was never any
mention.

"Remaining in such dire afflictions, unable to bear oppression exceed-
ing human endurance, we investigated the treachery of that dog Alexis
Adashev and all his accomplices, yet we punished them with mercy. We
did not inflict the death penalty on anyone but banished them to various
places. The priest Sylvester, seeing his advisers in disgrace, left of his own
free will. We did not dismiss him in order to disgrace him but because we
did not wish to judge him here. I wish to be judged with him in the world
to come, before the Lamb of God…. I have allowed his son to remain un-
molested to the present day, he is merely debarred from our presence.
Laymen we punished according to their treachery. At first we ordered the
death penalty for no one, only ordered everyone to shun Sylvester and
Adashev and not to have any communication with them. An oath was
demanded from all of them in this regard; but these accomplices, whom
you call martyrs, transgressed our decree and their oath on the cross. Not
only did they not keep away from these traitors, but they helped all the
more, scheming in every way to return them to their former dignity and to
plot all the more fiercely against us. Since their malice proved unquench-
able … the guilty received judgment according to their offenses."

In this version of events we find neither circumlocution nor contradiction. Both the motives and the sequence of events are clear. Ivan himself
explains how his dislike for the magnates caused him to befriend Adashev,
a man of relatively humble origins. For spiritual counsel, for moral
guidance, the priest Sylvester was admitted, a man better qualified than all
others. Submission to Sylvester in all things personal and moral was
complete, but Sylvester got together with Adashev and built around
himself a numerous and powerful party that aimed at Ivan's complete

submission in all things. Ivan's disagreements with Sylvester and his supporters were made out to be disobedience to the word of God, for which
punishment would follow directly. At the time of the tsar's illness Sylvester, Adashev's father and their friends acted in a way which forced
Ivan to doubt their loyalty to him and his family. They aroused or exac-
erbated dislike of the tsaritsa and her brothers and made no secret of their
own dislike.

Ivan also referred to a later clash. It occurred, according to his list of
grievances, on the return from Mozhaisk with the sick tsaritsa. "How am
I to recall the hard journey to the capital from Mozhaisk with our ailing
tsaritsa Anastasia? Owing to one single little word was she considered
worthless." This piece of information is devoid of details and remains as
obscure as the references to the affair of Kurliatiev and Sitsky, or the many
other allusions Ivan made in his correspondence with Kurbsky. The
remark nevertheless points clearly to the conflict between Anastasia and
Sylvester, Adashev and their cohort. "On account of a single little word on
her part did she appear worthless to them; on account of her single little
word they became angry." That clash, evidently, was the final, decisive
event in the struggle. We know the date of Ivan's journey with the sick
tsaritsa: it was in November 1559. By the following spring we find Adashev already in honorable exile among the forces dispatched to Livonia.
Sylvester must have retired at the same time.

It is curious to note here the residuum of Sylvester's moral influence
over Ivan, who represents Adashev as the more guilty. "We investigated
the treachery of that dog Alexis Adashev and all his accomplices."
Sylvester retired voluntarily. Ivan reiterates that he did him no harm, that
he did not want to judge him but would stand with him before the judgment of Christ. Usually unrestrained in abusive expressions, only once
throughout his correspondence with Kurbsky did Ivan allow himself an
abusive expression at Sylvester's expense. Recalling his disagreements
with the priest over advice about political matters, Ivan ventured to call
him an ignoramus.

Worth noting is the information Ivan provides about the various stages
of disgrace. First came banishment of a few and taking of oaths from the
remainder not to communicate with those banished, but the oaths were
not honored, and Sylvester's and Adashev's collaborators attempted to
restore them to their former importance. Then came the punishments.

Actually it is hard to imagine the numerous and powerful party of Sylvester and Adashev remaining dispassionate observers of their own fall,

not attempting to regain their previous positions. That could have been achieved only by restoring Sylvester and Adashev to their former importance.

QUESTIONABLE EVIDENCE

The actual information about the transfer of Adashev from Fellin to Dorpat and Sylvester from the St. Cyril to the Solovetsk monastery, is more reliable than the explanations. The explanations which Kurbsky offers us are particularly dubious. Livonian towns wanting to give themselves up to Adashev, the St. Cyril monks admiring Sylvester, and this causing envy and apprehension among their enemies!

Finally, it is important to note that Ivan, in listing Sylvester's and Adashev's offenses, makes no mention whatever of poisoning Anastasia. This again undermines the credibility of Kurbsky's testimony. According to Kurbsky it was Sylvester's and Adashev's enemies that dreamed up the idea about the tsaritsa having been poisoned, convinced Ivan of it and thus initiated their fall from favor. If Ivan really believed the poisoning, and if this was the crux of the accusations, what kept him from mentioning it in his letter to Kurbsky? Only in his second letter, when he is attempting to refute a reproach for having lost his moral purity, does Ivan address the following question to Kurbsky. "Why did you separate me from my wife? Had you only not taken from me my young wife, there would have been no 'sacrifices to Cronus.' .... Had you not sided with the priest against me, none of this would have happened! It was all your doing."

Thus what is most important to Kurbsky at first receives no mention from Ivan. He mentions something later but only in passing, in the vaguest terms, and only in order somehow to justify himself against the reproaches of immoral behavior. The discrepancy is easy to explain. Ivan felt no need to hide the chief reasons for his actions. It was his fight with Sylvester, Adashev and their comrades for authority that led to their removal. Then it was the attempt among the supporters of Sylvester and Adashev to resurrect their leaders' former primacy that led to further disgraces and punishments. These were exactly the two things Kurbsky wanted to conceal. To do so he confused the sequence of events. What should have come first he placed afterwards, and he presented a disingenuous explanation.

IVAN'S DEPRAVITY

Ivan did not deny the executions. They followed in the wake of the maneuvering on behalf of Sylvester and Adashev, initiated by their supporters.

We are probably correct, therefore, to accept Kurbsky's testimony about the execution of a certain widow, Maria Magdalene, and her five sons. The widow was Polish by birth and converted to Orthodoxy in Moscow. According to Kurbsky she was accused of complicity with Adashev and of witchcraft. Kurbsky extolled her Christian behavior. Then there were the executions of Adashev's relatives, first his brother Daniel with his twelve sons and father-in-law Turov, then the three Satin brothers, whose sister was married to Alexis Adashev, and finally Ivan Shishkin and his wife and children, also Adashev's relatives.

We cannot of course vouch for Kurbsky's information in all its details. We do not know, for example, whether in fact Daniel Adashev was executed together with his twelve sons. Yet on the basis of Ivan's own admissions we are justified in accepting the information supplied by Kurbsky and other contemporaries as an indication of Ivan's moral depravity at the time.

We have watched how the basis for this depravity was laid in his younger years. Later his marriage, the impression produced by the fires, and the influence of Sylvester and Adashev tempered his passions and cleansed his soul, but soon thereafter Ivan became agitated anew by suspicion and anger resulting from the behavior of Sylvester and his cronies at the time of the tsar's illness, from the formation of two opposing parties at court, and from the hatred of Sylvester and his party for Anastasia. Finally Sylvester and Adashev were banished, but their supporters remained and asked to be restored to their former positions. Ivan had to act against them, had to impose punishments. It resurrected the terrifying days of the Shuiskys, Kubenskys and Vorontsovs.

A vacuum formed around Ivan. Those to whom he was accustomed, whom he loved, moreover those he respected disappeared or, worse, grew apart with antagonizing reproaches on their lips and in their eyes. He felt no respect for the new men who took their places. Just then a new blow—Ivan became a widower. He was left completely alone. He stood face to face with his passions, passions that demanded immediate satisfaction, and Ivan's nature prevented him from stopping once his immediate passions were served. Ruled by his impressionable, passionate nature, he shifted from vice to virtue and from virtue to vice with great rapidity.

EXECUTIONS

Two executions present themselves as products of this moral depravity, those of Prince Mikhail Repnin and Prince Dmitry Obolensky-Ovchinin.

Ivan, according to Kurbsky, invited Repnin to a banquet, wishing to befriend him. When the rest of party in festive mood donned masks and began to dance, Repnin with tears in his eyes tried to tell Ivan that such behavior did not befit a Christian tsar. Ivan responded by placing a mask on Repnin, saying "Enjoy yourself, join in the fun!" Whereupon Repnin ripped off his mask and stamped on it. "That I should perform such mindless unbefitting acts," he declared, "I, a boyar." Ivan in a fury drove him away. A few days later he had him killed—in church, beside the altar, during the reading of the gospels. The same night Ivan gave orders to kill Prince Yury Kashin as he entered church for matins. They killed him on the very threshold of the church.[29]

Kurbsky does not give any explanations for this latter killing. We mention these executions because Kurbsky wrote the following in his first letter to the tsar. "Wherefore have you spilled the sacred blood of your commanders in the Lord's churches and stained the thresholds of the churches with their martyr's blood?" Ivan in his answer did not deny the executions, but he did write "We have not spilled any blood in churches.... We have not stained church thresholds with blood."

The young Prince Obolensky-Ovchinin, the nephew of Grand Princess Elena's lover, according to one source[30] was executed for having got angry with the young Fedor Basmanov, Ivan's favorite. "I and my ancestors," he told him, "always have served the sovereign's interests, but you! You serve in vile sodomy." Kurbsky's silence about the reason for Obolensky-Ovchinin's execution renders that source suspect. Kurbsky also contradicts its author regarding the way in which Obolensky-Ovchinin was killed.

MORE BANISHMENTS

The closest to Sylvester and Adashev among the boyars was Prince Dmitry Kurliatiev. He and his wife and daughters were banished to a monastery. Kurbsky says they all were tonsured forcibly, even the infant daughters, and after a few years were strangled.

Prince Mikhail Vorotynsky was banished to Beloozero with his family. Some information has come down to us regarding the fate of these disgraced dignitaries. At the end of 1564 the Vorotynskys' custodians wrote that over the preceding year the exiles were short two fresh beluga sturgeons, two fresh stellate sturgeons, a half pud[31] of grapes, a half pud of raisins, and three buckets of cream. Orders were given to send the missing supplies. Vorotynsky begged to be sent his official perquisites of a bucket of French liqueur, a bucket of Rhine wine, a bucket of brown sugar, two hundred lemons, ten grivenki[32] of peppers, a grivenka of saffron, two grivenki of carnations, a pud of beeswax, two tubes of fruit pastilles and five fresh salmon. The monies the prince received annually amounted to fifty rubles for himself, the princess and their children, and forty-eight rubles twenty-seven altyns for their twelve servants.

SURETY PLEDGES

We do not know of what these were accused, or if they were sentenced to death or merely confinement, but we do know the accusations against certain other dignitaries who fell into disgrace and later were pardoned. In 1561 a written promise not to defect was extracted from Prince Vasily Glinsky for having *committed a misdemeanor*. In 1562 twenty-nine men pledged surety for Prince Ivan Belsky that he would not flee to another realm or appanage principality, whereupon yet another one hundred and twenty had to pledge surety to guarantee the guarantors. Then, in the same year, the same Belsky asked pardon for his crime, that he "violated his oath on the cross and despite the salary from his sovereign committed treason by communicating with King Sigismund Augustus, by receiving a charter of safe conduct for himself from the king, and by desiring to desert his own sovereign." Despite this, the tsar "granted his favor to his slave and pardoned his guilt." In writing Belsky pledged "to serve my sovereign and later his eldest son when he ascends the throne. Whichever of my sovereign's children may reside on appanage principalities, I promise not to transfer my allegiance to them. I further promise never to transfer my allegiance to any appanage prince whomsoever."

The following year, 1563, Belsky and six other boyars had to stand surety for another would-be deserter, Prince Alexander Vorotynsky. As was customary, another fifty-six had to stand surety for these guarantors. The next year, 1564, the boyar Ivan Vasilievich Sheremetev was bound by a similar double guarantee. Kurbsky writes that Ivan tormented Sheremetev to learn where his wealth was hidden. Sheremetev answered that "it has been transferred into heavenly treasure, to Christ through the hands of the poor." Ivan relented and ordered the heavy fetters removed and the man transferred to a less harsh prison. On the same day, it appears, Ivan gave orders to strangle Sheremetev's brother Nikita although the evidence, particularly about the death of Nikita Sheremetev, is questionable. As for the fate of Ivan Sheremetev it is known that, having given his pledge, he remained for a long time in his former location and later accepted tonsure at the St. Cyril monastery at Beloozero. We first saw Sheremetev as an adviser to the Shuiskys and an active participant in the overthrow of Prince Ivan Belsky.[33]

KURBSKY DESERTS TO THE ENEMY

It was difficult for the magnates in Moscow to desert. For the commanders fighting on the borders in Livonia it was far easier. One of the most famous, Prince Andrei Kurbsky, seized the opportunity. He deserted to Lithuania, to King Sigismund Augustus, who welcomed him with honor.

Kurbsky was one of the closest allies of Sylvester and Adashev but according to his own testimony he enjoyed Ivan's particular favor to the end of 1559. The tsar, when he sent Kurbsky to Livonia for the second time, told him, "I must either march myself against the Livonians or send you, my dear friend. Go and serve me faithfully."

Kurbsky's relationship with Ivan was bound to change once Sylvester and Adashev were removed. The execution of their friends and relatives deepened the estrangement. According to some sources it was Kurbsky's unsuccessful battle with the Lithuanians at Nevel that forced him to save himself from Ivan's wrath and desert. In his letter to Ivan, Kurbsky wrote about the reasons for his departure. "What evil and persecution have I not suffered from you! What misfortunes and ills have you not brought upon me? What iniquitous tissues of lies have you not woven against me! I cannot recount the various misfortunes I have received at your hands because of their multitude.... I did not beseech you with humble words, did not plead with tearful sighs, did not petition the church hierarchs for any sort of mercy from you."

Ivan answered, "Why did you sell your soul for the sake of your body? Did you fear death on account of the *false* word of your own friends and spies? .... From these devilish rumors you have filled yourself with rage against me! .... Because of *my one small angry word* you have destroyed ... your soul." Elsewhere Ivan wrote, "Evil and persecution you have not received from me without cause, and misfortunes and ills we have not brought upon you. Whatever minor punishment came to you was for your criminal behavior, for you were in collusion with our traitors. False accusations and treacheries of which you are not guilty I have not imputed to you. For whatever offences you committed we inflicted punishment on you according to your guilt. If you cannot enumerate the disgraces inflicted by us owing to their multitude, then how can all the universe recount your treacheries?" And so forth.

It is evident from this that the matter did not arise just because of one angry word. Kurbsky was actually thrown into disgrace and suffered punishment for his connections with Sylvester and Adashev "because you were in collusion with our traitors." What punishment would a commander who was not yet recalled, who continued to lead armies, likely suffer? Possibly the confiscation of some of his property. In the event it may well have been an *angry word* about the Nevel battle that decided Kurbsky to flee, for from Ivan's words it is evident that Kurbsky's friends informed him of the tsar's anger. They let him know that in this regard his life was in danger.

From the information about Kurbsky's flight we know that he received two letters. One came from King Sigismund Augustus, the other from Senators Nicholas Radziwill, the Lithuanian hetman, and Evstafy Wolowicz, the Lithuanian underchancellor. In these letters the king, the hetman and the underchancellor invited Kurbsky to leave the Muscovite realm and come over to Lithuania. Later Kurbsky also received charters from the king and from Radziwill. The king promised his favor and Radziwill confirmed that he would be given a fitting upkeep. Kurbsky left for Lithuania when he received a charter of safe conduct from the king, and the senators swore that the king would fulfill his promises. Wolan, a noted Lithuanian scholar of the time, in extolling the achievements of his benefactor Hetman Radziwill, counted as one of the most important his success in turning Kurbsky from Lithuania's enemy into a distinguished resident.

Kurbsky was one of the best educated, most widely read men of his time, in this regard not inferior to Ivan. Quite possibly their exceptional devotion to reading, their exceptional bookishness, formerly served as the strongest link between them.

KURBSKY'S FAMOUS CORRESPONDENCE WITH IVAN

Kurbsky had no wish to leave quietly, to part from Ivan in silence. He invited him rather to a literary duel. Ivan, unable by nature to refuse, answered. So began the historically valuable correspondence. Not only does it contain the protagonists' personal and contemporary attitudes, it also speaks of ancestral legends and reveals the historical links between events. Besides his letters to Ivan, Kurbsky also wrote in Lithuania a work dealing with contemporary affairs, justifying and praising his own side and blaming Ivan for everything. This work has the same significance for us as his correspondence with the tsar.

As we saw, the chief dissatisfaction of the princes and the descendants of the early retinue[34] with the new order of things lay in the fact that the Muscovite rulers had ceased their ancient custom of doing nothing without the retinue's advice. They were particularly incensed with Grand Prince Vasily III, whose adviser Bishop Vassian Toporkov gave the very same advice to Vasily's son Ivan IV.

After discussing Toporkov's role in transmitting the practice from grandfather and father to son, Kurbsky writes, "O truly diabolical voice, full of all kinds of evil, pride and forgetfulness! You forgot, O bishop, that which is written in the Second Book of Kings, when David took counsel with his magnates when he desired to count the people of Israel. All the magnates advised him not to count ... but the king did not listen to his counsellors.... Did you forget what misfortune God inflicted as a result of his failure to listen to his counsellors? Almost the whole of Israel perished! ....[35] Did you forget what pride and following the counsel of young men and forsaking that of the old brought to foolish Rehoboam?"[36] Introducing many more examples from Holy Scripture, Kurbsky expresses his notion thus. "If a tsar is honored by his realm but nevertheless cannot receive all of God's gifts, he must seek good and useful counsel not only from his advisers but also from ordinary men, for the gift of the spirit is granted not according to worldly wealth or the strength of the realm, but according to righteousness of the soul. God does not value might and pride, but sincere righteousness as much as anyone of good will can accept." Kurbsky then praises Ivan III for accomplishing his great victories because he listened to his advisers, although in another place he calls Ivan III a wicked tyrant and a destroyer of his relatives and his retinue. Neither Kurbsky nor Ivan paid attention to such contradictions, as is natural with those writing under the influence of passion who jump to every possible position in order to defend their basic premise.

Kurbsky could not forget that he was a descendant of the princes of Yaroslavl and Smolensk. In speaking of the aristocrats fallen victim to Ivan IV and to his father and grandfather, Kurbsky did not neglect to bring in their genealogy. He did not neglect to point out who belonged to the ancient princely aristocracy, descendants of this or that prince. In one of his letters to the tsar he writes, "I do not understand what more you want from us. Not only have you killed by various deaths the clan princes, descendants of the great Vladimir, not only have you confiscated their property, movable and real, which your grandfather and your father did not manage to plunder. I can say ... that we have not denied your most arrogant majesty the tsar our last shirts."

It is evident from these words that in Kurbsky's mind Ivan's actions represented a consummation of the actions of his father and grandfather, a consummation of the struggle of the Muscovite sovereigns with the clan princes. His words make it clear that the descendants of the princes did not like the new title "tsar" appropriated by Ivan, since the title set the Muscovite ruler apart from the other clan princes.

Kurbsky uses the words "Your most arrogant majesty the tsar." Best of all he expresses the feelings that the princely descendants had for the Muscovite rulers. In the following passage, attempting to clear himself of the charges that he took part in the poisoning of Tsaritsa Anastasia and that he considered raising the appanage prince Vladimir to the throne, Kurbsky writes, "Though I be greatly sinful and unworthy, nonetheless I was born of noble parents of the clan of the grand prince of Smolensk, Fedor Rostislavich[37] ... and princes of this clan are not accustomed to eat the flesh of their kin nor drink the blood of their brothers, as with *certain others* long has been the habit. It was Yury of Moscow under the Horde that first dared raise his hand against the saintly Grand Prince Mikhail of Tver.[38] There were others after him. Still fresh in our memory is the fate of the princes of Uglich and the Yaroslavichi,[39] and others of the same blood, how they were wiped out and destroyed in whole families. O hard on the ears and horrible! Torn from their mothers' breasts, they were shut up in gloomy prisons and tormented. What happened to that blessed grandson Dmitry *crowned by God in perpetuity!*[40] Your tsaritsa is a close relative of me,[41] the God-forsaken one.

"You mention your cousin Vladimir as though we wanted him for the throne. I never even thought of that, for he was not worthy. Yet even then I guessed your future attitude towards me, when you forcibly made my cousin marry that cousin of yours, taking her into your family, from time immemorial a bloodthirsty clan."[42]

The Muscovite grand princes in principle had acknowledged the boyars' and free servitors' right of departure.[43] Starting with Ivan III, however, they tried to prevent them from exercising that right by means of sworn pledges and guarantees. Kurbsky's words show us clearly how the princes and descendants of ancient servitors themselves viewed these "accursed" charters in which they were forced to forego their valued right. "You call us traitors," he writes, "but you forced us against our will to kiss the cross *as is your custom.* Should anyone not swear allegiance, he dies a bitter death. My answer to you is that all wise men are agreed that should anyone make a vow against his will, he who has kissed the cross is not at fault but rather he who forced him to do so, even if there is no persecution; and if anyone under fierce persecution does not flee, he is a murderer of himself, acting against the word of the Lord, 'if they persecute you in this city, flee ye to another.'[44] Our Lord God showed an example to His faithful, fleeing not only from death but from the malevolence of the God-destroying Jews."

We have seen how Ivan, embittered against the magnates from his youth, came to put more trust in his crown secretaries, new men devoid of ancient lineage and pretensions. Such officials not only handled clerical and administrative affairs but even served as commanders such as, for example, Vyrodkov and Rzhevsky.[45] The institution was none too pleasing to Kurbsky, as we can see from his remark about crown secretaries. "The grand prince relies much on his scribes, whom he chooses not from among the nobility, not from the nobly born, but mostly from priests' sons or commoners; and this he does out of hatred for his magnates."

We have, besides Kurbsky's statements, the views of two other deserters on the topics of the right of departure and crown secretaries. They are contained in a letter to the vicegerent of Dorpat, Morozov, written by a former musketeer captain Timofey Teterin, together with one Mark Sarygozin. Teterin fell into disgrace and was forced to take monastic tonsure. He escaped from the monastery to Lithuania. Teterin and Sarygozin sent the following answer to the letter of reproach that Morozov sent to the Lithuanian commander Prince Polubensky. "You call us traitors unjustly. We could act like dogs and howl about it but we do not wish to be so foolish. We would indeed be traitors if we forsook our sovereign's salaries without enduring any persecution, but we are guilty only in the sense that we have long left unfulfilled the commandment of Christ and the apostles and did not run from our persecutor, for we have indeed fled from many unbearable tortures and from abuse of the Angelic Form.[46] You, Sire, should fear God more than your persecutor. You have no right to call traitors Orthodox Christians those who unjustly have suffered torment and persecution. Your honored vicegerency in Yuriev [Dorpat] is no better than my cell in Timokhino. For five years you were vicegerent of Smolensk, and now the sovereign has made you vicegerent of Yuriev and its surroundings, but he has taken your wife as hostage and has not yet sent you even a penny of your salary. He ordered you to feed two thousand but has not paid you half a grain. It would not be proper to beg. No one would believe you! The *grand prince* (Teterin refuses to call Ivan tsar) has some new confidants, crown secretaries who give him only half of anything while pocketing large portions for themselves. Your fathers would not have kept their fathers as slaves, but here they are owning land and trading with your heads. For your sins God has taken away your senses. You have stuck out your necks for your women and children and family estates, but you are going to lose your heads. We ask you, Sire, what is it like for women and children whose husbands and fathers have been put to death in various and unjust ways?"

IVAN'S PROUD RESPONSE

Let us now turn to Ivan's answers. First of all he speaks about his right to the autocratic throne as an ancient, unalterable, abiding right. "Our autocracy began with St. Vladimir. We were born to the tsardom and we did not usurp what was not ours." This right of his he contrasted to Kurbsky's obsolete and indeed forsaken claim to the Yaroslavl principality.[47]

Kurbsky's basic argument concerned the tsar's obligation to consult with his boyars. Under Ivan and before him, according to Kurbsky, things were fine whenever he heeded their advice. Whenever he banished his advisers and attempted to rule by himself, everything went wrong. Ivan's basic argument was just the reverse, that the tsar should not be subject to any outside influences whatsoever. "Is that a leprous conscience—to hold my own realm in my own hand and not to let my servants rule? Is that contrary to reason—to refuse to be ruled by one's subjects? Is that illustrious Orthodoxy—to be ordered about by my own slaves?.... The Russian autocrats from the beginning have themselves ruled their entire realms, not the boyars and magnates."

Ivan considered himself as much the defender of the new order of things as the descendant of Muscovite sovereigns. He explained to the descendant of Yaroslavl princes the aim of his rule and the superiority of the new order. Referring to the words of the Apostle Paul, the tsar compared old and new Russia to the Old and New Testaments. "Just as then in place of the cross they had need of circumcision, so do you in place of your sovereign's rule need self-discipline.... Zealously I endeavor to guide people to the truth and to the light in order that they may know the one true God, Who is glorified in the Trinity, and the sovereign given to them by God; and in order that they may cease from internecine strife and a froward life, which things cause kingdoms to crumble.... For if a tsar's subjects do not obey him, never will internecine strife cease.... Or is this sweetness and light— to cease doing good deeds and by means of internecine strife and contumacy create evil?"

Thus did Ivan arrive at the very highest concept of autocratic power, "truth and light for the people through God and the sovereign who is given to them by God." He gave the historical basis for this concept. Internecine strife and the tearing apart of the land ended with the consolidation of united rule and autocracy. The consequence of insubordination was strife. With such an exalted concept of the significance of the tsar, Ivan felt that answering the letter from Kurbsky, a former subject turned traitor, was a weakness unbefitting a tsar, but he was a man of feeling and therefore could not resist answering. A confession of this weakness is evident in the following words. "Hitherto Russian rulers were answerable to no man, but they were free to reward and punish their subjects. They did not litigate with them before any judge. Although it is unfitting to discuss their misdemeanors, we have done so all the same."

To Kurbsky's accusation of cruelty Ivan answers, "We are free to reward our servants and likewise free to punish them." To the charge of having accused his subjects falsely, he answers "Even if my accusations are false, from whom else can you expect the truth? Why should I lie? .... From a desire for the old appanage power of our own subjects? Or their miserable rags? Or that we have a sudden desire to consume them?"

Kurbsky belonged to the priest Sylvester's party and particularly reproached Ivan for sending the priest away. Ivan gives the following answer to that reproach. "Do you consider it pious illustriousness when a kingdom is ruled by an ignorant priest? .... Every kingdom ruled by a priest falls to ruin. What is it you want? What happened to [Byzantine] Greece? Do you counsel us that destruction?"[48]

Kurbsky, defending his opinion about the necessity of counsel, draws on examples from Holy Scripture. Ivan studied this source of examples no less than Kurbsky and he answers his rival, "Remember that God, having led Israel out of slavery, did not appoint a priest to rule the people, nor several governors, but only Moses, whom he placed over them like a tsar. He did not allow him to perform priestly offices but entrusted the task to his brother Aaron, whom he forbade from interfering in secular matters. When Aaron did begin to exercise authority, he led the people away from God.[49] See, how priests should not take over the affairs of tsars. Thus did Dathan and Abiram attempt to seize power and perished—and what destruction did they bring on Israel![50] A fitting fate for you boyars! After this Joshua the son of Nun was judge over Israel when Eleazar was priest.[51] From that time, until Eli the priest, the judges ruled and ... saved Israel. When Eli the priest took upon himself the office of priest and ruler, even though he was just and good, because of the wicked behavior of his sons ... both he and they perished of an evil death and all Israel was conquered ... until the days of King David."

Ivan, having such an exalted notion of his own importance, was greatly hurt by Kurbsky's rude tone of voice. Kurbsky, referring to his own descent from one of the tsar's relatives, contrasted the valiant clan of the Rostislavich princes of Smolensk with the Muscovite princes, "from time immemorial a bloodthirsty clan." In a furious outburst Ivan reminds Kurbsky about his duty to respect the tsar's person with an example from Byzantine history. "You dog, do you not recall how the three patriarchs assembled with a multitude of the clergy against the impious Emperor Theophilus and sent him a many-worded scroll? Yet such blasphemies as yours they did not write, even though Tsar Theophilus was impious."[52]

If Kurbsky in his letters spoke as the descendant of princes who had lost their possessions, Ivan in his letters revealed more than once the strength of the impression produced upon him by the behavior of the magnates during his illness. Justifying his punishment of the magnates, the tsar claimed they were worse than all other traitors in history. He mentioned that Emperor Constantine executed his own son;[53] that Fedor Rostislavich, Kurbsky's ancestor, spilled much blood in Smolensk on Easter Day,[54] and that King David executed those who betrayed him.[55] It followed that the Muscovite boyars should be punished likewise because they, "breaking their sacred vows rejected him who was given to them by God, him who was born to rule in their land, and did as much evil as could be done, in all ways, by word and deed and secret scheme. Why should they be punished any less severely?"

In another place the tsar says, "As in Israel when certain men conspiring with Abimelech, the son of Gideon's concubine, massacred in one day Gideon's seventy lawful sons in order to place Abimelech upon the throne,[56] so did you too, you dogs, in your treacherous manner, wish to destroy the legitimate successors to the tsardom and raise to the throne a distant relative, though lawfully born. Are you thus well-wishing and do you thus lay down your life for me when like Herod you wanted to kill a suckling babe, to extinguish this light by death and to place a stranger upon the throne? Is this how you lay down your life for me and wish me well?"

Kurbsky, the boyar and descendant of Yaroslavl princes, considered that the new order of things and the beginning of evil could be traced to Ivan III. He called the whole clan of Muscovite princes bloodthirsty. Ivan also knew his history. He knew when and how began the struggle that was left to him to carry to such an awesome extreme. If Kurbsky on the one hand termed Ivan "cruelty born of lawlessness and lechery," Ivan on the other hand felt justified in describing Kurbsky as a congenital traitor, born of a generation of vipers.

"You are accustomed," says the tsar, "by the example of your forefathers to practise treachery, just as your grandfather Prince Mikhailo Karamysh,[57] together with Prince Andrei of Uglich[58] plotted treachery against our grandfather Grand Prince Ivan III. Thus too did your father, Prince Mikhailo, together with Grand Prince Dmitry, grandson of Ivan,[59] many a time plot destruction and murder against our father Vasily [III]. Thus too did the grandfathers of your mother, Vasily and Ivan Tuchko,[60] utter many an upbraiding and reproachful word to our grandfather the great sovereign Ivan [III]. Thus too did your grandfather, Mikhailo Tuchkov, at the death of our mother Grand Princess Elena, pronounce many a haughty word concerning her to our crown secretary Elizar Tsypliatev. Since you thus are born of a generation of vipers, therefore do you spew forth such venom."

We have seen how Kurbsky and similar fugitives considered their vows inoperative because they were extracted under duress. In Ivan's view the renegades destroyed not only their own souls but also those of their forefathers when they broke their oaths. "Were you not shamed by your servant Vaska Shibanov?" writes Ivan, referring to him who delivered Kurbsky's letter. "He preserved his honor before the tsar and before all the people, standing at the very gates of death. Because of his oath on the cross he did not renounce you but, praising you, was prepared to die for you. You have not imitated his piety. Because of one angry word from me have you destroyed not only your own soul but the soul of your forefathers, for God placed them in our grandfather's service and they, having given their souls, served unto their death and ordered you, their children, to serve the children and grandchildren of our grandfather."

PSYCHOLOGICAL IMPACT OF KURBSKY'S DEPARTURE

Kurbsky's departure and his correspondence cost Ivan dear. The adherents of the fallen party of Sylvester and Adashev had no desire meekly to suffer the persecution directed at them by the tsar. One of their most important members, previously one of those closest to Ivan, went over to an enemy sovereign. Not only did he reappear as a leader of that sovereign's forces in the war against Moscow but, even worse, he dared to send the tsar a document full of reproaches and cries for revenge. The descendant of Fedor Rostislavich, prince of Smolensk and Yaroslavl, poured out his heart in his document to Ivan. He reproached the tsar for murdering, imprisoning and driving away the *strong of Israel*. He forgot to what he was exposing those of similar origin and position. He now emerged as spokesman for those princes and commanders, those strong of Israel, who had not been executed, imprisoned or driven away but who remained to fill the court of the Muscovite tsar!

Kurbsky, in Ivan's eyes, was no simple deserter who left his homeland simply because he feared personal disgrace. He was the spokesman of an entire party. He reproached Ivan not merely on his own behalf but for many others in whose name he threatened him with celestial vengeance. Ivan knew how large Sylvester and Adashev's party was, how numerous the swarm of people who cherished their ancient right to give advice and, at the first grievance, to secede. He touched that hostile party, that swarm, and lo! It expressed its intentions through one of its chief representatives.

What purpose now did those written oaths and guarantees serve? It yet might be possible to prevent the departure of magnates residing in Moscow and the country's inner districts, but how to restrain those on the borders? Whom could he send to lead the army? Even domestically, if there were already so many embittered, where did safety lie? It is not hard to understand the direction such thoughts must have led a passionate, impressionable, alarmed man. "I have many enemies, I am not safe, so I must take measures to protect myself and my family; in the event of failure, I must prepare my refuge in a different land." Such thoughts came to dominate Ivan's mind.

IVAN ABANDONS MOSCOW

He prepared for battle. First he had to test his opponents' strength. He had to know if the people would come to their defense or abandon them.

On December 3, 1564, a Sunday, the tsar left Moscow with his entire family for the village of Kolomenskoe. There they celebrated the holiday of St. Nicholas the Miracle Worker [December 6]. This departure was unlike previous occasions when he left for pilgrimages or for his various diversions. This time he took along icons and gold crosses studded with precious stones, vessels of gold and silver, clothes, money, his entire treasury. Those boyars, nobles, privy counsellors and chancellery officials ordered to accompany him were told to bring their wives and children. Those courtiers and junior boyars from other cities whom the tsar selected to accompany him were ordered to bring their men, their horses and all their military service equipment.

Bad weather and impassable roads kept him in Kolomenskoe for two weeks. Then when the rivers froze he travelled to the village of Taininskoe, from Taininskoe to the Trinity monastery;[61] and from Trinity to Alexandrov

Village.[62] In Moscow Metropolitan Afanasy, Archbishop Pimen of Novgorod, Archbishop Nikandr of Rostov, the boyars, the lords-in-waiting and all the chancellery officials were bewildered and depressed at this momentous and unprecedented action by the sovereign.

Just one month later, on January 3, 1565, their bewilderment was ended. From his village the tsar sent a list to the metropolitan which spelled out the treacheries of the boyars, the commanders and even the chancellery officials, including the treacheries and damages they perpetrated against the realm before he came of age. The tsar lashed out angrily at his men of God—the archbishops, the bishops, and the whole clergy, at his boyars, his majordomo, and his master of the horse, at the lords-in-waiting, treasurers, crown secretaries, junior boyars and all the chancellery officials. He claimed that after his father died the boyars and all the officials did much harm to the people. They robbed his treasury without any thought of adding to it. Boyars and commanders appropriated parcels of the sovereign's land for themselves or for friends and relatives. They appropriated estates and great patrimonies and awarded themselves government salaries and tax-farming privileges. They amassed great fortunes but showed no concern whatever for protecting the ruler or the realm or indeed the whole of Orthodox Christianity from enemies. Instead they oppressed Christians and themselves evaded service. Whenever the tsar tried to punish boyars or officials or servants, the clergy banded together to protect the boyars and courtiers. The tsar, with great sorrow in his heart, was unable to bear their many perfidies and left his realm. He went to settle somewhere else, wherever God should point the way. To the leading and ordinary merchants and to all the Orthodox Christians of Moscow, the tsar sent another document with orders for it to be read aloud. In it the tsar assured them that his anger and his reproaches were in no way directed at them.

When the letters were read out, sobs and howls broke out among both boyars and commoners. "Alas! Woe! We have sinned before God. We have angered our sovereign by our many sins before him. We have turned his great mercy into anger and rage! To whom can we turn now? Who will care for us? Who will save us from the onslaughts of foreigners? How can sheep be without a pastor? When wolves see sheep without a pastor, they devour them!" They entreated the metropolitan to take the remaining clergy and mollify the tsar, begging him not to abandon his realm. He could govern and rule them as he pleased. As for the evildoers in the government who were guilty of treason, let the Lord show the tsar His almighty will as to who should live and who should die. "We shall all follow you, our prelate, to bow our heads low before the sovereign and weep." The leading merchants and all the townsfolk spoke. "If only the tsar had not left his realm and his people to the ravages of wolves. If only he had saved them, especially from the hands of the powerful. We will not protect the evildoers and traitors within the government. We will exterminate them." The clergy and boyars appeared at Alexandrov Village. They revealed to Ivan their general decision and earnest supplication. He might rule as he wished, if only he would take the government once again into his own hands.

OPRICHNINA SET UP

Ivan granted their supplication on certain conditions. He must be allowed to punish all who were guilty of treachery and disobedience, to execute them and seize their possessions for the treasury. He also must be allowed to set up for himself an *oprichnina* [63] as his own separate domain. It would have its own court and establish its own particular rules. Its boyars, lords-in-waiting, majordomos, treasurers, crown secretaries, gentry, junior boyars, court table attendants, aides, petty officials and residents—all would be appointed specially. For food, drink and fodder, the oprichnina palaces would have especially appointed stewards, brewers, chefs, cooks, bakers, all sorts of craftsmen, grooms, huntsmen and all the servants required for the necessary jobs. Finally, the tsar must be allowed to appoint a special corps of musketeers for himself.

Ivan also designated the towns and districts to supply the sovereign's upkeep, from which would be paid the salaries of the boyars, the gentry and all court servitors appointed to the oprichnina. If these receipts were insufficient he would take over other towns and districts. Counting the princes, gentry and junior boyars, both at the court and in the towns, the oprichnina would comprise altogether a thousand men. Estates would be granted to them in those townships taken over by the oprichnina. All who owned estates in those areas, whether by inheritance or in return for service, if they were not chosen for the oprichnina would be removed and given lands elsewhere. Even in Moscow itself certain streets and suburbs were included in the oprichnina. Only those boyars, gentry, and officials selected to serve in the oprichnina could live there. The previous inhabitants would be transferred to other streets.

As for the rest of the Muscovite realm, to be called the zemshchina, all matters relating to the army, the law courts, and the government were turned over to those boyars ordered to remain outside the oprichnina. Ivan ordered Princes Ivan Dmitrevich Belsky, Ivan Fedorovich Mstislavsky, and all the rest there, including grooms, majordomos, treasurers, crown secretaries and other officials, to carry on according to custom and to rule as of old, referring the most important matters to the boyars. If there were questions of conscription or other extremely important matters involving the zemshchina, the boyars should bring them to the tsar.

For his own support the tsar demanded a hundred thousand rubles from the tax office. If any boyars, commanders, or officials were disgraced or sentenced to death for high treason, their properties would revert to the treasury. In all these things the clergy, the boyars, and all the officials had no choice but to agree to the tsar's demands.

These changes resulted in the execution of Kurbsky's colleagues, those who had plotted mischief with him against the tsar or his wife and children. These included Prince Alexander Borisovich Gorbaty-Shuisky with his young son Peter and his relatives, the two Khovrins, Prince Ivan Sukhoy-Kashin, Prince Dmitry Shevyrev, and Prince Peter Gorensky, caught while attempting to escape. We know nothing about other victims, apart from ill-defined charges of association with Kurbsky. We do not know of what Princes Ivan Kurakin and Dmitry Obolensky-Nemogo were found guilty, only that the latter was accused of having been involved with the attempt to place Prince Vladimir on the throne.

Some boyars and junior boyars lost their possessions, others were banished to Kazan. The boyar Ivan Petrovich Yakovlev begged forgiveness for his offences and was pardoned in return for a surety. Prince Vasily Semeonovich Obolensky-Serebriany and his son were restored to favor, as were Lev Matveevich Saltykov and his two sons. In the following year, 1566, Prince Mikhail Ivanovich Vorotynsky begged forgiveness for his offences. In return for double surety he was forgiven and allowed to return from his exile in Beloozero. In the same year Prince Ivan Petrovich Okhliabinin and Boyar Ovchin-Pleshcheev also were pardoned; the former promised never to leave or accept tonsure as a monk.

We have an idea what all this cost Ivan. As a result of Kurbsky's departure and subsequent correspondence, the withdrawal to Alexandrov Village, the anxious awaiting of the results of his documents sent to Moscow, Ivan was barely recognizable when he returned to Moscow. He went completely bald; even his beard fell out.

The course of action that Ivan thought up, or at least adopted—according to some sources, the architects of the oprichnina were Vasily Yuriev, Alexis Basmanov and some others—also corresponded to the shattered condition of his spirit. Frightened by Kurbsky's departure and by the challenge thrown at him in the name of all his colleagues, Ivan came to suspect every one of his boyars. He jumped at the means to free himself from them, free himself from the necessity of continual daily association with them. It was obviously impossible to disgrace them all without evidence and without specific charges, or to imprison or exile them all, nor could he take away their duties or their ranks or their voices in the council, replacing them with new men of no standing, *youngsters* as they were termed. Ivan had been unable to advance his former favorite Alexis Adashev beyond lord-in-waiting and equally unable to push his new favorites any further. If he was prevented from removing all the old aristocracy from his company, one means yet remained, namely that *he* could leave *them,* which is exactly what he did.

The boyar council was given authority in practically all matters. Only matters of raising conscripts and of extreme importance had to be referred to the tsar. Old magnates were left with their old duties at court. Ivan did not wish to see them around him and therefore demanded a special court for himself with special boyars, lords-in-waiting, and so forth. Even so, Ivan could not be completely free of the old aristocracy if he had to live in the old palace, so he demanded a new palace. He could not avoid meeting old aristocrats during holy day excursions and the like if he remained in Moscow, so he quit Moscow and moved to Alexandrov Village.

It is easy to imagine the disruption created by removing the head of the realm from the realm, "the land" as it was called. In vain did Ivan assure the leading merchants and ordinary townsmen of Moscow to remain at ease, that he held nothing against them. The leading merchants and common folk understood clearly that their superiors, those to whom they had to refer all matters, were the same old magnates. At the same time they heard the tsar solemnly labelling these magnates ill-wishers and traitors, saw him removing himself from them to surround himself with a crowd of new people. They saw that the supreme authority rejected its own practical apparatus through which it had to act, calling that apparatus unsatisfactory for itself yet satisfactory for the realm. If the tsar left that apparatus in its previous situation yet severed the connection between the sovereign and the realm, calling the administrators of the land his enemies, it followed necessarily that he also alienated the land itself. Despite reassurances of good will, hostility to the land itself was bound to emerge sooner or later, either directly through the person of the tsar or through his new retinue, the oprichniks.[64]

The oprichnina was a product of hostility. It goes without saying that it could not have a beneficial, soothing influence. The tsar set up the oprichnina because he suspected the aristocrats of being his enemies. He wanted to surround himself with those completely devoted to him. In order to please the tsar, an oprichnik had to demonstrate his hostility to the old magnates. In order to preserve his importance and his privileges, an oprichnik had to abet and inflame the tsar's hostility to the old magnates.

It did not stop there. Was there any way to guarantee that among such a collection of people most, if not all, would not abuse their privileged position of immunity? Who among the governors of the zemshchina, if he came under suspicion or fell into disgrace, could possibly expect that his case would stand up in court against an oprichnik? Who among the suspected or fallen could possibly consider lodging a complaint against one of the tsar's close, trusty men, who could always convince a suspicious, irascible tsar that the complaint was spurious, that it was merely the result of spite against the oprichnik, that it demonstrated a desire to revolt against the tsar—a tsar who could rely only on his devoted oprichniks to protect him from his enemies?

Not all oprichniks were equally close to the tsar or enjoyed his un-divided trust, yet each of them, from highest to lowest, considered it his primary duty to stand up for his fellows. This was true for the entire crowd, the entire retinue of favorites! It is hardly surprising, then, that we find such outspoken complaints about the oprichnina from contemporaries. The oprichniks, for their part, hardly remained voiceless. They denounced boyars for breaking oaths sworn on the cross, or for growing rich and idle on the tears and blood of the towns and districts. They decried the lack of justice in the Muscovite realm. They complained that some worked their way into the tsar's favor only because they were magnates, not by virtue of their military service or any other sort of expertise; such people, they declared, were sorcerers and heretics and deserved to suffer cruel punishments. They advised the tsar to take the income from the entire tsardom for his own treasury, to pay his warriors from it and gladden their hearts, to draw them closer to him and to trust them in all things.

Muscovy's enemies tried to use the dissatisfaction produced by the oprichnina. Unsuccessful attempts to do so led to new executions and further consolidation of the oprichnina. A certain Kozlov, a native of one of the Moscow districts, moved to Lithuania and married there. Sigismund Augustus sent him as a courier to Ivan. He reported back to the king that he had managed to incline all the Muscovite magnates to betrayal. He was sent again to Moscow, this time entrusted with documents from the king and the hetman Jan Chodkiewicz for Princes Belsky, Mstislavsky and Vorotynsky, as well as the boyar Ivan Cheliadnin, master of the horse, inviting them to come over to the king's side.

The documents were seized. Ivan ordered the named boyars to write—
rather, he himself wrote for them—antagonistic replies, which were sent
back with Kozlov. Somehow Belsky, Mstislavsky and Vorotynsky managed to avoid disaster. The elderly Cheliadnin was not so fortunate. In
1568 he was executed together with his wife and his collaborators, Princes
Ivan Kurakin-Bulgakov and Dmitry Riapolovsky, three princes from
Rostov, Princes Peter Shcheniatiev-Patrikeev and Ivan Turuntay-Pronsky,
and the treasurer Tiutin. Cheliadnin as we saw had taken part in stirring up
the people against the Glinskys following the great fire.[65] The Rostov
princes incurred Ivan's wrath by attempting to leave for Lithuania together
with their entire families following the tsar's illness. During that illness
in 1568 Shcheniatiev-Patrikeev and Turuntay-Pronsky supported Prince
Vladimir.

METROPOLITAN PHILIP

The Russian church energetically supported the Russian autocracy until
the Muscovite autocrats entered their final struggle with the remnants of
antiquity, the cluster of princes and retainers. Then the church took upon
itself a sacred duty, to restrain violence amid the struggle, to prevent the
triumphant principle from being used for evil ends. The church was as
zealous as ever in helping the tsar crush the pretensions of princes and
retainers, yet it recognized those very aristocrats as members of the fold
and volunteered to protect them. It became an established tradition for the
metropolitan and the clergy in general to intercede for the disgraced and
even to attempt to place them under their protection.

Metropolitan Makary, although he had attained his position as a result
of the triumph of the Shuiskys, at the request of the young Ivan had petitioned the Shuiskys on behalf of Fedor Vorontsov.[66] He suffered much
abuse for his efforts, yet outlived the Shuiskys, outlived the disturbances
following their demise, and managed to avoid a collision with Sylvester.
If we can believe Kurbsky, he even stood up for Sylvester during his disgrace. He witnessed the revival of executions and died in 1563. He tried
several times to quit the metropolitanate but was kept on by the tsar and by
the church hierarchy.

Makary's successor was Afanasy, a monk from the Miracles monastery
and formerly the tsar's confessor. Having just set up his oprichnina and
claiming an unfettered right to execute evildoers, Ivan accused the clergy
of protecting the guilty and demanded they renounce their custom of intercession. Afanasy, who witnessed the creation of the oprichnina, nevertheless was granted permission to mourn for the boyar Yakovlev and for

Prince Vorotynsky. In 1566 he quit the metropolitanate for reasons of ill-health.

Archbishop German of Kazan[67] succeeded Afanasy as metropolitan. His arguments, according to Kurbsky, displeased Ivan's favorites. German was dismissed and in 1566 the abbot of the Solovetsk monastery, Philip, son of the boyar Stepan Kolychev, was summoned to replace him.[68] Philip agreed to become metropolitan only on condition that the oprichnina be abolished. Ivan became angry. In the end Philip gave in. He accepted that his duty lay not in opposing the tsar's will but in soothing his anger at every possible opportunity. Philip promised in writing "not to intervene in the tsar's oprichnina or his domestic life and after his installation not to leave the metropolitanate on account of the oprichnina or the tsar's domestic life."

Philip may have agreed not to interfere in the oprichnina but he did not renounce the right to intercede. When executions followed the Kozlov affair and the oprichnina began to create an uproar, the magnates and the people implored the metropolitan to get involved. He knew the people were accustomed to seeing an intercessor in the metropolitan and had no wish to remain silent.

In vain did Ivan try to avoid a meeting with the metropolitan, fearing his intercessions. Sooner or later they had to meet in church, and it was there that the terrible scenes of exorcism took place. "Just keep quiet, that is all I ask of you, Holy Father, keep quiet!" said Ivan, trying to control the angry spirit that ruled him, "Keep quiet and give us your blessing!" "Our silence," Philip replied, "would burden your soul with sins and bring death."

Ivan My supporters have risen against me and seek to do me harm. Our counsels are none of your business.

Philip I am the pastor of Christ's flock!

Ivan Philip! Do not contradict our sovereignty, lest my anger strike you down! Better that you relinquish the metropolitanate.

Philip I did not ask for this position, did not seek it through others, did not try to purchase it through bribery. Why did you deprive me of my peace?

Ivan left the church in deepest gloom which frightened his oprichniks. They decided to destroy Philip. They found collaborators among the clergy, among the hierarchs in Novgorod, Suzdal, and Riazan, in the archpriest of the Annunciation cathedral and in the tsar's confessor.

The confessor denounced Philip to Ivan, openly and in private. The oprichniks sent to the Solovetsk monastery and summoned Paisy, Philip's

Archangel Michael tower, Solovetsky monastery.
Built 1582–1594. Architect: Trifon.
Source: V.V. Kostochkin, *Drevnerusskie goroda* (Moscow, 1972).

successor as father superior. It was his denunciations that became the basis of accusations entered in the ecclesiastical court. Philip had no defenders, for everyone held his tongue.

On November 8, 1568 the oprichniks dragged Philip in disgrace out of the Dormition cathedral. The congregation ran tearfully after him. The Otroch monastery in Tver was designated as the place of Philip's exile. In 1569 Ivan, passing through Tver on his expedition against Novgorod,[69] sent his most trusted oprichnik, Grigory Maliuta-Skuratov,[70] to ask Philip for his blessing. Philip refused, saying that he blessed only good men and good works. The oprichnik strangled him. Thus fell unconquered a great shepherd of the Russian church, a martyr to the sacred custom of intercession. His elected replacement was Cyril, archimandrite of the Trinity monastery.

DEATH OF PRINCE VLADIMIR

Many perished for their support of the tsar's cousin Prince Vladimir. His turn came in 1569. We have mentioned the written oath extracted from him in 1553. In the following year, 1554, another tsarevich, Ivan Ivanovich, was born. The tsar extracted yet another written promise from his cousin to serve this tsarevich in the event of the tsar's death. The extent of Ivan's mistrust for his cousin since his illness is demonstrated by the following section of Vladimir's promise. "I agree to live in Moscow at my own court and have with me at my court altogether ... (the number is erased) servitors and no more; all my servitors I shall keep on my own estate."

Ivan restricted Vladimir's conduct still further. Should a domestic quarrel ever break out between Ivan Ivanovich and any of his brothers, Vladimir had to promise "not to befriend or communicate with any other of your sons who might become hostile to Tsarevich Ivan. Should your son Tsarevich Ivan send me against such a brother, I agree to go against him and carry out whatever is required on the orders of your son, Tsarevich Ivan, without any scheming. I agree never to accept into my service any of your son's serving princes with their patrimonies, nor any of his boyars, chancellors, junior boyars, or any other of his followers whatsoever. Should any of your boyars, chancellors or others insult me during your reign, Tsar Ivan, I agree not to try to avenge any such insults. I agree to take no action in any matter without consulting those of your son's boyars mentioned in your testament, and I agree to make no decisions about any matter without first speaking to your son and his mother.

"Should my mother Princess Evfrosinia attempt to turn me against your son Tsarevich Ivan or against his mother, I agree not to listen to my mother but to inform your son Tsarevich Ivan and his mother of her words, truthfully and without scheming. Should I ever find out that my mother is attempting on her own without informing me to work some sort of evil against your son Tsarevich Ivan, against his mother, or against his boyars and chancellors as named in your testament, I agree to inform your son and his mother about it truthfully and without scheming; this I shall not conceal in any way, according to my oath upon the cross. Should God take away your son Tsarevich Ivan and should you have no other children remaining, I agree that your authority be transferred entirely to your tsaritsa, Grand Princess Anastasia, according to your testament and by my oath upon the cross." Only one month later Ivan extracted a third written promise from Vladimir containing several additional clauses. The appanage prince promised to keep not more than one hundred and eight servitors with him at his Moscow court.

In 1563, according to the chronicler, the tsar unleashed his anger on Princess Evfrosinia and her son. Ivan received a note from Savluk Ivanov, a chancellor in Prince Vladimir's service. Ivanov wrote to the tsar about various matters of state, including the information that Princess Evfrosinia and her son were plotting many wrongs against the tsar, and that in order to carry them out they were holding him, Savluk, in fetters in prison. The tsar ordered Savluk brought to him. Many investigations followed as a result of what he had to say, and many wrongdoings came to light. The tsar informed Princess Evfrosinia and her son of their wrongs, in the presence of the metropolitan and the church hierarchs. Afterwards Evfrosinia took the veil, and all of Vladimir's boyars and servants were transferred elsewhere. We have seen how Ivan's father used this method in dealing with one of his brothers.[71] In 1566 the tsar confiscated his cousin's appanage estates. In place of Staritsa and Vereia he gave him Dmitrov and Zvenigorod. According to one foreign source,[72] in 1568 Vladimir considered becoming a subject of Sigismund Augustus just before he perished in January 1569.[73]

EXECUTIONS AT NOVGOROD

A terrible fire raged within Ivan, for which there was no shortage of fuel. In the summer of 1569 a certain Peter from Volhynia appeared before the tsar. He reported that the people of Novgorod intended to surrender to the Polish king. He said they even had written a document to that effect and placed it in the Holy Wisdom cathedral behind the icon of the Virgin. Ivan dispatched someone he could trust to Novgorod together with the man from Volhynia. They actually did discover a document behind the icon and brought it to the tsar. The signatures of Archbishop Pimen and other leading citizens appeared genuine. Some said that this Peter was a vagrant who had been punished by the people of Novgorod. In revenge he composed the document himself, signing it with exceptional artistry in the hand of the archbishop and other citizens. Ivan decided to crush Novgorod.

In December 1569 he set out from Alexandrov Village. Already at Klin, at the beginning of the Tver district, he began to wreak his vengeance. From Klin all the way to Novgorod he laid everything waste. Tver especially suffered. On January 2, 1570, the advance regiment of the tsar's retinue appeared before Novgorod. They were ordered to construct a strong barrier around the city so that none should escape. The boyars and junior boyars of this advance regiment attacked the monasteries outside the town and confiscated the monastic treasuries. About five hundred fathers superior and monks were taken into Novgorod and flogged before the tsar's arrival. Other junior boyars rounded up the priests and deacons from all the Novgorod churches and turned them over to the care of the bailiffs, ten to each, who held them in iron fetters and flogged them every day from morning to evening; they extracted a ransom of twenty rubles for each. The ecclesiastical and residential buildings of the foremost parish churches were sealed, as were the warehouses of all the wealthier men. The leading merchants, officials and traders were seized and turned over to bailiffs. Their houses and possessions were confiscated and their wives and children placed under arrest.

On January 6 the tsar himself arrived with his son Ivan and the entire court, including some fifteen hundred musketeers. He stopped at Gorodishche, the trading quarter. The following day the first orders appeared. The arrested fathers superior and monks were to be flogged to death with canes and their bodies transported back to the monasteries for burial.

On the third day, a Sunday, Ivan proceeded to the Novgorod citadel for mass at the Holy Wisdom cathedral. On the bridge over the Volkhov he was met, as was customary, by Archbishop Pimen who attempted to bless him. The tsar would not approach the cross but said to the archbishop, "You reprobate! You are not holding the life-giving cross but a weapon, a weapon you would use to wound our heart. You and your accomplices, the people of this city, wish to turn over our patrimony, this great and blessed Novgorod, to a foreigner, to the Lithuanian king Sigismund Augustus. Henceforth you are not a pastor, not a teacher, but a wolf, a destroyer, a traitor, the torment of our purple mantle and our crown!"

Saying this, the tsar ordered Pimen to proceed with the crosses to the Holy Wisdom cathedral to conduct mass. Ivan and all his followers attended, after which they dined with the archbishop in his refectory. The tsar sat down to table and began to eat. Then suddenly he uttered a terrible shout as a prearranged signal to his princes and boyars. They began to plunder the archbishop's treasury and his whole court. They seized his boyars and servants and, having stripped the prelate himself, placed him in confinement, where he was given only two dengas' worth of food a day.

The majordomo Lev Saltykov, the confessor Archpriest Evstafy, and the boyars burst into the cathedral and seized all the sacred objects in the sacristy. The same was done in all the churches and monasteries. Meanwhile Ivan, with his son, left the archbishop's residence and went back to his quarters in Gorodishche where he held court.

They brought before him all the people of Novgorod who had been placed under guard. They began to torture them by burning them with some sort of "clever fire-making device" which the chronicler terms a grill. The accused were attached to sleds, dragged to the Volkhov bridge and thrown into the river. The women and children were thrown in from a high bank, hands and feet tied together, infants tied to their mothers. Lest anyone escape, junior boyars and musketeers patrolled the river in small boats with boathooks, spears, lances and axes. Anyone rising to the surface was snagged with the boathooks and jabbed with the weapons until he or she sank again into the depths. This went on every day for five weeks.

When he had finished administering his justice and meting out punishment, Ivan began a tour of the monasteries around Novgorod. In each he gave instructions to plunder the cellars and warehouses, to burn the grain and hay in the granaries and in the ricks, and to slaughter the cattle. After visiting the monasteries he gave orders for his men to go down all the trading streets and alleyways in Novgorod, seize all goods and raze all the storehouses and shops to their foundations. Then he began a tour of the suburbs where he gave orders to destroy all houses, slaughter all inhabitants without exception, men and women, and wreck homesteads and mansions, smashing in the windows and the gates. Meanwhile he sent armed bands out in all directions to the fifths,[74] to various settlements and village districts up to two hundred and fifty versts away with orders to plunder everything, to turn it all into a wasteland. The devastation lasted six weeks.

Finally on the morning of February 13 the tsar gave orders to bring before him the leading citizen of each street in Novgorod. When they were assembled they stood trembling, emaciated and cheerless like corpses, but the tsar gazed at them kindly and tenderly. "Inhabitants of Lord Novgorod the Great," he said, "those of you who remain among the living! Pray to the Lord God, to the Virgin Mother, and to all the saints for the power of our pious tsar, for my children the blessed tsareviches, Ivan and Fedor. Pray also for our Christ-loving army so that the Lord God may grant us victory and supremacy over all our enemies, visible and invisible. May God pass judgment upon that common traitor of yours and mine, the prelate Pimen, and his wicked advisers and accomplices. All this blood lies upon them, the traitors. You need not grieve about this now. Live gratefully in Novgorod. I leave in my place as your governor my boyar and commander, Prince Peter Danilovich Pronsky." The same day Ivan left Novgorod by the Pskov highway. The prelate Pimen and the priests and deacons who were not yet flogged, as well as the disgraced people of Novgorod whose cases were not yet decided, were sent off under guard to Alexandrov Village.

The impression that the massacre made upon the people of Novgorod is demonstrated by the following incident. On May 25, 1571 a large crowd assembled for mass at the church of St. Paraskeva in the trading quarter. After the service the bells in the bell tower began to ring. A sudden nameless dread fell over the people. Everyone—men, women, and children— ran off in all directions. They collided with one another, knowing not where to flee. Merchants threw open their shops and with their own hands gave away their goods to the first people they came across. We find precisely the same story of such a panic in the chronicles under the year 1239 following the massacres committed by Batu Khan.[75]

From Novgorod Ivan headed for Pskov, where the inhabitants feared the same fate as had befallen Novgorod. Following the orders of the commander Prince Tokmakov, every inhabitant stood before his dwelling with his wife and children, holding out bread and salt. When they saw the tsar they all fell to their knees. Ivan did not remain long in Pskov. He ordered his men to ransack the possessions of the citizens, excepting the clergy of the parish churches. He seized the treasuries of the monasteries and churches, their icons, crosses, shrouds, vessels, books and bells.

TRAITORS EXECUTED

The affair did not end with Novgorod and Pskov. The tsar, after his return to Moscow, began an investigation into the communications that Archbishop Pimen and the officials of Novgorod had maintained with the boyars Alexis Basmanov, his son Fedor, the treasurer Nikita Funikov, the keeper of the seal Viskovaty, Semeon Yakovlev, the crown secretary Vasily Stepanov, Andrei Vasiliev and Prince Afanasy Viazemsky.

The communications involved turning Novgorod and Pskov over to the Lithuanian king, deposing Ivan, and placing Prince Vladimir Andreevich on the throne. Since the details of this *case of investigation into treachery* have not survived, the historian has no right to make a judgment about the proceedings. The results, however, are known. Executed were Prince Peter Obolensky-Serebriany, Viskovaty, Funikov, and the boyars Ovchin-Pleshcheev and Ivan Vorontsov, son of Fedor, already known to us. Many others, some one hundred and eighty, were pardoned. What is most extraordinary is to find the names of Ivan's leading favorites among the condemned: names like Basmanov and Viazemsky. Viazemsky died under torture. Alexis Basmanov, it is said, was killed by his son Fedor on Ivan's orders. Pimen of Novgorod was banished to Venev.

IVAN'S TESTAMENT OF 1572

We know the condition of Ivan's spirit and the shape of his thoughts following the actions just related. To the year 1572 belongs the only testament of his which has come down to us.[76] In the testament the tsar expresses his conviction that he and his family are not solidly on the Muscovite throne. He considers himself an outcast, waging a battle against his enemies. He sees no speedy end to the battle and therefore is giving instructions to his sons as to how they should live until the battle is over. The testament begins with Ivan's confession. The following words are noteworthy. "The body is exhausted, the spirit ails, spiritual and bodily sores multiply, and there is no physician to cure me. I waited for someone to grieve with me, but none came. I did not seek comforters, for they returned me only evil for good, spite for love."

The admonition to his children begins with Christ's words, "This I tell you, to love one another." "Live yourselves in love," he continues, "but learn the military arts as much as possible. Since you must rule people and reward them but also *protect yourself from them,* and since you must learn to secure their loyalty in all things, you should also learn to love and reward well those who serve you truly; protect them from others so they suffer no oppression from anyone, for then they will serve you more truly still. For those who are evil you should bring about disgrace but in stages, employing reason in place of anger.

"You should learn all things, things to do with God, with the saints, with monks, with soldiers, with judges. Learn about living in Moscow and every custom of its life. Learn about all the ranks held, here and in other states. All these things you should know yourselves.

"Similarly you should learn about all traditions, how people live, how they would like to live, to what extent they will keep from changing. That way people will not be able to order you around but you them, for if you do not know about all these things you cannot rule your own realm; others will do it for you.

"Because of my many transgressions I made God so angry that I was hounded by the boyars; because of their willfulness I was driven away from my own property and had to wander about the country. For my sins, many misfortunes are left for you to bear, but for the Lord's sake do not waste yourselves in grieving.... Until God takes mercy on you and frees you from these misfortunes, stay together. For people should serve you united, and the land should be united, and there should be one treasury for all. That will be more profitable for you.

"My son Ivan, protect my son and your brother Fedor as yourself. See that he lacks nothing and is kept satisfied in all things so that he feels no anger against you, but do not give him either his own appanage principality or his own treasury.

"My son Fedor, *until you are settled* do not ask my son Ivan, your elder brother, for a principality or a treasury, or to live your own life. Be wise, for my son Ivan should be able to support you without any loss. You should both live together and manage all things together; that would be the most advantageous for you both.

"My son Ivan, keep and protect and love and support my son Fedor, your younger brother, and wish him as well in everything as you wish for yourself. You should not find fault with him but let him be his own man, for better or for worse. Should he be guilty of something in your sight, you should scold or punish him, but not fall out with him permanently. You must never allow quarrels to come between you, for Cain killed Abel, and you should not follow their example. If God grants that you rule over the realm and your brother Fedor over an appanage principality, you must not try to take the principality away from him; you should not speak ill of him to anyone. Wherever your lands border upon his, maintain the boundary firmly and with justice. Do not provoke him unjustly or indulge his human weaknesses, for even though a man acquire much land and wealth, he cannot avoid a three cubit grave. That is where everything ends.

"As for you, my son Fedor, obey my son Ivan as your father in my place and listen to him in all things as you would to me. Submit to him in everything and wish him as well as you would wish me, your parent. Do not contradict him in anything but live according to his word in all things, just as now you live according to mine. If God grants that he rule over the realm and you over an appanage principality, do not try to take over the realm that is under him. Plan no evil against him with anyone. Remain as one with him, everywhere, for better or for worse.

"*Until my son Ivan comes to rule this realm and you your appanage principality,* be loyal to your brother my son Ivan and never converse with those who would do him treachery or ill. Should they entice you with glory, wealth or honors, or promise you cities or rights which would set you above my son Ivan, or summon you to rule over the realm, you should refuse absolutely to listen. Do not do anything Ivan does not wish, for as Ivan my son instructs you, so you must do, and not be tempted by anything. Wherever my son Ivan sends you on his service, or orders you to send your men on his service, you must go on his service and send your men as my son Ivan instructs you. Wherever Ivan's lands border upon yours, observe the boundary faithfully. Be concerned for justice and do not provoke him unjustly or indulge his human weaknesses, for a man may acquire great wealth or lands, yet still cannot avoid a three cubit grave....

"You, my son Fedor, be submissive to my son Ivan, your elder brother, in all things and wish him well, as you would me or yourself. Obey his will in all things even to blood and death. Do not contradict him in anything. Should Ivan become angry at you or if he aggrieves you somehow, *even then do not contradict your elder brother; do not raise arms or seek to defend yourself against him.* Beg his pardon so that he may forgive you. His anger will subside, and he will come again to favor you according to my instructions. Should you be guilty of anything, beg his pardon and be loving to him. If he hears your entreaty, so much the better; if he does not, still do not attempt to defend yourself."

These instructions draw our attention first of all to the tsar's desire for unity between his children. He wants them not to part company until such time as the elder of them, Ivan, can crush all sedition and become established on the throne. If not, he felt, an appanage prince would become the most potent weapon in the hands of the disaffected. Secondly Ivan in his testament is not content with a vague command to the younger son to obey the elder in place of his father. He delineates the implications of this filial obedience. The younger must obey the will of the elder with his blood and even his death, never contradict him in anything, and in case of being aggrieved by his elder brother never dare raise arms against him or even defend himself.

Ivan here is abolishing the legality of internecine strife in the ruling family by placing the younger brother in an absolutely subordinate relationship to the elder. Now the younger brother can no longer say to the

Ivan IV the Terrible
Reconstruction by N.N. Gerasimov published January 1964
following exhumation on April 23, 1963.

elder, as did the Olgovichi of old,[77] "You are our elder brother, but if you do not give us what we want we will seek it ourselves." In his instructions Ivan seeks to dictate relationships among crown princes.

Ivan was not convinced of a happy outcome for his family in the struggle, as the following words of his testament bear witness. "Do not forget us or our parents or grandparents, whether you remain in the capital city of Moscow or wherever you may be, *even if you should find yourself persecuted or exiled.* Remember always the holy liturgies, the requiems, the lamentations, and the charities to the poor and needy." Ivan bestowed upon his son "the mantle of the Russian tsardom, with the crown of Monomakh and the entire regalia of the tsar, which was given to our forefather, *Tsar* and Grand Prince Vladimir Monomakh, by the Byzantine emperor Constantine Monomachus from the city of the tsars.[78] I am also bestowing on my son Ivan all the crowns and regalia that I have had made, the staffs and cloaks and the German scepter. I am also bestowing on my son Ivan my own Russian tsardom, which my father Grand Prince Vasily bestowed upon me and which God gave me."

Here we find an important abrogation compared to the dispositions of previous rulers. The appanage prince Fedor received no part of the city of Moscow. For his appanage principality he received fourteen towns of which the most important was Suzdal, but it exemplifies Ivan's notion that an appanage prince must not think of having any sort of independence. "My son Fedor's appanage shall be subject both to Ivan and the tsardom."[79]

Finally, Ivan gave his sons the following advice about the oprichnina. "The oprichnina that I have established is left to the disposition of my sons, Ivan and Fedor. However they may profit thereby, let them do so. The model is there at hand." Although Ivan gave his sons the choice of continuing the oprichnina or abolishing it, during his reign its abolition was hardly expected, for one evil gave rise to another.

GRAND PRINCE SIMEON

In 1571 Prince Mstislavsky made the following written statement. "I, Prince Ivan Mstislavsky, did not keep my faith. I betrayed my sovereign and his children and his lands, the whole of Christian Orthodoxy, the whole Russian land. I and my comrades summoned the godless Crimean khan, Devlet-Girey." The tsar pardoned Mstislavsky in response to the plea of Metropolitan Cyril and twenty-four other clergymen but extracted a surety pledge. Three boyars promised to pay the treasury twenty thousand rubles in the event of Mstislavsky's desertion. A further two hundred and eighty-five guarantors were brought in as witnesses. Ten years later Mstislavsky once again begged forgiveness for himself and his two sons for having been guilty of so many crimes against the tsar.

Such documents indicate that there was some doubt as to whether the government of the zemshchina could be entrusted as before to Mstislavsky and his friends. Although the tsar did not want to be involved in the zemshchina government, still it was necessary to place at its head someone who was by title and origin superior to the princes and boyars, yet at the same time had nothing in common with them; in other words, someone reliable.

Thus we find in one of the chronicles under the year 1574 the following information. "In the Kremlin square, near the Immaculate Virgin gate, the tsar executed many boyars, the archimandrite of the Miracles monastery, an archpriest and many of all ranks. Their heads were thrown into Mstislavsky's courtyard. At the same time Ivan produced Simeon Bekbulatovich[80] and made him tsar of Moscow. He crowned him, referred to himself as 'Ivan of Moscow' and left the city to live on Petrovka street. He gave his entire imperial rank to Simeon, while he himself travelled about simply, like a boyar, in sleighs. Whenever he was in the presence of Tsar Simeon he sat well removed from the tsar's place, together with the boyars." Indeed documents have come down to us in which all manner of decrees about zemshchina matters are produced in the name of *Simeon, Grand Prince of All Russia* as tsar, where Tsar Ivan himself is called the *Sovereign Prince of Moscow.*

Simeon did not reign in Moscow for more than two years. According to the chronicles, Ivan sent him away and gave him Tver and Torzhok to rule.[81] The division into oprichnina and zemshchina remained, but the name "oprichnina" aroused such hatred that the tsar found it necessary to abandon it. Instead of the term "oprichnina" we find "court." In place of "oprichnina towns" and "oprichnina commanders" we find "court towns" and "court commanders."[82]

Meanwhile executions continued on various occasions, such as after the attack of the Crimean khan, when Mstislavsky admitted that he and his friends had summoned the khan, and on the occasion of the illness and death of the tsar's bride,[83] on account of which many old boyars perished, including the famous commander Prince Mikhail Vorotynsky, whom we last saw incarcerated in the St. Cyril monastery of Beloozero, Prince Nikita Odoevsky, the boyar Mikhail Yakovlevich Morozov, Prince Peter Kurakin, and others less famous. Kurbsky says that Vorotynsky was put to the torture because of a slave's denunciation whereby he was accused of sorcery and evil intentions against Ivan. After enduring his tortures the old man was again carried off into imprisonment at Beloozero but died on the way. Contemporary Russian witnesses say that Ivan kept this cast of mind to the end of his life, this quickness to anger and destruction. In the last eight years of his life, however, we can find no indication of any more executions.

IV

POLOTSK, POLAND, CRIMEA AND TURKEY

RUSSIAN VICTORIES IN LIVONIA

In 1559 Master Kettler, despairing of the Livonians saving themselves on their own, concluded a close alliance with Sigismund Augustus. Encouraged by the pact and receiving help in the form of men and money from Germany, from the duke of Prussia and from the inhabitants of Riga and Reval, Kettler took the offensive. He defeated the Muscovites under their commander Zakhar Pleshcheev near Dorpat and lay siege to the city itself.

The besieged Russians launched a not very successful sortie, yet this was the full extent of the Livonian success. Winter came on and the allied division contributed by Duke Christopher of Mecklenburg withdrew. Kettler tried at least to take Lais with his Livonians but was repulsed twice by the Russian garrison commanded by the musketeer captain Kashkarov. According to the Livonian chronicles Kettler could do nothing against the brave resistance of the enemy, and with shame and losses had to withdraw to Oberpahlen. He encountered severe difficulties reaching it since the roads were in no condition for transporting his heavy artillery. Once there his infantry, demoralized by their lack of success and at not having been paid, mutinied. They were pacified with difficulty and dispersed to their winter quarters. The heavy artillery was sent on to Fellin.

The snowless winter did not restrain the Russians. Princes Ivan Mstislavsky, Peter Shuisky and Vasily Obolensky-Serebriany pushed on during the winter of 1559-1560 as far as the Gulf of Riga without meeting any resistance and captured Marienburg. In the spring a Russian division set off for Estonia and defeated the Livonians near Werpel. To the east partisan volunteers from Pskov wreaked havoc in Livonia, taking captives and driving off cattle. The Livonians managed to catch only a few of them.

In the spring Prince Andrei Kurbsky arrived in Livonia. He routed the old master Fürstenberg near Weissenstein and Fellin. A large Muscovite division of sixty thousand men under Mstislavsky and Shuisky set out to capture Fellin. A force of twelve thousand under Prince Barbashin marched towards the coast on rumors that Fürstenberg intended to send a rich treasury to Hapsal. The Livonians' best commander Landmarshal Philipp Bell set out to attack Barbashin with only five hundred soldiers, hoping that the element of surprise would equalize their strengths.

He was mistaken. His entire detachment was destroyed. Bell himself, according to Kurbsky the Livonians' last defense and hope, was taken captive along with eleven commanders and a hundred and twenty knights. Kurbsky speaks with great respect of Bell's bravery, sharp thinking and eloquence, as well as of the fond regard that others had for him. The Russian commanders treated him in comradely fashion. They sat down to table together and enjoyed his highly intelligent conversation.

Kurbsky has preserved for us Bell's remarks about the history of the Order of Livonian Knights and his explanation for its collapse. "While we remained within the Catholic faith and lived moderately and chastely, the Lord protected us from our enemies on all sides and helped us in all things, but since we have deserted the faith of *the church,* dared to overturn the laws and the holy commandments, adopted a newly contrived faith, indulged in excesses, and turned aside onto the broad easy road to perdition, the Lord clearly is punishing us for our sins and sentencing us for our lawlessness by delivering us into the arms of you, our enemies. Without much effort or sacrifice have you taken our lofty cities, our strongholds, our illustrious palaces and courts, all of which were fortified by our forefathers. Without having planted them yourselves, you are enjoying our gardens and vineyards. What can I say about you? You took it by the sword! Others have entered freely without swords, gaining access to our wealth and storehouses without effort merely by promising us help and protection. Fine help! Here we stand, captured by our enemies, but do not think that you humbled us by your own strength. God delivered us into the hands of our enemies for our sins."

Here Bell wept bitterly and moved all the Russian commanders to tears. Wiping his tears, he added the following with a more cheerful countenance, "Nevertheless I thank God and rejoice to be captured and made to suffer for my beloved homeland. Should I happen to die for it, my death will be dear to me." When the commanders sent Bell off to Moscow they begged the tsar not to take his life. The prisoner, however, responded to

Ivan's stern questions with equal sternness. Among other things he said, "You took our homeland unjustly and bloodthirstily, hardly befitting a Christian tsar." Ivan flew into a rage and ordered Bell's head cut off.

The Russians besieged Fellin. The Livonians defended it bravely even when the outer walls fell, but when the Russians began shooting fireballs and set the town ablaze, the defenders called a truce despite the fact they still controlled the virtually impregnable citadel, three other collateral fortifications, eighteen huge siege cannon, four hundred and fifty medium or small guns and a great many supplies of all sorts. The reason, according to Livonian sources, was that the garrison's pay was several months in arrears, and they refused to serve any longer. In vain did old Fürstenberg promise them his entire personal fortune. The garrison turned over the city to the Russians, arranging free passage for themselves. Fürstenberg himself was sent to Moscow where the commanders promised he would receive the tsar's mercy. The promise was kept. The old man was given an estate at Liubim, a town in the Kostroma district, where eventually he died peacefully.

The Livonian chronicles give an interesting detail of the victory parade in Moscow when Fürstenberg and the other Livonian prisoners were marched through the streets on display before the citizens. "It's your doing, you Germans!" a Tatar prisoner is reported to have shouted. "You were the first to give the grand prince the birch rods to scourge us, and now he is scourging you." By birches the Tatar meant the weaponry the Russians had borrowed from the Germans.

Several other cities followed Fellin's example. The Russian forces devastated the country unhindered, everywhere outnumbering and annihilating any Livonian detachments daring to come out to meet them, but Mstislavsky was unable to take Weissenstein. His unsuccessful attempt ended the campaign of 1560.

LIVONIA DISINTEGRATES

Although the conquest of the Order's territories was far from complete, despite the Russian successes, nevertheless the blows Ivan directed against the Order hastened its disintegration. Bishop Menninghausen of Øsel[1] entered into secret negotiations with the Danish king Frederik II.[2] He sold him his territories of Øsel and Pilten for twenty thousand reichsthalers and departed with the money for Germany even though he had no right to dispose of those lands without the knowledge and approval of the Order's authorities. The Danish king did not keep the territories for himself. He was bound by his father's will to give his brother Magnus certain lands in Holstein; instead of these, he gave him his newest purchase.[3] In 1560 Magnus appeared in Arensburg,[4] and many Livonian aristocrats, assuming that Denmark would not abandon him, enlisted in his service.

The appearance of this new face in the Baltic produced new troubles. When the nobles of the land were gathered together in Pernau[5] and Magnus arrived to take up the position of administrator of Øsel, the Livonian diet instead of arriving at some sort of decision beneficial to the country became the scene of violent arguments between Magnus and Master Kettler over the lands Magnus intended to rule. The affair nearly led to war. Meanwhile the Russians took Fellin.

At the Russian withdrawal from Weissenstein an internecine war actually did break out, although not between Magnus and Kettler. The peasants revolted. They claimed that although the nobles in times of peace burdened them with terrible obligations, in times of war they did not protect them from the enemy; therefore they were refusing to obey them any longer. They burned castles and attacked nobles, but finally were defeated in their siege of Lode castle and only then were pacified.

In Reval meanwhile the citizens watched helplessly as Muscovite soldiers led away from under their very walls their cattle and even their people. They sent envoys to the Swedish king, Erik XIV, son and successor of Gustav Vasa,[6] to ask for a loan of money and to find out what they could expect from him in the event of a Muscovite siege. Erik answered that he was not in the habit of giving money away uselessly, but if Reval wished to place itself entirely under his protection, he was prepared to accept it, not for ambition but for Christian love, and to avoid ending up with such an intolerable neighbor as Muscovy. He would guarantee them all their former rights and protect them with all the means at his disposal.

Reval considered the offer. They could expect no help from the emperor or the empire, and none from the master. Poland was far away and also sent no help when it was needed, besides which Polish customs, language and faith were different from their own. Because of the distance between them Reval, unlike Riga, had few trade connections with the Poles and Lithuanians and was in no way dependent upon them. Thus there was no advantage at all in a union with Poland, only a more rapid final destruction. Denmark previously had refused their supplication. A union with Sweden was preferable by reason of religious affinity and proximity. It was easy to receive aid and to trade over the open sea. Reasoning along these lines, in June

1561 the people of Reval swore fidelity to the Swedish king, who for his part promised to preserve their traditional rights.

Reval's motives for uniting with Sweden demonstrated why Livonia, conversely, preferred to join Poland. "We do not live off Poland and Lithuania," said the citizens of Reval, "the way Riga does." Riga was indeed tied by commercial interests to Lithuania, in particular by means of the Dvina river.[7] The Livonian nobility no less than the merchants of Riga wished for a union with Poland, for nowhere else did their fellow nobles occupy so envious a position. Kettler therefore opened negotiations with Nicholas Radziwill, governor of Wilno, concerning the unification of Livonia with Poland. In November 1561 the matter was settled. Livonia turned itself over to Poland, preserving all its traditional rights. In return for signed obligations to Poland, Master Kettler was made duke of Courland and Semigallia.

An interesting account has survived of the reasons why the Poles considered Livonia's annexation necessary. "Of all the parts of our present kingdom, none has a greater number of cities, fortresses and castles than Prussia. Yet Livonia, in its wealth of fortified places, equals or exceeds Prussia. The Polish realm is greatly in need of fortified places since it is surrounded on the north and east by wild and barbaric peoples. Livonia is favored by its coastal position and its abundance of ports. Should Livonia belong to the Polish king, he also would rule the sea. All of Poland's leading families can testify to the benefit to the realm of ports. The prosperity of private individuals increased extraordinarily from the moment the kingdom received the Prussian ports into its realm. Now our people are second to none in Europe in the splendor of their dress and adornments and in the abundance of gold and silver. The royal treasury has grown rich from the collection of duties. Besides, see how the might and strength of the kingdom will increase through the annexation of such an extensive country! How easy it will be to deal with Muscovy then, how easy to restrain the enemy when the king has such fortresses! The main reason why we should accept Livonia is that if we reject it, this glorious fertile country with its ports, cities, fortresses and navigable rivers will go over to our dangerous neighbor. Either we must wage a war with Muscovy, constantly and with all our might, or we must conclude an honorable and advantageous peace, but the conditions of such a peace could not be called either honorable or advantageous if they involved ceding Livonia to Muscovy. If we have to drive the Muscovites out of Livonia for once and for all, why should we then not take Livonia for ourselves? Why should we turn down the rewards of victory? Like the Muscovites we must also drive away the Swedes, whose might is a danger to us. First of all we must settle with Muscovy."

This exposition of the reasons why Poland should take possession of Livonia demonstrates why Muscovy sought the same thing. Poland had the Prussian ports on the Baltic while Muscovy had none. That is why Ivan was not interested in partitioning Livonia with Sigismund Augustus, keeping only what he had won so far. His conquests, with the exception of Narva, were all inland and held little significance for him. The Poles wished to deal with Muscovy before turning against Sweden. In Moscow, similarly, there was no desire to take on two enemies at once. In the negotiations which Ivan reopened with Sweden, therefore, he made no mention of Reval.

These talks were not amicable, but for a different reason. The young king, Erik XIV, could not accept with indifference the humiliating custom whereby he was obliged to communicate through Novgorod vicegerents rather than directly with the tsar. In 1560 Erik sent an envoy to demand that the peace treaties written in his father's reign and ratified only by the seals of the Novgorod vicegerents be ratified by the tsar's seal, and that henceforth he deal directly with the tsar. He also demanded the abolition of the conditions set out in the former documents whereby the Swedish king was prevented from helping the Polish king or the Livonian master against Muscovy. In order to frighten Ivan and make him more amenable the Swedish envoys declared that the emperor and the Polish and Danish kings were trying to talk Erik into a coalition against the tsar over Livonia.

"Do not imagine," retorted the Muscovites, "that our sovereign would ever break our ancestral traditions by altering the peace treaties. King Gustav in his youth acted in the same haughty manner as your sovereign now, also seeking to communicate directly with our sovereign. How much innocent blood of his own people was shed because of this pride, how much of his land was subjected to devastation? Yet he was a reasonable man. Although he was at fault, after consulting his magnates and sage counsellors he asked forgiveness for his wrongdoing. Your reasoning we cannot understand. Why have you put on such airs? You yourselves must realize that it was because of wrongdoing on the part of the Livonians that this unpleasant business so quickly arose, and now who can tame it? Consider the lands of Kazan and Astrakhan. Those once great realms became puffed up with pride and tried to abandon the old ways, bringing down upon them our sovereign's anger. You know well what happened to them on account of their misdeeds. Now we see your sovereign King Erik has learned nothing from anywhere, sitting in his ancient land. It appears to us that either your king is very young, or his older counsellors have been dismissed and he takes counsel only from the young, for only such advice could have produced such words." When the envoys said that it could not possibly be difficult for the tsar to communicate directly with the king, the boyars answered, "The most difficult thing in the world is to break ancestral traditions."

Tradition was not broken, and on his return the translator for the Swedish legation complained to the king that the legation had been shown much dishonor in Novgorod and Moscow. When in order to ratify the peace Muscovite envoys were sent to Sweden representing the Novgorod vicegerents, Erik had his revenge. "We suffered much dishonor and many damages from the king," the envoys reported to Moscow. "In Vyborg they made scurrilous speeches and cursed us. They gave us no food, and since we were not allowed to unload any of our own supplies from the ships, we had to spend the whole day locked up without food." When they arrived in Sweden they were given rooms without stoves or benches and were forced to travel on foot to see the king. When they were summoned to dinner, the king gave orders to set before them only such meat dishes as were allowed during St. Peter's fast, fully aware that they only got a fasting meal while under guard. When greetings from the Novgorod vicegerents were pronounced, the king neither stirred from his place nor raised his headpiece. Three times the envoys were summoned to the king, three times they were turned back.

IVAN PROPOSES TO POLISH KING'S SISTER

These discourtesies were of little consequence since the tsar turned his entire attention to Lithuania. At first Ivan tried to settle the matter peacefully, by means of marriage to one of the king's sisters. Besides the possibility of using this relationship to achieve a peaceful agreement over Livonia, Ivan may have had another aim. With the death of the childless Sigismund Augustus the Jagiellonian house of Lithuania would become extinct.[8] The sister of the last Jagiellonian would carry with her to Moscow the right to succeed to Lithuania. As we shall see, Ivan cared little for Poland.

He asked the metropolitan whether he could marry a sister of the king, considering the degree of consanguinity between them as a result of his aunt Elena's marriage to the bride's uncle Alexander. The metropolitan assured him that he could, and they began to plan in Moscow how the princess should be met and where she should live before her conversion to Orthodoxy. It was decided that the boyars would not mention the conversion in their negotiations with the Polish lords. Should the Polish lords themselves say that the princess must remain a Roman Catholic, they were to object and point out former examples like Vytautas's daughter Sophia, or the sister of Algirdas, who accepted conversion into the Greek faith.[9] If the lords did not agree, the negotiators should drop the matter.

Fedor Sukin was dispatched to Lithuania with the proposal. "In your travels along the road to Wilno," he was instructed, "try to determine clearly the differences between the king's two sisters. Find out how old they are, how tall, how *in body,* the manners of each, and which is fairer. Whichever is fairer, speak about her to the king. If the elder princess is no better looking than the younger and over twenty-five, do not speak about her but only about the younger. Take care to ascertain whether she is sickly or very thin. If one is sickly or very thin or has some bad habit, do not speak about her; speak about the one who is healthy and not thin and without defect. Even if the elder is over twenty-five, if she is fairer than the younger, speak about her. If it is impossible to tell which is fairer, speak about the princesses without mentioning names. If they agree to give one in marriage to the tsar and grand prince, Sukin must look at them immediately and draw their faces and send the sketches to the tsar. If they are unwilling to show him the princesses, request *portraits.*"

Sukin decided that the younger princess, Katarzyna, was the fairer. He therefore made the proposal to the king to give her in marriage to the tsar. The Polish lords answered for the king that when the father of the princesses died he entrusted his family to the emperor.[10] The king, desiring to conduct the matter according to his father's wishes, insisted upon conferring with the emperor and the other kings and with his friends and relatives, as well as the duke of Brunswick and his cousin the king of Hungary. Besides, the Polish council of lords was not in session just then. The king had to confer with it too, since the princesses were born in Poland and their dowries were there. "We perceive from your words," replied the envoy Sukin, "that your sovereign is unwilling to entertain the proposal seriously, since he would postpone such an important matter for so long." So ended the first negotiation session.

When the envoys were summoned for a second time Sigismund Augustus declared that he agreed to give his sister Katarzyna in marriage to the tsar. The envoys asked permission to pay their respects, but the lords answered, "The matter has not been settled completely, and until then it is not permitted for commoners to see a king's sister or daughter."

"If," replied the envoys, "we have neither seen our sovereign Princess Katarzyna, nor paid her our respects, what are we say to our sovereign on our return? It appears to us that the king does not wish to give his sister's hand to our sovereign."

They were told that they were not allowed to see the princess openly, since all the Polish courtiers were with her. If word got out that the Muscovite envoys had seen the princess, explained the lords, the king would face a furor over it in the Polish council of lords, but if the envoys wished to see her, they could look at her secretly when she entered the church. At first the envoys did not agree but later acquiesced. The matter ended without consequence. The king was willing to agree to the marriage of his sister to Ivan only if it furnished him with an advantageous peace treaty. The king's envoy, Jan Szimkowicz, appeared in Moscow to demand that a peace be concluded before the matter of a marriage could be decided. Magnates from both sides could meet for negotiations at the border, but prior to this meeting there could be no more fighting in Livonia.

Sigismund Augustus wanted to press his advantage, just as Ivan III earlier pressed a similar advantage when the Lithuanian king Alexander sought the hand of Ivan's daughter Elena. The grand prince similarly demanded the conclusion of peace before discussing marriage. Although the search for a marriage alliance emanated this time from the Muscovite side, Ivan IV's position was in no way similar to that of Alexander, who had to conclude a peace at any price, whether or not ratified by marriage to Elena. Ivan did not agree to negotiations at the border. In Moscow, as we have seen, it was considered the most difficult thing on earth to break ancestral traditions, and these demanded that peace negotiations be conducted in Moscow.[11]

Hostilities were initiated in Livonia by an offensive led by the Lithuanian hetman Radziwill against the Russians. In September 1561 after a five-week siege he took Tarwast. The Russian commanders defeated the Lithuanians at Pernau and then destroyed Tarwast, abandoned by the Lithuanians. The year 1562 witnessed devastating raids from both sides, yet communications between the two courts were not broken off. Sigismund Augustus had neither the means nor the desire to wage active war. He preferred to play for time with negotiations.

At the beginning of 1562 the king's envoy, an official named Korsak, arrived in Moscow bearing complaints that Ivan was offending the king and was not serious about peace. He requested a truce until further notice. "In your entire letter," Ivan answered Sigismund, "we could not find anything written honestly. You wrote only falsehoods, piling injustices upon us.... Previously you sent us Jan Szimkowicz, but then you wrote to the Perekop [Crimean] khan that Szimkowicz was sent not to conclude an agreement between us but to prevent one. Before that you sent a letter to Perekop in which you spoke against us with many unseemly words. If things are in such a state, what more can we expect from you? We have observed enough utter falsehoods in you."

Ivan's reproaches were justified. Sigismund Augustus never gave up inciting the Crimean khan against Moscow. He wrote to him that Ivan despite his truce with Lithuania was now waging war against Livonia, the king's protectorate. The king wrote that he did not wish to break his promise by starting a war with Muscovy while the truce was still in effect, but that it was a perfect time for the khan to attack Moscow since practically all Muscovite forces were tied down in Livonia.

Meanwhile the Lithuanian lords, acting under an old precedent, wrote to the metropolitan and boyars to get them to incline the tsar to peace and to concede Livonia, which from time immemorial belonged to the Polish kings and the Lithuanian grand princes. Acting on the tsar's instructions the metropolitan wrote back, "Earlier the bishop and commander of Wilno sent their envoys and couriers to us several times, and we answered them that we were churchmen and had nothing to do with such matters. Similarly now we tell you that such matters are the responsibility of the God-crowned autocratic and sovereign tsar's boyars, who may communicate with the Lithuanian lords. As Christian pastors we have reminded our blessed autocrat that he should be in peace and tranquillity with his neighbors. We implored the sovereign, who has not scorned our petition and is sending a safe conduct for the Lithuanian envoys."

"We need only recall history," replied the boyars, "and the fact that the Lithuanian hetmen Daniel and Movkold, the children of Rogvolod, seized the Lithuanian principality. They also paid tribute to Kiev, to the great sovereign Mstislav, son of Vladimir Monomakh. Therefore not only all the Russian land but also the Lithuanian land is our sovereign's patrimony. Beginning with the great sovereign Vladimir, who illuminated the Russian land with holy baptism, up to the time of our present great sovereign, our sovereign autocrats were not appointed to rule their states by anyone, whereas your sovereigns are elected. Which has the stronger right, a hereditary or an elected sovereign? You decide.

"With such words being spoken on both sides there can be no good outcome, only the spilling of Christian blood. We have reminded you about Lithuania only because you wrote unseemingly in your letter, quarrelling about the antiquity of our sovereign's royal patrimony.... That the Livonian land formerly paid obeisance to our sovereign is well known, not only to us here but also in many other lands. It behooves us point out how Jagailo hired the Livonian Germans against his uncle the Lithuanian grand prince Kestutis, which is well known to you.[12] Look in your chronicles and you will find it. You also know how Vytautas, fleeing from Jagailo, likewise hired the Livonian Germans, how Jagailo and Vytautas went to Marienburg, in German territory, and how many of their men the Germans killed, also how the Livonian Germans made peace on their own terms with Jagailo and Vytautas."

CAPTURE OF POLOTSK

Nothing was to be accomplished by these or any other words, only by action. At the beginning of 1563 Ivan himself advanced on the Lithuanian borders with a large force. The object of the campaign was Polotsk, an important city in its own right and especially in regard to Livonia on account of its commercial links with Riga along the Dvina.

On January 31 the city was besieged. On February 7 the stockade was taken. On February 15, after seven hundred yards of the wall were destroyed, the city capitulated. The bishop and one of the king's closest advisers, the Polish commander Dowojna, were taken to Moscow along with their possessions, the royal treasury, and property of the Lithuanian lords and merchants which included much gold and silver, to be presented to the tsar. Jews were drowned in the Dvina, but over five hundred of the king's mercenaries were presented with furs and released, being told they could enter the tsar's service or go to the king or to other lands, since they were strangers from other lands.

Informing the metropolitan about the capture of Polotsk, Ivan directed him to say, "The prophecy of the Russian saint, the miracle worker Metropolitan Peter,[13] that the hands of the city of Moscow would be raised over the shoulders of its enemies, has been fulfilled. God has poured His ineffable mercy upon us, unworthy though we are, and delivered our inheritance, the city of Polotsk, into our hands."

The tsar returned to Moscow as triumphantly as he had from Kazan. At the St. Joseph monastery he met his elder son, Tsarevich Ivan. At the last lodging before Moscow, in the village of Krylatskoe, he met his younger son Tsarevich Fedor, his brother Yury, Archbishop Nikandr of Rostov and other bishops, archimandrites and abbots. The metropolitan and all the Muscovite clergy met the tsar at the church of St. Boris and St. Gleb on the Arbat. Ivan bowed before them, saying that, by the grace of the Virgin, by the prayers of the great miracle workers, and by their own prayers, the Lord God had sent His mercy from on high and delivered his patrimony, the city of Polotsk, into his hands. The clergy wished him many years in his patrimony. They gave great thanks and praise that by his supreme effort the holy churches were cleansed of the iconoclastic Lutherans and that the remaining Christians were gathered together again into Orthodoxy.

Three commanders were stationed in Polotsk, Princes Peter Shuisky and Vasily and Peter Obolensky-Serebriany. They were instructed to "fortify the citadel without delay, sparing no efforts. Where necessary clear out the old and dig new moats, so there are only deep and steep moats. Where the old stockade was destroyed by fire, give immediate orders to build a stronger one with three or four walls. Do not on any account allow into the citadel Lithuanians, whether local or from elsewhere, neither servicemen nor landowners nor peasants. Then on a particular holiday in great celebration you may invite Lithuanian burgomasters and officials to the Holy Wisdom cathedral. You may allow them inside the citadel, a few at a time, but be sure to post additional guards with commanders at all points. On no account allow anybody, whether gentry or merchants, into the citadel without the knowledge of the boyars and without warders. Only the priests of the churches with their families are allowed to live within the citadel, and no strangers may live with them. Keep the citadel well lighted. The commanders must stay within at night with their regiments. Do not let anyone go about at night without a lantern.

"Entrust the government to Lithuanians. After determining all the local customs and habits, let them make decisions according to their customs. Have the court established outside the citadel, in the stockaded town. Select reliable leaders from among the trustworthy gentry and instruct them to decide all matters in the court with dispatch. Make them swear to judge fairly and not take bribes or presents. Assign to them chancellery officials to hold court in conjunction with the burgomasters. None of the servicemen, gentry, or traders remaining in the town quarter must be allowed to have any sort of offensive weapons. Those whom commanders consider unreliable should be sent off on some pretext to Pskov, Novgorod or Velikie Luki, and from there to Moscow."

The king sent a reprimand to the Crimean khan when he learned of the capture of Polotsk. Why had he promised the king to attack Moscow in the winter and then failed to do so? The Muscovite tsar, being secure from that quarter, had invaded Lithuania in full force and captured Polotsk.

PEACE TALKS WITH LITHUANIA

The king's council sent word to the boyars requesting the Muscovite armies to desist from further hostilities, and that Lithuanian envoys be received in Moscow on the feast of the Dormition [August 15]. Ivan ordered a cease-fire and communications were re-established.

At this moment Prince Dmitry Vishnevetsky[14] quit Muscovite service for unknown reasons and again went over to Lithuania, but he did not remain there long. The following instructions were issued to the courier Klobukov who was sent to Lithuania. "If they ask about Vishnevetsky answer, 'He came running to our sovereign like a dog and ran off like a dog. He is no loss whatever to our sovereign or our country.'"

Nevertheless Moscow hardly received calmly the news of the flight of the daring cossack who had shown the tsar such fine service against the Crimeans and who could now lend his services to the king against the tsar. Klobukov was ordered to determine "the terms under which Prince Vishnevetsky was received into the king's service. Did the king grant him an income, and does he live at court? In what capacity does he serve the king? Also find out about how Alexis and Gavril Cherkassky were received at court and what the king paid them. Should Alexis Cherkassky come to the courier and declare he wishes to come back to the tsar, answer that his request will be referred to the tsar."

The king as before tried to stall for time so as to gather his forces and rouse the khan. Now, after the capture of Polotsk, he had less hope than ever of concluding a favorable peace or even a truce. He sent a courier with a proposal to extend the armistice from the feast of the Dormition to that of the Annunciation [March 25]. The tsar refused and would only extend the term to December 6 of that year, 1563.

The king informed the khan. He also notified him that the negotiations with Moscow would concern only the prisoners taken at Polotsk. A peace would not be concluded; the khan should therefore proceed immediately during the winter against Muscovy, whose forces would all be concentrated against Lithuania. Should an armistice be concluded it would not extend further than July. The king's envoy asked the khan whether he, the king, should send emissaries to the sultan to urge him to act against Ivan too.

These particular communications remained unknown to Moscow, but others came to light. When the Lithuanian envoys, the border official Jerzy Chodkiewicz and Marshal Wolowicz, arrived in Moscow the boyars greeted them with reproaches. Why did the commander of Trotsk castle send a document to the junior boyar Prince Kropotkin in Tarwast inviting him to desert? Why did he write about Ivan's supposed brutality?

Letters from Sigismund Augustus to the Swedish king urging him into war with Moscow also were intercepted. Ivan ordered his envoys to say to the Lithuanians, "Is it justice that our brother plots with the Swedes against us? If he wants to lower his dignity by calling himself an equal brother to the Swedish king, that is his business; he can call his water carrier a brother if he chooses to. Is it justice that our brother writes to us that the Livonian land is his patrimony, but to the Swede that he will defend the wretched inhabitants of that conquered and devastated land? This means that it is not his own land! He calls us a lawbreaker, yet he chooses to ignore the godless illegalities allowed in his country (Ivan refers here to the spread of Protestantism in King Sigismund's realm). Our brother writes to the Swede that the Muscovite Christians are enemies, that it is impossible to have lasting peace, friendship or union with them. Are such reproachful words seemly? The bishops and the Polish lords also display an unseemly pride. Formerly they communicated with our boyars in letters, calling themselves their brothers, but now they venture to communicate with the metropolitan, who has the same rank as our own brother and cousins. It is hardly proper for our subjects to write as brothers to our metropolitan."

The envoys replied that the metropolitan could communicate with the bishop of Wilno, but not with the Polish lords, since he was on a par with the bishop. The boyars answered that the bishop was not equal to the metropolitan. Above the bishop was an archbishop, and yet above him a metropolitan. The boyars reproached the envoys also for breaking the last truce. Prince Mikhail Vishnevetsky, a cavalry captain, violated the truce when he led Akkerman Tatars against the Muscovite borderlands; he advanced on Novgorod Seversk with cossacks, Lithuanians and Akkerman Tatars.

When peace negotiations commenced, the boyars demanded Volhynia, Podolia and Galicia. The envoys answered that these were Polish, not Lithuanian. As Lithuanian envoys, they could not speak about other lands;

they would have to speak to the Polish envoys. Ivan gave up Podolia, then Volhynia, then Kiev and the cities along the Dnieper. Negotiations came to a halt over the disposition of the Polotsk district and the territories of the Order. The envoys conceded Polotsk, since it was occupied by Russian forces, but not its district or the Order's territories. Ivan ceded Courland, naming the Dvina river as the boundary between his and the king's territories, and on this basis he was prepared to conclude an armistice for ten or fifteen years, but the envoys refused. Then Ivan, gripped by his natural passion, broke all tradition and ordered the envoys brought before him in person. "I, a Christian sovereign," he said, "am demeaning myself by speaking directly with my brother's servants. What our boyars should have said to you, I myself will say. Do you have instructions from our brother about amity and an honest agreement? Tell us, how are we to resolve this matter fairly?"

"Gracious sovereign," Chodkiewicz replied, "grand prince! Permit me before your person to speak to you through our clerk, Michael Haraburda. I have grown up from youth under my own sovereign, and my Russian language gets mixed up with Polish, so it is impossible to know from my words what I am trying to say."

"Yury! Speak before us without hesitation," replied Ivan. "If you say something in Polish, we shall understand. You say that we are referring to towns which are in Poland, but this is old business. Kiev belonged to our ancestor Grand Prince Vladimir, and all those cities belonged to Kiev. Since the time of Grand Prince Vladimir our ancestors the great sovereigns, the Russian grand princes, ruled those cities and lands, which were acquired by your sovereign's ancestors through the misfortunes of our forefathers when Batu Khan attacked the Russian land.[15] We are not talking to our brother about foreign territory, we are speaking of our own patrimony, that which has belonged to us from time immemorial. Neither do we abase our brother's dignity at all, even though our brother still does not write our imperial name in full, thus taking away that which God has given us. For we claim what is ours, not anyone else's. All sovereigns write out our name in full, even those superior to your sovereign. If he refuses to do so, that is his business, he himself must know the reason why, although our ancestors could trace their origins to Caesar Augustus. We received from our ancestors the right to rule as sovereigns in our own realm. Who can take away what God has granted? We write our own name in documents as God gave it to us. If our brother does not describe us in his documents using our full title, we do not need his description."

The boyars, in conversation with the envoys, explained the genealogy of the Muscovite sovereigns. Caesar Augustus ruled the universe and stationed his brother Prus on the banks of the Vistula as far as the Nieman river. To this day it is named the Prussian land after him. From Prus to the great sovereign Riurik it was fourteen generations. Ivan declared that he did not care whether or not the king called him tsar, and perhaps not, although its usage might have removed one of the obstacles to peace. There remained a more important obstacle, namely Livonia.

Chodkiewicz refused the tsar's conditions and left empty-handed. Resumption of hostilities brought a reverse for the Muscovites. In its disadvantageous position, not far from Orsha on the Ulla river, the Muscovite army under Shuisky was defeated by Hetman Radziwill. Shuisky was killed in the fighting along with the two Paletsky princes. Two commanders, Zakhar Pleshcheev and Ivan Okhliabinin, were taken prisoner. A few of the junior boyars were killed. The rest managed to escape since the engagement took place towards nightfall. Yet the Lithuanian army made as little use of this second battle at Orsha as they did of the first. Kurbsky's desertion did not bring over other commanders. The commander of Polotsk, Prince Peter Shcheniatiev, rejected Radziwill's proposal to give up the city. The Russians captured Ozerishche and repulsed the Lithuanians from Chernigov. Kurbsky's actions in the Velikie Luki district consisted only in devastating some open positions. The campaign in Livonia proceeded with intermittent success.

Negotiations were reopened. Again a courier came from the bishop and the lords to see the metropolitan and boyars and *pick a quarrel.* In accordance with the earlier declaration that it was improper for the metropolitan to communicate with a bishop, the courier was not allowed to see the metropolitan. He presented his message only to the boyars, who answered that the tsar wanted peace and was calling a halt to hostilities.

The tsar sent the courier Zhelninsky with a safe conduct for the Lithuanians. He was issued the following instructions. "If the question arises about Andrei Kurbsky and why he deserted the tsar, answer, 'Although his sovereign gave him a generous salary, he committed treason. The sovereign wished to punish him, so he betrayed the sovereign. This was no wonder. Even if they do not go as far as Kurbsky in fleeing the realm, such traitors are of no concern to the Muscovite realm. By the grace of God and the health of our sovereign, the Muscovite realm does not lack men. Kurbsky betrayed our sovereign. He ran like a dog and disappeared like one.' If there are questions about the Germans in Dorpat, and as to why the tsar gave orders to move them to towns in Muscovy, answer, 'The sovereign gave orders to transfer the Germans because they communicated with the Livonian master and thus betrayed the tsar, telling him to come to the city bringing many men.' If you are asked where your sovereign went during the winter and why he disgraced many, answer, 'The sovereign was in his village during the winter. He disgraced the boyars and courtiers who committed great treason against him. For their great treacheries he ordered them executed." Zhelninsky was forbidden to speak to Kurbsky and the other traitors if he met them.

When the Lithuanian courier Jurjaga arrived in Moscow, the bailiff was similarly given instructions as to what to say to him. "If he asks, 'What is this oprichnina that we hear your sovereign has?' answer, 'Our sovereign has no oprichnina whatsoever. He lives at his own court. Those of his servitors who truly serve him live close by; those who serve him falsely live further away. The talk of such ignorant men who call it an oprichnina is not to be believed. The tsar is free to place his court and mansions wherever he pleases. Whom would he want to avoid?'"

Jurjaga arrived with news of the impending arrival of the plenipotentiaries Chodkiewicz and Tishkevich. When they arrived in Moscow the bailiffs were given the following instructions. "If the ambassadors ask about Prince Mikhail Vorotynsky and about his disgrace, tell them that only God is without sin and not one of the sovereign's servants is blameless. Prince Mikhail offended the sovereign, who had to bring disgrace upon him. Now the sovereign has reinstated him and given back to him his former patrimony, the cities of Odoev and Novosil, and more besides."

The ambassadors refused to conclude a permanent peace but tried to talk about an armistice. They were willing to concede Polotsk and all the lands in Livonia occupied by the Muscovite army. The tsar refused. He demanded Riga and other cities, although he conceded to the king Courland and several towns on the near side of the Dvina.

The ambassadors disagreed. They declared that a peace could be concluded more easily at a personal meeting between the tsar and the king at the border. Ivan readily agreed to this proposal. He demanded that the ambassadors immediately set down the details of the conference and the entire ceremony. The ambassadors refused to decide such an important matter on the spot and requested that a date be set for the arrival of new ambassadors.

The tsar, consulting his boyars, decided not to speak about such a conference with ambassadors. The matter could only be dragged out by such talks, and it was impossible to determine whether the king himself wanted to attend such a conference. He would only delay matters. Better for the tsar to send his own ambassadors to the king for talks about the fate of the Livonian land and the Polotsk district. They would find out whether or not the king wanted to come to a decision with the tsar over Livonia. The ambassadors could also find out in Lithuania all the local news, such as whether or not the king was in agreement with the emperor and the Poles and what his intentions were. While the tsar's ambassadors were with the king, the tsar would give orders to assemble supplies and artillery in preparation for a grand campaign against Livonia.

ASSEMBLY IN MOSCOW CONSIDERS NEGOTIATIONS

The king's willingness to concede all the towns and lands captured by the Muscovite forces made Ivan reconsider. The essential question he faced was whether it was worthwhile continuing a difficult war, the outcome of which was questionable. The defeat at Orsha and Kurbsky's defection offered little encouragement. An armistice meant keeping all conquests, which included Yuriev [Dorpat] and Polotsk. Such an armistice would be glorious. Besides, the king was in poor health and childless. Perhaps the whole of Lithuania could be united to Muscovy without war!

On the other hand giving up the idea of gaining the seacoast meant abandoning the chief aim of the war. It would allow the Lithuanian king to keep Riga and other important Livonian towns, gathering gratuitously the spoils won by Russian arms. It was difficult and vexing for Ivan. He was unwilling to decide this question alone. The opinions of the disgraced boyars, whom he suspected of infidelity and malice, were hardly adequate. He wanted to find out what other classes thought about the war.

He did not think he could find this out through the oprichniks, who stood as antagonists to the rest of the population, nor would it be possible through the zemshchina boyars, from whom he did not expect the truth. To consult the whole country through elected delegates was not an innovation for Ivan. In his youth he had summoned such representatives to the platform on the Red Square in order ceremoniously to absolve himself of blame for the people's earlier misfortunes and thrust the blame upon the boyars.

So in the summer of 1566 the tsar gave orders to convene a great assembly. He called for representatives from the clergy, the boyars, the lords-in-waiting, treasury officials, chancellery officials, the service gentry of the

first rank, the service gentry and junior boyars of the second rank, holders
of service estates in the western areas near the Lithuanian border, the
Toropets and Lutsk districts, as men most familiar with local conditions,
the chancellors and administrative officials, factors and the leading merchants of Moscow and Smolensk.

He presented them with the conditions under which he considered
making peace with the king, and asked their advice. The clergy, consisting
of nine hierarchs, fourteen archimandrites and abbots, and nine elders,
advised, "How great is our sovereign's humility! He gives up to the king
five cities in the Polotsk district, sixty or seventy versts on the other side
of the Dvina, the city of Ozerishche, the township of Uswiat in Livonia,
sixteen towns in Courland beyond the Dvina, and fifteen Livonian towns
on this side of the Dvina, together with their districts and dependent areas.
He gives back the Polotsk prisoners of war without payment or exchange
while he buys back his own. The justice of our sovereign is indeed great
compared to that of the king!

"No more must be given up. Better indeed to claim those Livonian cities
which the king took under his protection, Riga, Wenden, Wolmar, Rannen-
burg, Kokenhausen and other cities which touch our frontier cities of
Pskov and Yuriev. If the sovereign does not claim these cities, they will
become forever the king's, from whence will arise destruction of the sovereign's churches in the Livonian cities. Not only will there be great oppression in Yuriev and other Livonian cities and in Pskov, but matters also
will become very difficult for the traders of Novgorod the Great and other
cities.

"The king intervened in the Livonian cities and held them unjustly.
When our sovereign intervened in the Livonian land to punish its wrongs,
he took the master and the bishop and many people captive but blessed the
Livonian towns with Orthodoxy and built churches within them. The
remaining Germans realized their impotence and turned themselves and
all their cities over to the king. Had our sovereign not intervened in the
Livonian land, could the king have taken even one Livonian city? The
Livonian land from the time of our sovereign's ancestors, from the great
sovereign Yaroslav, son of Vladimir, belongs to him. Is this the king's
justice, that in the middle of a truce with our sovereign the king's men come
and capture our town of Tarwast and hold its people captive?

"Our advice is that it would be disadvantageous for our sovereign to
give up those Livonian cities that the king took under his protection. Better

to claim them, but whether or not the sovereign does claim them is up to him, as God instructs. We must pray to God for him, the sovereign, but it would be improper for us to give advice.

"The king's ambassadors wish to ascribe to the Polotsk land fifteen versts upriver along the Dvina and five versts downriver on the Polotsk side, but no land across the Dvina, thus making the Dvina the border; but how then would it be possible for the city to exist without its hinterland? Villages and hamlets cannot exist without their fields and other amenities. How can a city exist without any of its districts?"

The boyars, lords-in-waiting and chancellery officials for their part said, "Only God and our sovereign know how God reveals His will to him. It seems to us that the Livonian towns by no means should be relinquished to the king, for it would subject Polotsk to a state of siege. If the Polotsk land across the river is relinquished, Polotsk's trading quarters across the river will belong to the king. On this side of the Dvina the Polotsk district consists of inferior places; all the best places are across the Dvina. If during the years of the armistice the Lithuanians construct a town across the Dvina, when the armistice runs out Polotsk cannot last. If soldiers appear in the king's Livonian towns, Pskov will be imperilled, not to speak of Yuriev and the other towns. Better for the sovereign not to make peace on the basis of these immoderate demands, since that would allow the king to replenish his army.

"Our sovereign was much inclined to every Christian good and so acted, but the Lithuanian ambassadors were acting in bad faith. They made excessive demands and beyond that said nothing. Therefore it is better now, begging the Lord's mercy, for the sovereign to treat the king with a measure of his own justice. The king has not captured a point of vantage over the sovereign, who is more blessed by God than ever before.

"As far as a conference is concerned, we boyars, lords-in-waiting and administrative officials are of the following mind. Dismiss the suggestions of the Lithuanian ambassadors for a conference. It would be improper for boyars to meet with the Polish lords on the border, for this would be unprecedented. If the king wishes to meet with our sovereign and come to an agreement, let the sovereign's wishes for a Christian peace be expressed. It is well known how the Lithuanian ambassadors speak about a conference in order to deceive us while they gather troops and conspire with the Poles, fortifying the Livonian land and garrisoning it with soldiers. From all accounts the king needs more time and is at odds with the emperor. Should Poland go to war against the emperor, the Lithuanian land could not hope for any help from the Poles. Taking into account all these diplomatic considerations, it would not be wise to make peace with the king. We shall pledge our own lives to the tsar, realizing the king's deception, and keep our faith in God. God humbles the proud. We have expressed our thinking to the sovereign as it appears to us, but God will advise the sovereign in all things."

The keeper of the seal and chancellor Ivan Viskovaty expressed his opinion separately. He felt it would be possible to conclude an armistice with the king without demanding the Livonian cities, but only if the king withdrew his soldiers and did not prevent the tsar from acquiring them; and if he promised also not to come to their aid even after the armistice expired.

The service gentry and junior boyars agreed with the clergy and boyars. The service gentry from Toropets declared, "We the sovereign's slaves would sacrifice our lives for even one desiatina of land in the Polotsk or Ozerishche district. We are ready to die for Polotsk. We, the sovereign's slaves, are mounted and ready and will die fighting for the sovereign. Our sovereign is more just than the king. Had the sovereign not fought for the Livonian land, the king would never have been able to intervene, but now he is intervening. In our opinion the sovereign must maintain his claim to the Livonian cities. We, his slaves, are ready to do the sovereign's bidding." The rest answered in the same vein.

Hearing these opinions, Ivan sent the boyar Kolychev-Umnoy[16] to Lithuania. He was instructed to refuse an armistice, not only if Livonia remained unsecured, but also if the king refused to grant him the title of tsar of Livonia or if he refused to extradite Kurbsky. His instructions were, if the Lithuanian lords asserted that the tsar should give them Tsarevich Ivan to rule their realm, he must answer that he had no instructions to that effect, and without instructions how could he speak about such an important matter? If this matter was important to their sovereign or to the lords, they should send envoys to the sovereign, but God alone knew what their sovereign wished them to do.

If anyone asked why the sovereign ordered a court for himself situated outside the city, Kolychev was to answer that it was in order for the sovereign to maintain his composure. If someone tried to say that the tsar set up his court for the sake of separation or in order to punish the boyars he was to answer that the sovereign had no need to set up courts for this purpose. He was free among his people to reward the good and punish the evil. From whom should he wish to separate? If anyone tried to say that the tsar was unmerciful and executed people, or if they tried to speak about Prince Vasily Rybin or Ivan Karamyshev, the ambassador was to answer that the sovereign was merciful but punished evildoers everywhere. Regarding those two, the sovereign discovered they had plotted evil against him and his land.

If in response to his demanding, as part of his ambassadorial mission, that the king hand back to the sovereign Andrei Kurbsky and the junior boyars who went over with him, the council of lords said that extraditing such men was never done under any previous sovereign, he was to answer that the sovereign demanded their extradition because they were causing quarrels between sovereigns and urging further spilling of Christian blood. If they asked what treacheries Prince Kurbsky committed against the sovereign, he was to answer that Kurbsky had contrived every evil against the sovereign, against Tsaritsa Anastasia, and against their children. He called himself the rightful owner of Yaroslavl, over which he wanted absolute rule.

Kolychev reported back to Ivan that his proposals were rejected, that the Muscovite ambassadors were treated most dishonorably in Lithuania and were not fed, and that the king sent his courier Bykowski to Moscow with a declaration of war.

Bykowski met Ivan on the road to Novgorod. The tsar received him in his tent, dressed in his armor, with all those around him similarly armed. After complaining about the poor treatment Kolychev received, Ivan said to the courier, "You should not be surprised that we are sitting in battle array. You came to us with arrows from our brother Sigismund Augustus, so that is why we are sitting in this fashion." Bykowski answered with his own complaint. Moscow's ambassadors, Kolychev-Umnoy and his companions, did nothing good. After it was agreed that the lords would not start a war before October 1, 1567, and after they started to draw up the document, the Russian tsar's commanders refused to accept it because therein Chodkiewicz was called the administrator of Livonia. Calling upon God as his witness that the war was not over that, the king declared war through Bykowski, though he promised to receive a Muscovite ambassador.

The tsar and his son Tsarevich Ivan listened to the king's letter. After consulting the boyars they decided to hold Bykowski because the document presented to them contained antagonistic words. Bykowski's possessions and the goods of the merchants travelling with him were confiscated by the treasury.

HOSTILITIES RENEWED

Ivan proceeded to Novgorod. He would have opened the campaign from there, but on the advice of his commanders he decided to confine himself to a defensive war. At the start of 1568 Hetman Chodkiewicz besieged the Muscovite fortress of Ulla but was forced to lift the siege for the following reasons, as he later explained to the king. "Arriving at the enemy fortress of Ulla, I besieged it for three weeks, using every means against it. Seeing that our rank and file soldiers and platoon leaders were afraid of the enemy, fearing death, I ordered them to attack at night so that they would not see if their comrades were killed and would not be afraid, but this did not help. Other cavalry captains advanced, though not very quickly, indeed just barely dragging themselves along, but the common soldiers all tried to hide in the woods, in the ditches, along the river banks. Despite appeals, promises and beatings (it went so far that I actually bloodied my hands), they refused absolutely to attack the fortress. The more we urged them on, the more they ran and hid. As a result the night and morning were spent absolutely uselessly. The same thing with the cossacks I hired; they got as far as the moat, then turned and fled.

"Then I made up a detachment of Germans, gunners, and my servants, among whom was a Muscovite named Orel who defected to me from the fortress. They built a siege ramp against the wall and set fire to the fortress, but our soldiers would not help them in the slightest, would not even shoot so as to keep the besieged army from putting out the fire. Seeing this, I myself dismounted and went up to the spot from which the soldiers were ordered to advance upon the ramp. I tried to give them encouragement. I wanted either to demonstrate the service due to your royal majesty or sacrifice my own life, but unfortunately neither happened. After lengthy reminders, requests, threats and beatings, when nothing helped, I gave orders to throw up another ramp Tatar fashion, log upon log. The ramp was built successfully, but the bravery of the Muscovites and the cowardice of our men ruined everything. Some Muscovites jumped out of the fort and, to our shame, burned the ramp. Our men not only failed to protect it but did not even dare fire one shot and later fled from the entrenchments.

"When I got to the artillery emplacements I could not find any troops, not in the forward trenches, not even, except for a few cavalry captains, in the second or third trenches. We had to dismount four cavalry companies and get them to guard the cannon, but there was no hope for the infantry."

When Ivan returned to Alexandrov Village he wrote to the boyars in Moscow. He ordered them to discuss the Lithuanian affair and write to him at his village, advising him whether to make peace with the king. At the same time he gave orders to treat Bykowski well.

The boyars answered that he should send Bykowski back to the king with a document pointing out the king's injustice in detaining and dishonoring the tsar's ambassadors, Kolychev and his companions, which contravened accepted tradition. The document should point out the king's other misdeeds but subsequently should be written a little more gently so as not to break off relations. If the king wished to send a courier or emissary, he should be given free passage. Bykowski and the merchants should be given back their goods or the cash equivalent.

The tsar replied with a second question, whether or not he should make peace, and if so, on what basis. The boyars answered that the time to decide was when the king renewed relations, in the light of his communication. The tsar should not relinquish Livonian land as set out in the previous resolution. Ivan ordered the boyars to do what they thought best. He did not return all their possessions to Bykowski and the merchants, and when the courier complained, Ivan answered, "What we gave you came from our treasury. Go with that. You came to us with a declaration of war, so you should be satisfied that we did not give orders to spill your blood. If there are to be communications about serious matters between us and our brother King Sigismund, make that your only business."

Ivan wrote in the document to the king that he was inclined to go to war against him because of his discourteous document, but an outbreak of plague restrained him. He explained Bykowski's detention by quoting an ancient saying that those who bring a declaration of war will not fill their bellies by it.

KING'S ILLNESS HALTS OFFENSIVE

Bykowski's return greatly relieved the Lithuanians. The king's deteriorating health forced them to consider making important concessions. A courier arrived in Moscow with a request for safe conduct for plenipotentiaries. The king sent his regards and called Ivan *tsar*. Ivan told his keeper of the seal to find out in conversation with the courier the significance of this news. The courier answered that the lords of the council ordered him to do so to show honor to the tsar.

As a result of the honor the courier was awarded Bykowski's confiscated goods. A safe conduct also was issued, but no sooner had the courier departed than news arrived that the Lithuanian commanders, the Polubensky princes from Wolmar, had seized Izborsk.

The tsar sent orders to his commanders to take Izborsk back from the Lithuanians, orders which were fulfilled at once. The junior boyar Miasoyedov was sent to Lithuania with a complaint against the Polubenskys and a demand for the release of the captured commander of Izborsk. Miasoyedov was instructed to investigate as to "why is it being said in Lithuania and Poland that Tsarevich Ivan is acceptable as ruler of the grand principality of Lithuania and of Poland, and why is this rumor being spread among the people? Is it a ruse or do the Lithuanians truly want it, and do all the people want it, and why is the rumor not made an outright declaration instead of being spread as a rumor?"

Miasoyedov was also given the following instructions. "If Prince Andrei Kurbsky or any other of those who have betrayed the tsar try to speak to you, answer, 'What can be said to a traitor? How much evil have you not wrought with your treachery and unscrupulous behavior? God grants victory from on high to the sovereign against his enemies and destroys your treachery.' Say no more than that, and go away. To an unimportant traitor say nothing, rather single him out, spit in his face and go away."

IVAN AS CANDIDATE FOR POLISH THRONE

In 1570 the Lithuanian plenipotentiaries Jan Krotoszewski and Nicholas Tawlosz arrived. During the negotiations arguments again arose over the Polotsk boundaries, as a result of which they failed to come to any agreement. In order to facilitate their business the ambassadors asked for permission to talk directly to the tsar.

They declared to Ivan that it would be particularly to his advantage to conclude a peace. When Ivan asked why, the ambassadors answered, "Our sovereign's council of lords of the Polish kingdom and that of the Lithuanian grand principality have consulted over the fact that our sovereign has no children. If the Lord God takes our sovereign from this world, neither council intends to choose a sovereign for themselves from the Muslim or other lands. They would prefer to choose a sovereign from a Slavic family and willingly, not involuntarily. Thus they send their respects to you, great sovereign, and to your descendants."

"We have heard such rumors previously," the tsar replied. "By God's mercy and the prayers of our ancestors our realm is complete, so why should we want yours? If you want us, you had best not irritate us but do as we instructed our boyars to tell you, so that Christendom might remain at peace." Ivan then delivered a long speech taking up forty-four pages in the diplomatic book, in which he related to the ambassadors in proper order the history of relations between Muscovy and Lithuania in his reign, concluding by saying that the war was not his doing but the king's.

When Ivan finished, the ambassadors said they did not understand fully certain phrases, for they did not know all the Russian words; would the tsar therefore order his speech written down for them? Ivan answered that their clerk heard and understood it all, and could relate it to them. The clerk was afraid and said, "Merciful sovereign! It is impossible to remember such great things. Your intelligence is a sovereign gift from God and is superior to the normal human mind."

An armistice was concluded for three years, with everything to be left as it was. During those three years they would conduct negotiations for peace. Princes Kanbarov and Meshchersky were sent to Lithuania to ratify the armistice. They were issued these instructions. "If they try to say that your sovereign executed many in Novgorod, Pskov and Moscow, answer, 'How came you to know this?' If they say they know, say, 'If you know about it, there is nothing we can tell you, except that God revealed to our sovereign the treachery of the evil affair in which you communicated through a spy to those who wished to betray our sovereign, and therefore such a fate befell the traitors. It was an absurd undertaking. When Prince Simon Luvgeny and Prince Mikhail Olelkovich were in Novgorod, even then Lithuania could not hold it. Whenever we cannot hold a place, we do not try to do so.'

"If you are asked why your sovereign executed the treasurer Funikov, the keeper of the seal Viskovaty, chancellors, junior boyars and many minor officials, answer, 'God revealed to our sovereign the communications between these traitors, the traitor Kurbsky and you, lords of the council. Therefore they were executed. Their blood lies on those who perpetrated such treachery. It was thanks to Lithuania that things did not go well for Novgorod and Pskov.'"

The instructions also told the ambassadors how to act in the event of Sigismund's death and the choosing of a new king. "If the king dies and in his place they enthrone a sovereign from another realm, do not ratify the armistice with him but demand that he send envoys to Moscow. If one of the lords of the council accedes to the throne, you ambassadors are not to attend court. If they force you to come to discharge your embassy, when you enter the chancellery remain seated, do not bow or present your credentials, but say, 'He is like our brother, and we were not sent to such a man. It is not fitting for our sovereign to communicate with a slave, with our brother, not even through us the high ambassadors.'"

The Muscovite ambassadors sent some welcome news to Moscow. "The king has removed all restrictions from Wilno. He has dropped his claim to Wilno, saying that wherever Polotsk goes, there Wilno should go also. Wilno, in position and approach, is no stronger than Polotsk; Muscovites approaching it would not be turned back. Both councils of lords wish the tsar or the tsarevich for the kingdom. They do not want to choose a king from among the Turks for he would be a Muslim, and there would be oppression by the Turks. If they took a king from the emperor, there would be little in it for them since he is a poor protector of his friends, but the tsar is a sovereign valiant and strong. He could provide protection from the Turkish sultan and from all countries and even call upon his own realm for reinforcements. They wanted to petition the tsar about the tsarevich until a certain Evstafy Wolowicz dissuaded them, acting through the dark counsels of the king, who thought of nominating as his successor his relative, a Hungarian crown prince, but the prince died. In Warsaw it was said that there was no point in looking for any other than the Muscovite sovereign. The lords were said to be ordering clothes on the Muscovite pattern, and many were wearing them already. They were collecting velvets and damasks for gowns also made in the Muscovite style for the royal princesses. The king's sister wanted very much to marry the tsar."

IVAN'S LIVONIAN VASSAL MAGNUS

Election as king of himself or of his son held little temptation for Ivan. Even one of lesser intelligence must have realized that it was most unlikely. One thought occupied Ivan's mind, the acquisition of Livonia. He finally decided to offer Polotsk to Lithuania in return for Livonia, but would the king agree? Even if Sigismund Augustus and the Sejm agreed to yield the Livonian cities entrusted to them, those cities might then turn to other defenders. Reval was already in Swedish hands. Even without defenders the coastal cities could long hold out against the Muscovite army. In short, gaining direct rule over Livonia would demand more blood, more time.

Ivan hit upon the thought of indirect rule, of giving Livonia a German ruler who would accept a vassal relationship with the Muscovite sovereign such as the duke of Courland maintained with the Polish king. In 1564 Ivan proposed to his captive the elderly Master Fürstenberg to return to rule Livonia if he would swear, on behalf of all the ranks and towns, fidelity to the tsar and his descendants as his hereditary supreme sovereign. Fürstenberg, unwilling to break the vow he made to the Holy Roman

empire, rejected the proposal. At least that was how the story is related in
the Livonian chronicles.

The Polish court received different information at the end of 1564. It
was reported from Moscow that an envoy from the grand master of the
German order, nominally restored in Germany, was petitioning for
Fürstenberg's freedom on the following conditions. (1) Upon his return to
Livonia, Fürstenberg restore all the Greek Orthodox churches. (2) All the
chief fortresses in Livonia remain under Muscovite control. (3) The master
make no decisions without the approval of six Muscovite officials, to be
seated on his council. (4) If ever the master lacked troops, he would request
them only from Muscovy, not from any other realm without the tsar's
approval. (5) On Fürstenberg's death it would be up to the tsar to appoint
his successor. News of this arrangement with Fürstenberg greatly upset
King Sigismund Augustus, but in January 1565 different news arrived.
Fürstenberg died while preparing to move to Livonia.

At that time two captive Livonian nobles, Johann Taube and Ehlert
Kruse,[17] were enjoying the tsar's particular favor. They continually encouraged Ivan's notion of giving Livonia a special ruler who would be a
vassal of the Muscovite tsar. When Fürstenberg died they pointed out two
capable of succeeding him, namely Kettler, Fürstenberg's successor and
presently duke of Courland, and Magnus, the Danish prince and ruler of
Øsel.

Taube and Kruse set off for Dorpat in order to bring the matter more
quickly to a head. From there they wrote to Kettler but he refused. Then
they turned to Magnus who finally accepted the proposal, arriving in
Moscow in 1570. Ivan proclaimed him king of Livonia and bridegroom of
his kinswoman Yevfimia, daughter of his first cousin Prince Vladimir. The
captive citizens of Dorpat were allowed to return to their homeland.

Magnus gave his oath of fidelity in the following terms. (1) Should the
tsar himself go to war and summon King Magnus to go with him, he must
supply fifteen hundred horsemen and as many foot soldiers. If the tsar did
not go on campaign himself, Magnus was not required to go either, and
Magnus's army would be paid by the tsar's treasury. If Magnus led his
army separately from that of the tsar, his rank would be superior to that of
any Muscovite commander. Should Magnus not wish to take part personally in a campaign, he was obliged to pay the tsar's treasury three thalers
in lieu of each horseman and half that amount for each foot soldier. If the
tsar himself did not lead his forces in person, Magnus was not required to
contribute either men or money until such time as the whole of Livonia

was completely at peace. (2) Should Magnus wage war in Livonia and the tsar sent there some Muscovite commanders, the king must confer with the commanders but would have supreme command of the forces. (3) Magnus, his descendants, and all the inhabitants of Livonia were granted all former rights, freedoms, laws, and customs. (4) They could preserve their own religion with its Augsburg creed.[18] (5) The Livonian cities might trade duty-free in the Muscovite districts, although without any special protection, and in return King Magnus must allow free transit to Muscovy to all merchants from overseas with their goods; likewise to all artisans, tradesmen and military personnel. (6) If Riga, Reval and other Livonian cities did not recognize Magnus as their king, the tsar accepted an obligation to help him against those cities and against all enemies. (7) Upon the death of Magnus and his descendants, a successor was to be chosen with the general approval of all Livonians.

SWEDEN STEPS IN

The armistice that Ivan and Sigismund Augustus concluded limited the new king of Livonia by preventing him from taking any action against cities occupied by Polish garrisons. Reval, the second richest and second most important city in Magnus's kingdom, was not occupied by Poles but by Swedes.

We have seen how Ivan preferred to conserve his strength for his most dangerous enemy, Lithuania. For this reason he kept the peace with Sweden despite the seizure of Reval. In 1563 Ivan concluded with King Erik a new armistice to last for seven years. Erik again insisted that he be allowed to deal directly with the tsar but again received a decisive rebuff. The tsar gave orders to write back to Erik about the absurd and disagreeable nature of his writings. In the document were many strange and derisive expressions, reproaching Erik for his folly. Erik was informed that the only time his kingly authority would prevail was when his majesty the tsar and his court were floating around the Swedish islands. He was told that the royal request to confer directly with the tsar was as far from reality as heaven is from the earth. Soon afterwards, however, very friendly direct relations emerged between the two sovereigns. Let us consider for a moment Erik's character. In certain respects it serves to explain Ivan's.

Gustav Vasa left four sons. The eldest, Erik, became king. His three brothers received dukedoms. John obtained Finland, Magnus Øsel and Östergötland, and Karl Södermanland. Erik's understanding of the difficulties of his position are evident in the following conversation between himself and his favorite, the Swedish magnate Persson. "My dear departed father," Erik told Persson, "left me in a difficult position by dividing up the dukedoms among my brothers." "The late king," responded Persson, "justified his actions on the grounds that it would have been much worse had your brothers been made less powerful than the magnates. He preferred domestic quarrelling between the king and his powerful brothers to driving the royal house out of the country altogether and allowing the return of a different form of government. He knew well that in the event of quarrels among brothers Sweden would yet support its royal family but that the loyalty would be forfeited if the power of the magnates grew too strong. The best way to prevent that was to have powerful dukes standing over them."

Hence Erik, like Ivan, was ruled by a dread of boyars, and neither was in a position to do anything about it. In Erik's case suspicion and fear of the magnates did not entirely exclude suspicion and fear of his brothers. Soon the conduct of Duke John of Finland strengthened these feelings.

The occupation of Reval threatened to involve Sweden in a war with Poland since Sigismund Augustus, like Ivan, declared his right to all the Order's territories. When war finally did break out, the Swedish general Horn captured Pernau and Wittenstein from the Poles. At the time John of Finland declared himself on Poland's side. He advised his brother Erik to conclude a pact with Poland against Muscovy and to give back to Sigismund Augustus all the Livonian positions taken by the Swedes. Moreover John married Sigismund Augustus's sister Katarzyna, whom the tsar had courted unsuccessfully. John gave his brother-in-law a significant sum of money and, as a guarantee, occupied several places in Livonia. The conditions of the marriage agreement remained secret to Erik, but it was said that John promised to act as a free and independent sovereign.

Erik ordered the serving gentry in Finland to move into Livonia against the Poles; John he ordered to appear in Stockholm before a tribunal to answer for his pact with enemies of the realm. John replied by throwing the king's envoys into prison. He called the Finns to arms, demanded their personal allegiance as an independent monarch, and requested aid from Poland and Prussia.

The Swedish estates sentenced him in his absence to death. He was besieged by the king's army in Åbo and received no aid. After two months he was forced to surrender. He was taken to Sweden and imprisoned in Gripsholm castle, together with his wife who refused to be parted from him. Despite Persson's advice, Erik did not execute his brother.

For the rest, Erik fluctuated between terror and repentance. He removed himself from his magnates and surrounded himself with low-born favorites who, for their own personal advantage, made him more and more suspicious of others. He became gloomy and severe and eventually suffered fits of insanity and rage. The results can be seen in certain facts. In 1562 only one death sentence was passed in Sweden. In 1563 there were fifty, of which thirty-two were related to the case of Duke John. By October 1567 altogether two hundred and thirty-two were sentenced to death. Mere words or signs were reckoned to be crimes against the state. Yet at the same time, even during his fits, Erik displayed an energetic intellectual capacity. No one wrote as much or as quickly as he.

Finding himself at war with Poland and Denmark, Erik had to seek a rapprochement with the Muscovite tsar. It came about as a result of Erik's promise to surrender to Ivan his sister-in-law Katarzyna, wife of the imprisoned duke of Finland. The tsar in return ceded Estonia to the king, whom he promised to help in his war with Sigismund and in making peace with Denmark and the Hanseatic cities.

Ivan explained his desire to have Katarzyna in his hands. If Erik intended to wait to give her away until after proclaiming her husband's death, he would refuse to marry her or keep her as his mistress, but he wanted to have her in his hands in order to annoy her brother, his enemy the Polish king, and through her compel the conclusion of an advantageous peace.

Muscovite envoys appeared in Sweden, as was customary, to accept the king's promise to fulfill the agreement, but Erik was unable to fulfill it. He had freed his brother John from prison. In a fit of insanity it had seemed to him that he himself was imprisoned and his brother was ruling. The Muscovite envoys waited a full year. Magnates came to explain that the tsar's request could not now be fulfilled. Katarzyna could not be given away to him, for now that would be a sacrilegious matter and inglorious for the tsar himself. "Our sovereign," the envoys replied, "is taking Katarzyna, sister of the Polish king, from your sovereign for his honor. He wishes to gain an advantage over his enemy the Polish king, who is also your sovereign's enemy." When they tried under the pretext of giving them better accommodations to transfer the envoys from Stockholm to a village, the envoys refused to move voluntarily. Let the king do as he pleased. They had committed no offense against him, so why was he banishing the envoys to a village as if they had committed a crime?

Finally they were allowed to see the king, who said to them, "We have given you no answer up to now because the devil and some evil people have started some nasty business here. Besides which, the Danish war prevented us from doing so." Later Erik decided he should arrest a second brother. He gave instructions to tell the envoys he was giving them Katarzyna. One day a "young lad, an inhabitant of the royal household" arrived to see the envoys. It is a known fact that Erik, fearing the magnates, took young men from school and gave them various tasks. The young lad declared that the king sent him with orders to tell the envoys to take him with them to Russia. He was afraid of his own magnates, no longer free to act on his own.

On September 29, 1568 an uprising broke out against Erik, who summoned the Muscovite envoys and told them about it. "How long ago," asked the envoys, "did the matter begin?" "From the moment my envoys arrived with you from Russia," Erik replied. "I was in Uppsala then. The rebels plotted in secret, and I was locked up. I would still be their captive had not the Danes invaded my lands, but since the Danes did come the rebels let me go, since there was no one else to protect the country. After that things improved. If my brother John kills me or takes me prisoner, the tsar should not recognize John as king." Concerning Katarzyna, Erik said, "I promised such a thing in anticipation of John's death. Because of it I found myself in great enmity with my brothers, with the Polish king, with other sovereigns, with everyone, but in all else I am happy to befriend and oblige your sovereign. All my hopes lie with God and your sovereign, but how could we take away a living man's wife?"

The uprising ended in Erik's overthrow and the elevation of his brother John to the throne. During the uprising the soldiers burst in upon the envoys and robbed them. The new king sent to Moscow begging a safe conduct for his envoys. The charter was granted, but when the Swedish envoys arrived they were seized and told, "King John sent to the tsar and grand prince requesting a safe conduct for his envoys. Our sovereign instructed his Novgorod vicegerents to establish peace and amity according to previous customs, and the tsar and grand prince sent King John a charter of safe conduct, but King John did not observe this formal reply and the tsar's safe conduct. He sent his envoys with empty messages undeserving of the safe conduct. John writes to us to conclude a peace with him with the same conditions that his majesty the tsar would have granted to his brother King Erik. If King John were now to send Katarzyna, sister of the Polish king, to his majesty the tsar, the tsar would conclude a peace with him according to the agreement made with King Erik. Have you instructions concerning Princess Katarzyna with you?"

"We know nothing," the envoys answered, "about the message our sovereign King John wrote to the tsar. We were sent not to argue, for our sovereign wishes to establish peace and neighborly relations between us. We are only saying what our sovereign ordered us to say." The Muscovites told the envoys they would be banished to Murom, whereupon they begged the boyars to have the tsar alleviate their disgrace and order his Novgorod vicegerents to conclude a peace with their king. The peace would be as of old, with the exception that to the king's side should be ascribed those Livonian cities that tsar relinquished to Erik.

Just then Prince Magnus appeared in Moscow. According to the Swedish envoys he did them great harm and incensed the tsar against them. The boyars argued that the Swedish envoys be held while the tsar dealt with Livonian matters and heard the petition of the Danish prince Magnus on how best to handle these matters. Once they were settled, the tsar should deal with Swedish matters.

MAGNUS FAILS AGAINST POLAND

The tsar agreed and ordered the Swedish envoys to Murom. On August 21, 1570 Magnus arrived at Reval with a Russian force of twenty-five thousand and a large detachment of Livonians, including many volunteers from among the gentry and townsmen.

A request to the people of Reval to surrender had no effect, so Magnus laid a siege. It was impossible to starve the inhabitants out because Swedish ships supplied them with everything they needed. Bombardment of the city had little effect. Magnus sent his court chaplain into Reval to urge the besieged to surrender, but that did not help. Magnus, realizing his failure, lashed out at Taube and Kruse, accusing them of bringing him to Reval with false promises. After spending thirty weeks outside the city, on March 16, 1571 he burned the camp and laid waste the surrounding countryside. The Russian part of his army made for Narva. The Livonians tried to take Wittenstein but were unsuccessful. After that Magnus retired to Oberpahlen.

Taube and Kruse, frightened at being held responsible for the failure by the tsar, whom they promised an easy victory at Reval, travelled to Dorpat and from there corresponded secretly with the Polish king. They promised to rule Dorpat in his interests if he would receive them graciously and grant them the same benefits they enjoyed in Moscow.

Sigismund Augustus accepted their proposal. They persuaded Rosen, chief of the Livonian guard in Russian service at Dorpat, to turn against the Russians and attack them unexpectedly on a Sunday after dinner when they usually slept. At first the conspirators were successful. They overcame the Russian guards, opened the prisons and freed the prisoners, who grabbed the weapons of the slain and joined the conspirators, but when the conspirators called the inhabitants of Dorpat to arms, the citizens shut themselves indoors in terror.

The junior boyars and musketeers constituting the Russian garrison also blockaded themselves in houses, where they managed to arm themselves. The musketeers stationed in the trading quarter as well as Russian merchants came to their aid with all sorts of arms and soon cleared the city of Rosen's detachment. They did not spare the inhabitants, whom they suspected of complicity in the attempt. Taube and Kruse removed their families and belongings beforehand from Dorpat. The moment they knew the conspiracy had failed they set out for Poland, where the Polish king gave them a gracious welcome.

Magnus, hearing about the affair in Dorpat and fearing the tsar's wrath, sent a letter to Ivan with his assurance that he knew nothing about the conspiracy. He also considered it prudent to leave Oberpahlen and retire to his previous rulership on the island of Øsel. Ivan was quick to put Magnus at ease. His bride Yevfimia having recently died, Ivan offered Magnus the hand of her younger sister Maria.[19] He agreed, and their former relationship was restored.

QUEEN ELIZABETH OFFERS IVAN ASYLUM

Ivan's enemies well understood and appreciated Ivan's determination to acquire a Baltic territory. Sigismund Augustus, attempting to stop the trade with Narva, wrote to Queen Elizabeth in England, "The Muscovite sovereign daily grows stronger by acquiring the objects that are brought to Narva, not only goods but arms the like of which he never saw before. Not only are crafted items brought there, but craftsmen themselves are also coming. By these devices he is acquiring the means to defeat everyone. The strength of this enemy and the power that he exercises over his subjects is not unknown to your majesty. Hitherto we have been able to defeat him only because he was ignorant and did not know the arts. If navigation to Narva is continued, what will remain unknown to him?"

The English government paid little attention to the apprehensions of Ivan's neighbors and continued relations with Muscovy, concerned only to win more trading advantages for its merchants. The tsar in his amicable relations with Elizabeth had in mind something besides trade. Just as his friend Erik of Sweden asked the Muscovite envoys to take him to Russia, so Ivan asked Elizabeth to grant him asylum in England should he be driven out of his own country. Elizabeth answered him that if ever her dear brother the great emperor and grand prince needed to leave his own country as a result of conspiracy or attack by foreign enemies, she would welcome him and his wife and children with the honor befitting such a great sovereign. He would be assured of leading his life in complete freedom and tranquillity with all he brought with him, and he would have complete freedom regarding his faith. He would be granted a comfortable residence with sufficient income to live there as long as he wished.

CRIMEAN AFFAIRS

When Ivan turned all his attention to Livonia he needed to preserve the peace on his Crimean flank. He thought that after the accomplishments of Vishnevetsky, Rzhevsky and Adashev, and after the capture of Polotsk, the khan might be convinced of the hopelessness of fighting powerful Muscovy or forming a union with weak Livonia.

He made one attempt to find out whether Devlet-Girey could be inclined to peace. A plenipotentiary by the name of Afanasy Nagoy was sent to the Crimea bearing a message from the conqueror of Kazan and Astrakhan. Ivan did not choose to use the previous polite expressions. "From Ivan Vasilievich," he wrote, "by the grace of God great sovereign, tsar and grand prince of All Russia, of the Muscovite, Novgorod, Kazan, Astrakhan, German and other lands, to the great khan of the Great Horde, my brother Khan Devlet-Girey, courteous greetings."

The Crimeans also modified their former behavior concerning the Muscovites. Nagoy wrote that when he walked to and from the khan's residence no protection was provided him; the greeters and the porters provided no luxuries. The ambassador delivered his sovereign's message to the khan. "From the beginning our grandfather the great sovereign Ivan and your grandfather Khan Mengli-Girey preserved great friendship and love. To whomsoever God gave help over his enemies the other sent a *seuncha* (courier of victory), and they rejoiced together. Between them they rewarded and enriched their followers, they kept their enemies under their feet, and their friends rejoiced.

"This winter we went to do battle with our enemy the king. We mounted up and took with us all our soldiers from many lands. We arrived in the king's land and, God be praised, we took the city of Polotsk. We would have gone on to Wilno, but the king's great council petitioned our boyars to ask us to leave the country. Their sovereign the king sent his envoys to beg forgiveness for his wrongdoings. Our boyars went to our cousin Vladimir Andreevich and, together with him, fell at our feet and cried out, 'Great sovereign! Your faith and the king's are one and the same, why spill any more blood? You have conquered the land of your enemy, your soldiers have spoiled themselves with riches and captives, you have taken their finest city, your enemy has surrendered to you and wishes to place himself at your mercy!' We, not wishing to go against the supplication of our cousin and our boyars, returned to our own country."

"If they bring up Kazan," Nagoy was instructed, "ask what there is to say about Kazan, which is entirely at the sovereign's mercy. Many churches are built in the city and its districts. Only Russian people live in its trading quarter, and the tsar has given away many lands there to his princes and junior boyars as service estates. This winter in the tsar's service in the Lithuanian land there were fifty thousand men just from Kazan, not counting Russians. There were also two thousand men from Astrakhan, but the tsar will not take men from Astrakhan any more on such distant campaigns since it is too far for them to travel; the tsar has ordered them to serve locally instead, in Shavkal, Yurgench, Derbent and other places where the tsar's commanders might send them.

"If they refer in any connection to Grand Prince Ivan Danilovich Kalita and Khan Uzbek, even if the khan himself mentions it, answer that these events were before your time, as God and the khan must know. Should the princes speak of it without the khan, answer that such talk is not helpful, that the matter was a misfortune of the forefathers of your sovereign, but now, with God's will, they themselves know in whose land lies the camp of Khan Uzbek. It is well known who sends envoys and commanders against that camp and, according to the charter of Khan Uzbek, who is supposed to send gifts to whom—this they know. Khan Uzbek and Grand Prince Ivan by now have passed on; that which exists today is visible to all, and what is visible is stronger than what used to be. In all states God today raises up one but tomorrow another."

"The king yearly sends me treasure," the khan responded to Nagoy's message, "but your sovereign quarrels with me and does not send me treasure and presents such as previous khans received. If your sovereign wishes friendship with me, let him give me treasure such as was given to Khan Sahib-Girey as well as the treasure that the king gives me, and also presents in excess of the king's. If he does not give me treasure and presents, why should I make peace with your sovereign and lose thereby the king's treasure?"

"My sovereign will not send you any treasure," Nagoy retorted. "Our sovereign is not obliged to give anything to anyone. Our sovereign does not buy friendship. Let there be amity between you, but our sovereign will not countenance giving you presents." The khan complained that Ivan had ordered the khan's envoy in Putivl arrested and confined in Moscow. Nagoy answered that this was done on the order of traitors close to the tsar, but now these were disgraced. One of the princes told Nagoy, "The Tatar loves him who gives him the most; he is their friend."

Ivan's peace proposals gave the khan a chance to bargain with the king, who sent him his treasure of thirty-six wagonloads of trinkets. The khan sent word that if he was not sent twice that amount, he would conclude peace with the Muscovite and with him make common cause against Lithuania. The khan accepted the king's treasure, and in expectation of rich presents from the tsar made peace with him until he found out who would be the more generous. The tsar's new envoy, the chancellor and commander Matvey Rzhevsky,[20] did bring the khan presents that pleased him greatly. He showed both envoys, Rzhevsky and Nagoy, greater respect in return. He even gave them gifts, which never had happened before, and gave a charter of peace to the tsar.

TURKS FAIL TO TAKE ASTRAKHAN

The marauding nature of their horde prevented the Crimean khans from keeping long-range interests in mind for long. Frightened by Rzhevsky, Vishnevetsky and Adashev, tempted by rich gifts, Khan Devlet-Girey might put Kazan and Astrakhan out of his mind for the time being, but not so another ruler. Thoughts about these places, about Christian churches being constructed in an ancient Muslim refuge, upset him who considered himself the head of the Muslim world, the Turkish sultan.

Distance and other concerns prevented Suleiman I[21] from coming to the aid of Kazan and Astrakhan himself. He entrusted the matter to the Crimeans and the Nogay, but we have seen how they fulfilled their obligations. Now, having settled his other affairs and heeding the appeals of the Muslims, Suleiman decided to attend to the North and send an army to capture Astrakhan.

The plan frightened the Crimean khan more than anyone. Dependence on the Turks was a great burden to him. Fearing most of all an increase of Turkish might on the northern shores of the Black Sea and on the Don and Volga, he tried everything to deter the sultan from undertaking a campaign against Astrakhan. He knew that the burden of such a campaign would fall upon him. His Crimeans were inclined only to undertake plundering expeditions offering a sure prospect of spoils. Now they would be forced to undertake a difficult campaign of doubtful success. They would be forced to besiege a city and do battle with Russians who would not easily be subjugated. Even in the event of success they could not plunder their brother Tatars, and any Muscovite captives would have to be turned over to the Turks.

Nagoy reported to Ivan that in September 1563 the Turkish *khunker* (sultan) ordered Devlet-Girey to prepare supplies and horses for a spring campaign against Astrakhan. The sultan was sending his crown princes along with many men and janissaries to accompany the khan. He ordered the khan to prepare a thousand wagons for the artillery. The Turks would come by boat with the heavy artillery along the Don as far as the Ilovlia river, at the mouth of which they were to transfer the artillery and wagons to small boats in order to haul them up the Ilovlia. After a portage of about seven versts from the Ilovlia to the Cherepakha river (at present-day Kachalinsk), they were to go down the Cherepakha to the Volga, cross the Volga to the Nogay side at that point, and march overland to Astrakhan. The Cherkess, as well as the Nogay and the men of Astrakhan and Kazan, had begged the sultan to send troops against Astrakhan and were prepared to cooperate. The Astrakhan Tatars awaited only the arrival of the sultan's forces to capture the citadel.

The sultan was vexed with the tsar over one matter in particular. When Muslims from the Caucasus and other lands came to Astrakhan in the course of their pilgrimage to Mohammed's grave, the Muscovite commanders in Astrakhan would not let them in. Devlet-Girey sent back a courier to say that he was at peace with the Muscovite tsar. He attempted to discourage the sultan from sending soldiers to Astrakhan. "Even should you take Astrakhan now from the grand prince, you could not keep it, for the grand prince would take it back again. You would only lose men and gain no profit." Nagoy concluded his report with the following piece of information. "A master of the janissaries who lives with the khan among the other janissaries dined with Rzhevsky. We plied him with drink in order to get some news, and when he got drunk he told us that the Turk was certain to send many men in the spring to Astrakhan and has ordered the khan to go. The Turk has artillery, and for excavation work drills, spades, axes, shovels and troughs, all ready for the spring campaign. The khan does not want to go to Astrakhan and is trying to talk the Turk out of it."

The khan himself sent the same news to Moscow. According to his courier, the sultan ordered one fortress to be constructed at the beginning of the portage, another at the Volga end. Between these two points a canal was to be dug and water let into it so that the artillery might be transported along it. When they arrived at Astrakhan they were to construct a third fortress to subject Astrakhan to the sultan. After all this the khan announced that the sultan took his advice and called off the campaign.[22]

Satisfied with the khan's behavior and his treaty, Ivan sent a third envoy, Pisemsky, with presents and an accompanying note. "The very cloak that we wore when we gave our oath to you, our brother, we have taken from our shoulders and now send to you to wear as your own. The very goblet from which we have drunk we send you with a ladle so that you may drink from it to our health."

Yet to live in accord with the khan for long was impossible. Nagoy promised Devlet-Girey that the tsar would send him the same gifts that were sent to Sahib-Girey. The khan consented but his Tatar dignitaries disagreed, demanding such presents as Ivan's father had sent to Mahmet-Girey. Finally all agreed to the Sahib-Girey presents. Nagoy was preparing to leave the Crimea when a Lithuanian courier arrived with the news that the king was sending a double treasure and was undertaking to match the Sahib-Girey presents promised by the tsar, but only if the khan broke off relations with Moscow. This gave the khan a chance to bargain with the Muscovite ambassadors. He sent to ask Nagoy if he would guarantee that the tsar would send the Mahmet-Girey presents. Nagoy answered that he could not guarantee it.

At that point the khan, deciding that friendship with the king was more advantageous, and learning from the king that all the tsar's forces were on the Livonian frontier, attacked the Muscovite borderlands. Indeed, as a result of the treaty with Devlet-Girey the borderlands were denuded of forces. Not one soldier remained in Riazan. In spite of that, the people of Riazan, under the leadership of Ivan's favorite Alexis Basmanov and his son Fedor, repulsed all the Tatars' attacks. When the khan heard of the approach of Muscovite commanders he did not wait to meet them but retired. He suffered a significant loss of men because a separate detachment of his, having dispersed for plunder, was annihilated.

As a result Ivan once again either had to keep his eyes on his southern border or had to compete with the king in the Crimean auction and increase his gifts to brigands. The khan refused to modify his demands. In order to force the tsar to agree to the Mahmet-Girey presents he now demanded that Ivan turn Kazan and Astrakhan over to him. He also demanded that Ivan enthrone his son Adyl-Girey as khan in Kazan.

"How could that be?" said Nagoy in response to these demands. "Our sovereign has constructed churches in the city and in the trading quarter and in all the villages. He has sent Russians there and distributed the villages and districts of the Kazan territory among his junior boyars as service estates. As for the high and middle-ranking Tatar nobles from Kazan, he has awarded them villages and districts, some around Moscow, others around Novgorod and Pskov, as their estates. The tsar has built seven fortresses in the Kazan land, on the Sviiaga, the Cheboksara, the Sura, the Alatyr and the Kurmysh, as well as in Arsk and at Laishev."

The khan's couriers brought the demand for Kazan and Astrakhan to Moscow. They were told that such a demand was not made in good faith. At the table the couriers were given furs, as was customary, but thinner than those given previously. One of the couriers complained about it. "Why should we reward you," the tsar replied, "when your khan has broken his promise, attacked Riazan, and now demands Kazan and Astrakhan? Cities and lands do not come with bowl and bread."

Perhaps the khan would have forgotten about Kazan and Astrakhan had he not kept being reminded of them. As Nagoy wrote to Moscow, "Envoys from the Nogay[23] came to the Crimea seeking peace and an alliance between themselves and the khan. If he wanted to make war on Kazan and Astrakhan, they were prepared to go with him. Koshtivley, a Tatar nobleman from Kazan, arrived in the Crimea with the Nogay envoys. He said he was with the Nogay in Moscow where he met two lowland Cheremiss, Laish and Lamberdey by name, who begged the khan to march on Kazan or at least send his crown princes, for they all awaited his arrival. On his arrival they would all go over to him and cooperate in the capture of Kazan. Furthermore, the Cherkess reminded the khan that Tsar Ivan was building a fortress on the Terek, and that if he finished it, not only would the Terek be lost, but the Tiumen and Shevkal rivers too would be ruled by Muscovy." The khan answered the Cherkess that he was not strong enough to prevent the tsar from constructing a fortress. He had strength enough only to carry out surprise raids on the Muscovite borderlands.

In the autumn of 1565 the khan arrived at Bolkhov with cannon. Russian commanders with soldiers were posted there and executed a successful sally, not even allowing the Tatars to set fire to the trading quarter.

When two of the commanders, Princes Ivan Belsky and Ivan Mstislavsky, approached the main Crimean army the khan, true to character, fled.

Even after this attack the khan still sent couriers to Moscow with demands for Kazan and Astrakhan and for a lasting peace. He also requested rich presents in return for a truce. "Great sovereigns," the tsar replied, "do not make or listen to idle speeches." The tsar similarly did not allow the khan to repeat his former treatment of Muscovite envoys. We find, for example, the following instructions issued to his ambassador Aliabiev. "Should the khan mention how he sent the courier Mustafa to his brother the grand prince on serious business, and how the grand prince ordered Andrei Shchepotiev to seize him because Sulesh Murza seized Andrei's possessions as payment of our presents, but how he, the khan, was not ordering Mustafa to carry out the same seizure on you, answer him thus. 'Whatever presents our sovereign sent with Andrei Shchepotiev to you, these presents Andrei delivered to you, but Sulesh took Andrei's things by force, and when Andrei remonstrated to you against Sulesh you offered him no satisfaction. Andrei petitioned our sovereign, and the tsar authorized him to carry out the same seizure upon your courier. If you take something from me by force, my sovereign will order me to take double from your envoy, and furthermore because of this he will not send you any more envoys.'"

Nagoy resided a long time in the Crimea, refusing to leave without a conclusive peace treaty or an envoy from the khan. One day the khan asked him for a coat of squirrel fur for one of his princes. Nagoy did not give it. "You gave no fur coat," the Tatar nobles told him, "so our khan is holding you in disgrace and sending you away. The Crimea will not allow our envoy to be detained in Moscow. Our khan has many slaves who have perished in Muscovy." "If your khan sends us away with envoys," Nagoy replied, "we will go gladly, but if he tries to send us away without envoys and without business, we will not go. We prefer to die in the Crimea than go back without envoys."

Nagoy's presence in the Crimea was necessary for news, which became ever more important following revelation of dissatisfaction in Kazan and Astrakhan and the intentions of Constantinople. Nagoy, for example, informed the tsar that two Kazan nobles and all the lowland Cheremiss had begged the khan to send his son with soldiers. As soon as the crown prince arrived they would abandon the Muscovite sovereign and take over the stockade in Kazan. The men in all the villages serving Muscovy would be theirs; they could assemble sixty thousand lowland Cheremiss.

The Nogay princes also sent a request to the khan. "As long as we were horseless and naked," they said, "we had to serve the tsar and grand prince, but now we are mounted and clothed. If you send the crown prince to Kazan with an army let us know, for we are prepared to help your son."

The khan was in no position to take Kazan from the tsar, yet it was also difficult to consider making peace with Muscovy. The brigands understood the danger threatening them if Muscovy grew stronger. "The crown princes held a council," wrote Nagoy. "The crown princes, karachis, uhlans, princes, murzas[24] and all the land decided to make peace with the king and not to make peace with you, sire. 'Should you make peace with the Muscovite,' they told the khan, 'it would mean betraying the king. The Muscovite will wage war on the king, take Kiev, and start constructing fortresses along the Dnieper, and none of it shall remain for us. He already has conquered two Muslim realms and the Germans. Now he is sending you presents in order to finish his war with the king, but when he defeats the king, there will be no profit in it for our realm. You will derive no pleasure from his furs. He also gave furs to the people of Kazan, but the people derived no pleasure from them, for afterwards the Muscovites took Kazan.'"

The khan concurred with their opinion. He sent word to Nagoy that he did not wish to be at peace with his sovereign. Nagoy managed to secure an audience with the khan, who told him, "News has come to me that your sovereign wishes to build a fortress on the Terek river. If your sovereign wishes to remain in friendship and brotherhood with me he should not build a fortress on the Terek. He should give me the presents of Mahmet-Girey and I shall make peace with him. Should he construct a fortress on the Terek, you could give me a mountain of gold but I would not make peace with him, for he already has taken two Muslim realms, Kazan and Astrakhan, and is now building a fortress on the Terek and making himself our neighbor."

The khan sent a personal letter to Ivan saying much the same thing. The tsar, together with his boyars, composed an answer. Kazan and Astrakhan would not be given back. The fortress on the Terek was being built for the protection of Prince Temriuk, the sovereign's father-in-law.[25] If the khan so wished, let him send his crown prince to Moscow. The sovereign would give him the daughter of Shah Ali in marriage and also Kasimov.[26] The gifts of Mahmet-Girey would not be sent. The tsar would send a gift of three hundred rubles to keep the khan from breaking off relations.

To the proposal to seat his son in Kasimov the khan told Nagoy, "I asked your sovereign for Kazan and Astrakhan. Your sovereign does not give me them. What he offers instead, to seat a crown prince in Kasimov, is unsatisfactory to me. My son and I have what we have. Should your sovereign not give me Astrakhan, the Turk will take it."

Sultan Selim II,[27] Suleiman's successor, was indeed contemplating fighting for Astrakhan. "The Turk sent a letter to the khan in the spring (1567)," Nagoy reported. "The sultan received envoys from Khiva and Bukhara on their way to Mecca by way of Astrakhan. They complained to the Turk that the Muscovite tsar had captured Muslim realms, taken Kazan and Astrakhan and torn Islam asunder, imposing Christianity and warring against many other Muslim realms, and that in Astrakhan, from port duties levied on ships from many lands, he was making a huge profit at the rate of thousands of gold pieces a day. The Turk was directing the khan to proceed with his sons to Astrakhan in the spring, and he, the sultan, was sending Crown Prince Krym-Girey and Prince Kasim with artillery to take Astrakhan and make Krym-Girey khan there."

The khan himself told Nagoy, "Although I have quarrelled with your sovereign and been at peace with him, now someone mighty, the Turkish emperor, has raised himself against your sovereign, and is sending me against Astrakhan. Indeed all the Muslim states are rising up against your sovereign for having seized Muslim realms." "God gave Astrakhan to our sovereign," Nagoy responded, "and God and our sovereign will protect it. You yourself know that our sovereign rides his own horse and avenges his enemies' hostility." "How can it be," the khan replied, "that God entrusted these cities to your sovereign when we rely on the same God?" "In this age sovereigns exchange gifts," Nagoy answered, "but sovereigns do not dispose of realms; that is impossible."

As always the khan feared Turkish proximity more than that of the Muscovites. He wrote the sultan that it was impossible to go to Astrakhan in summertime because of the many waterless places, and to go in wintertime was equally impossible, for the Turks could not withstand the frost, besides which there was presently a famine in the Crimea and no available supplies. He would have to leave with his sons for Astrakhan early in the spring and begin operations on the fortress. If they did not take Astrakhan they could at least build a fortress across the river on the Crimean side, on the site of the old settlement, and from there operate against Astrakhan.

Later on the khan attempted yet again to dissuade the sultan entirely from a campaign against Astrakhan. "I have," he wrote, "reliable information that the Muscovite tsar has sent a force of sixty thousand to Astrakhan. If we do not take Astrakhan, dishonor will fall upon you, not upon me, but if you wish to fight the Muscovites, order your men to come with me against the Muscovite borderlands. Even if we do not take any cities at least we can ravage the land and cause much vexation."

The khan sent a courier to Moscow with news about the campaign of the Turkish army to Astrakhan. He proposed that the best solution would be for the tsar to turn over Astrakhan to him. "We do not wish," he wrote, "to allow the Turks free passage through our territory and therefore we write to inform you of it." "Since when," Ivan replied, "does one give back a fortress?"

In the spring of 1569 a Turkish force of seventeen thousand arrived in Kaffa. Kasim, pasha of Kaffa, was to lead them to Perevolok, construct a canal between the Don and the Volga, and then take Astrakhan or at least build a stronghold nearby. The khan, with fifty thousand of his Tatars, joined the campaign. Ships with cannon under the protection of five hundred soldiers sailed from Azov up the Don.

Among the captives manning the Turkish boats was a certain Simeon Maltsev. Originally sent from Moscow as an envoy to the Nogay, he was captured by the Azov cossacks, sold to the Turks, and impressed into galley service. "What misfortunes and sorrows did I not endure on the way from Kaffa to Perevolok!" wrote Maltsev later. "While I suffered my life in penal servitude, I praised the name of the sovereign above that of the great emperor Constantine. The ships took five weeks to Perevolok. The Turks were in great terror and despaired of their bellies. The janissaries of Christian origin—Greeks or Wallachians—were amazed that none of the sovereign's men or cossacks were on the Don. Had the Turks travelled such rivers in Frankish or Hungarian lands, they all would have been killed. The natural fortifications along the banks of the Don easily could be defended by only two thousand cossacks fighting bare-handed."

The Turks reached Perevolok in the middle of August. They began digging the canal but could not complete the work, so Kasim Pasha gave orders to drag the boats overland. The khan advised turning back. On his instructions the Tatars spread it among the Turks that even in the event of success the undertaking would turn out badly for them, since in the northern lands winter lasts for nine months and in the summer months night is no more than three hours long. The Turks therefore would either have to

stay awake all night or contravene their religious customs requiring them
to pray for two hours after sunset and again for two hours before sunrise.
Disaffection grew among the Turkish soldiers. Just then envoys appeared
from Astrakhan. They convinced the pasha that it would be useless to take
the boats with them. They promised to supply the Turks with as many boats
as they needed if only they would proceed immediately to Astrakhan and
take it from the Russians.

Easier said than done. When Kasim drew near to Astrakhan in mid-
September he decided not to attack it. Halting below the city on the site of
the ancient settlement he decided to construct a stronghold in which to
spend the winter and ordered the khan to return to the Crimea. When the
pasha's intentions became known in the army, a rebellion flared up. According to Maltsev, the Turks approached the pasha in a great furor, crying,
"We cannot winter here! We would die of hunger. Our sovereign sent us
off with supplies for three years, but when we left Azov you ordered us to
take rations for only forty days. The people of Astrakhan cannot feed us.
The janissaries have all given up. We are leaving with the Crimean khan.
You deceived the sovereign. Thanks to your *misinformation* he ignored
Khan Devlet-Girey. What the khan wrote to the sultan, what he said to us,
and even what he said to you at Perevolok, all has proved true."

Maltsev had other reasons to be pleased besides the developments
within the Turkish camp. "Near Astrakhan the Turks captured one Arseny,"
he reported, "a cellarer and assistant to the abbot of the St. Nicholas monastery. They put him next to me on the same chain. I studied him and then
asked him to speak. He had heard from the abbot that Prince Peter
Obolensky-Serebriany was nearing Astrakhan with thirty thousand soldiers on boats, and that the sovereign also had sent Prince Belsky overland
to Astrakhan with an army of a hundred thousand. He even had some
Nogay with him. The Persian shah had sent his regards to our tsar, saying,
'The Turks are looking for a road here by way of Astrakhan, but you, great
tsar, with your strong arm can help me against the Turk.' Our sovereign
granted the shah's request and sent him his ambassador Alexis Khoznikov
with a hundred cannon and five hundred muskets."

The following night the Turks themselves learned of the approach of the
Muscovite commanders, Prince Obolensky-Serebriany and Prince Zamiatnia
Saburov, with a large army. They learned that the Russians had intercepted
the Nogay who had gone over to the Turkish side. As Maltsev put it, everything around Astrakhan was trembling before the sovereign tsar, who
alone under the sun put fear into "both Busurmans and Latins."[28]

As a consequence of these tidings, on September 20 Kasim burned his wooden fortifications and fled from Astrakhan with the khan. After sixty versts he met a courier coming from the sultan. Selim was writing to instruct Kasim to winter over at Astrakhan, saying that he would receive strong reinforcements in the spring. In order to distract the Muscovite forces, the Crimean khan and the Turkish pasha, the sultan's son-in-law, should march on Russia.

Yet Kasim continued his flight. A month later the Turks reached Azov. The khan led them past the Cherkess along the Kabarda road, through the waterless places. The Turks, suffering in their deprivation, called Selim unlucky because the first thing he did after coming to the throne was to send his soldiers on an unsuccessful campaign. "We have had no great battles to exhaust us," they said, "yet should an enemy attack us now, not one of us would return home alive."

STEPPE DIPLOMACY

The khan achieved his goal. The Turks failed to establish a Muslim realm on the Volga. Yet he found himself in an embarrassing position regarding Muscovy. He used to invoke the sultan to threaten the tsar, but the sultan's undertaking had failed. Summoning a pro-Muscovite Crimean by the name of Prince Sulesh, the khan said to him, "What can I tell the Muscovite now? I do not know what to ask. I exhausted the Turks in the Astrakhan campaign. When I reached Astrakhan I did not cross the river, neither did I attack the city. I acted thus both for the Muscovite tsar and for myself. I did not want Astrakhan under Turkish rule. I further acted in my own interests by not allowing the Turk's men into the Crimea." The khan finally sent a courier to Moscow with a dispatch. He asked for Kazan and Astrakhan and demanded an exchange of envoys, Nagoy for Yamboldui, long detained in Moscow. He also demanded a thousand rubles, furs and gerfalcons.

Ivan, expecting a second Turkish attack, realized the khan's potential usefulness in that event and therefore answered him graciously. Rejecting the request for Kazan and Astrakhan, he wrote, "We would like to send you, our brother, the gifts of Mahmet-Girey, yet in Moscow there has been a great fire and the books in which those gifts were noted are lost. As for the account of the gifts to Mahmet-Girey that you have sent us, the oldest people here relate that they have never heard mention of so great an amount. Therefore you, our brother, should review this amount and let us know how henceforth we are to remain in friendship and brotherhood."

Constantinople remained the greatest threat. While it was difficult enough maintaining soldiers on the banks of the Oka to protect against the khan during the Livonian war, particularly in the absence of a standing army, it was even more difficult to maintain additional large regiments in distant Astrakhan. Ivan knew that come spring the sultan would launch a new campaign against that city, and that at the same time the khan would attack Muscovy. The slightest Turkish success along the lower reaches of the Volga would spark an uprising of dissatisfied inhabitants of the Kazan territory. Keeping his eyes ever on the shores of the Baltic, preparing for important events in Lithuania and Poland, all the while feeling insecure at home, Ivan was forced to use every means, even to the point of sacrifice, in order to keep the peace with the khan and the sultan.

Thus the tsar agreed to give the khan the Mahmet-Girey presents. In 1570 he sent his ambassador Novosiltsev to Constantinople under the pretext of congratulating Sultan Selim II on his accession to the throne. The ambassador was to remind the sultan of the previously friendly relations of his predecessors with Ivan's. More important, he was also to suggest that Islam suffered no oppression in the new Muscovite territories conquered from the Tatars.

After speaking of Kazan affairs under Ivan III, Vasily III and Ivan IV, Novosiltsev told the sultan, "It was because of Kazan's wrongdoings that our sovereign campaigned against them, and because of their wrongdoings that God also punished them. Those men of Kazan now serve our sovereign truly. They live in their own places and receive government salaries, and the tsar does not force them to renounce their faith, neither does he demolish their houses of worship. See how our sovereign has seated Crown Prince Sain-Bulat[29] in Kasimov and ordered mosques and cemeteries constructed according to Muslim law. Our sovereign does not infringe upon his freedom in any way. Were our sovereign intent on breaking Muslim law, he would not have permitted Sain-Bulat to settle in the midst of his own territory and live according to Muslim law."

The sultan sent a dispatch with Novosiltsev. He demanded that the Astrakhan road be opened, that the Russian fortress established in Kabarda territory be abandoned, and that travellers from every quarter be allowed through. In March 1571 a new ambassador by the name of Kuzminsky was sent to Constantinople. He bore a dispatch from the tsar to the sultan. "We wish to remain henceforth in brotherhood and benevolence with you, so we are showing you this token of brotherly love. We have given orders to abandon the fortress on the Terek river in the territory of

Kabarda and to remove our subjects to Astrakhan. As to what you wrote us about the road, you should understand that it was closed because many were using it to practice brigandage and caused much treachery and damage to our city of Astrakhan, but now for you, our brother, we have ordered that the road be opened to all travellers."

"If they say that purses were stolen in Astrakhan and corpses violated," Kuzminsky was instructed, "answer that this was done without the sovereign's knowledge by robbers, boyars' slaves and cossacks." Kuzminsky also had to speak on behalf of the tsar to the sultan's favorite Mahmet-Pasha. "If you desire our bounty and affection," he was instructed to say, "serve us. Ingratiate us with your sovereign by preserving amity between us and your sovereign so that our brother, Sultan Selim, remain in brotherhood and love with us, united with us against the Roman emperor and the Polish king and against all the Italian (Western European) rulers." No favorable reply was forthcoming. The sultan continued to demand the return of Kazan and Astrakhan and even vassalage.

CRIMEAN INVASION

Meanwhile reports of the hostile intentions of the sultan and the khan continued to filter through to Moscow. The entire summer of 1570 was spent in uneasy expectation of a Tatar attack. The army took up a position on the Oka. Twice Ivan himself travelled there on rumors of the khan's approach, but these proved false. Only small parties of Tatars showed up, and they were driven off easily. At the end of September the boyars claimed that the village cossacks were spreading lies about the appearance of a large hostile army, keeping the tsar standing in Serpukhov for nothing. The commanders kept their positions along the river only until the end of the first week in October. After that they returned home.

The alarm was sounded again in the spring of 1571. The commanders Princes Belsky, Mstislavsky, Vorotynsky and the two Ivan Shuiskys were dispatched to the Oka with a force of fifty thousand. The tsar advanced to Serpukhov with his oprichniks. This time the alarm was genuine. The khan attacked the Muscovite borderlands with a combined army of one hundred and twenty thousand.

Some junior boyars deserted to him in the steppes. There were two from Belev, two from Kaluga, one from Kashira and one from Serpukhov. "For two successive years," they told the khan, "there has been great famine and plague in all Muscovite cities. Many have perished, and the tsar has executed many others in disgrace. The rest of the soldiers and all the Tatars are in the German lands. The tsar is waiting in Serpukhov with his oprichnina, but their numbers are small. You should proceed straight to Moscow. We shall lead you across the Oka, and if you meet any soldiers whatsoever on the road to Moscow you may have us executed." Two baptized Tatars also went over to the khan and told him the same. The khan proceeded according to the directions of the traitors and crossed the Oka at an unknown location. The village cossacks, who in the previous year in their reports appear to have exaggerated the danger, now remained silent.

Ivan was cut off from the main army. He hastily retreated from Serpukhov to Bronnitsy, from there to Alexandrov Village and finally to Rostov, just as his predecessors Dmitry Donskoy and Vasily I did in similar circumstances.[30] He spoke about treachery, claiming that the boyars sent the junior boyars to the khan to lead him safely across the Oka. Prince Mstislavsky later confessed, in a document referred to previously, that he so directed the khan, but that is all we have by way of explanation of this affair.

Nevertheless the Muscovite commanders, once they learned that the khan had crossed the Oka, anticipated his action. They arrived at Moscow on May 23 and spread out throughout the suburbs to defend the city. The Tatars appeared on the following day, May 24, Ascension Day, and succeeded in setting fire to the suburbs. Under clear skies but with a strong wind the fire raged through the city in three hours, destroying the tinder-dry mass of wooden buildings. Only the Kremlin was spared. According to foreigners' reports, eight hundred thousand soldiers and civilians perished. Even allowing for exaggeration in the unreliable and indeed impossible estimates, the figure must have been enormous. At the alarming reports of the Tatars' approach many must have fled into Moscow from the outlying districts, and once the fire broke out they had nowhere to flee. The Tatars held the open field and nobody was allowed into the Kremlin. Most, we are told, perished when they tried to escape through the city gates furthest from the enemy. A huge crowd piled up there, filling up the adjacent streets, until they were several layers thick, those above trampling those below to death.

According to Russian accounts the number of people burned was countless. The metropolitan and the clergy sat it out in the Dormition cathedral. The leading boyar, Prince Belsky, suffocated in the stone cellar of his own palace. Who could count all the other princes, princesses, boyars and others who perished? Men were assigned to throw bodies into the Moskva river, until corpses dammed it up. Only corpses with living friends received a proper burial. The conflagration in the suburbs prevented the Tatars from looting. The khan, hearing of the approach of a large Russian force, decided not to besiege the Kremlin and departed with a great number of captives, according to some sources as many as a hundred and fifty thousand.

As Ivan was returning to Moscow, couriers from Devlet-Girey met him at the village of Bratovshchino on the road to the Trinity monastery. They handed the tsar the following message from the khan. "I burn and lay waste everything because of Kazan and Astrakhan. Relying on the greatness of God I turn the wealth of the whole world into dust. I came against you and burned your city. I wanted your crown and your head, but you never came to face us. You are still swaggering about, but now I am the sovereign of Muscovy! You would have known shame and ignominy had you come and faced us. If you would be our friend honestly and truly, give us back our realms of Astrakhan and Kazan. Even if you wanted to give us the wealth of all the world in treasure and money it would be insufficient. Our desire is Kazan and Astrakhan. I know my way about your realm and I shall remember it."

We have seen how difficult, dangerous, and inopportune for Ivan was the struggle against Turkey and the Crimea over Astrakhan, also how he was prepared to make important concessions in order to avoid the struggle. Now Devlet-Girey's ruinous attack, particularly its awesome results, must have alarmed the tsar even more. Success would embolden the khan. The Muscovites could expect another invasion soon. Indeed, Devlet-Girey was preparing for it.

He had to be held off as long as possible by prolonging negotiations and offering new concessions. Ivan, with his previous civility, communicated the following proposal to the khan. "You write about war in your letter, but if I write about it too we shall never reach an understanding. You are angry that we rejected your request for Kazan and Astrakhan. We would like to concede Astrakhan to you, only it is impossible to settle the matter immediately. First we must receive your ambassadors, since mere couriers cannot be trusted with such an important matter. We should agree upon a date, but until such time you should refrain from attacking our lands."

Ivan wrote to Nagoy so that he might say the same to the khan and his magnates. "Even if your conversation with the princes and nobles is not querulous but smooth and courteous, you must be firm about determining one thing, that if we turn Astrakhan over to the khan, how will he set a ruler over it? Would it not be possible to do so by the khan setting up his son in

Astrakhan and with him one of our boyars, as in Kasimov? There must be no violence at all directed against our subjects in Astrakhan. The roads leading to our realm from all lands may not be blocked. Is it possible for us on our own to enthrone the khan's son in Astrakhan?"

We also find an important concession contrary to accepted custom in the instructions issued to the courier sent with dispatches to the Crimea. "If they do not allow the courier to see the khan without paying a fee, and if they use these fees as an obstacle to the sovereign's business, the courier should pay a little, whatever he should happen to have. In return he must not leave the khan but speak about everything, peacefully, with bowing and not in discord, so that no particular words cause anger."

To the proposal about Astrakhan the khan replied, "As for your giving us Astrakhan but not Kazan, it seems useless to us. If the upper reaches of a river are yours, the lower reaches can hardly be mine!" In another letter the khan wrote, "I have now two or three daughters of marriageable age and two or three sons also preparing for marriage. For their happiness we require many articles and goods. In order to buy this dowry we ask from you two thousand rubles. Show your friendship! *Do not refuse!* Give!"

In his first dispatch written after the burning of Moscow the khan feigned unselfishness. He declared that the wealth of the entire world was nothing to him; he wanted only his Muslim territories. He was fighting for the sake of his faith. Yet he could not restrain himself for long from asking for money. Ivan remembered well the khan's earlier remarks and did not let slip a chance to take the khan at his word about what he really wanted. "Our brother Khan Devlet-Girey," he told the khan's courier, "could not have hoped to conquer our land. A sword cuts with time, but if it cuts too often it becomes dull and sometimes even sharp swords are broken. He requests of us Kazan and Astrakhan, but without negotiations and without ambassadors. How is such an important matter to be dealt with? As for what he wrote regarding his great needs, why should we be obliged to satisfy them? He warred against our land, and because of his war our land has become empty. It is impossible now to take anything from anybody." In his letter to the khan Ivan wrote, "In your letter you wrote us that in your eyes treasure and wealth were so much dust. How could we possibly fulfill such great requests in the face of your own letter? We have sent to you two hundred rubles, all that we happen to have."

Ivan was counting on the Tatar habit of forgetting about high principles when large sums were on the table. To this end he instructed Nagoy to beg the khan and the crown princes to abandon the matter of Kazan and

Astrakhan. If so, he promised not only to send the Mahmet-Girey gifts and to match those the Polish king was sending, but also to send both the Mahmet-Girey and the king's gifts combined.

SIGNIFICANT RUSSIAN VICTORY AT MOLODI

The khan understood Ivan's intention to play for time and put little faith in negotiations. In the summer of 1572, with a force of a hundred and twenty thousand men, he again marched on the Oka.

Ivan was in Novgorod, but a Russian force under Prince Mikhail Ivanovich Vorotynsky was stationed on the Oka near Serpukhov. The khan stationed a detail of two thousand men there to *hector* the Russians and keep them occupied. During the night he crossed the Oka with his main force. Vorotynsky gave chase and overtook them fifty versts from Moscow on the banks of the Lopasnia, at Molodi. It became the site of several violent engagements during late July and early August, all of which ended unsuccessfully for the khan. He was forced to flee after suffering many losses.[31]

After that the khan changed his tone. "I am told that the tsar and grand prince has a great and populous land," he wrote Ivan. "Travelling the length of his land would take nine months, the breadth of it six, and yet he will not grant me Kazan and Astrakhan! He could give me back those cities and still have plenty to spare. He will not give me Kazan and Astrakhan although he would give Astrakhan alone. I am ashamed of the Turk; he wages war with the tsar and grand prince but takes neither Kazan nor Astrakhan, indeed gets nothing out of it at all! The tsar at least offers me Astrakhan, yet until my dying day I may not trespass on his land. I shall not starve. On the left I shall have the Lithuanians and on the right the Cherkess. I shall fight against them, and from them I shall satisfy myself. For me it is only two months' journey to those lands and back."

Ivan also changed his tone. He replied to the khan that he could not rely on his promise to fulfill his needs only from the Lithuanian and Cherkess lands. "At present," he wrote, "we face only one sword, the Crimea; but Kazan could become a second sword, Astrakhan a third, the Nogay a fourth." The courier sent to the Crimea again was strictly forbidden to give presents. The dispatches, however, continued to express written courtesies.

Ivan continued to sting the khan over his first arrogant letter about Kazan and Astrakhan. "The presents I sent you were slight," wrote the tsar. "I did not send fine presents since you wrote that you did not need money, that wealth for you was so much dust."

NOTES

Additional information on personalities and topics found in the text and notes is available in George N. Rhyne and Joseph L. Wieczynski, eds., *The Modern Encyclopedia of Russian, Soviet and Eurasian History* (MERSH); Harry B. Weber, ed., *The Modern Encyclopedia of Russian and Soviet Literatures (Including Non-Russian and Emigre Literatures)* (MERSL); Paul D. Steeves, ed., *The Modern Encyclopedia of Religions in Russia and the Soviet Union* (MERRSU); and David R. Jones, ed., *The Military Encyclopedia of Russia and Eurasia* (formerly *The Military-Naval Encyclopedia of Russia and the Soviet Union*), all published by Academic International Press.

A comprehensive account of the period preceding the era covered in this volume, with illustrations, an extensive bibliography and background information, is Hugh F. Graham, *The Age of Vasily III* (Gulf Breeze, Fla., Academic International Press, 1976).

INTRODUCTION

1. A seminal work in this regard is the late Michael Cherniavsky's article "Ivan the Terrible as a Renaissance prince," *Slavic Review,* 27 (1968), pp. 195-211.

2. Literally a "hairdo," the unusual stacking of vaulted gables.

3. The exhumation was carried out in 1953. See V. Belitsyn, "The Disinterment of Ivan the Terrible," *Illustrated London News ,* 244 (May 1964), and Mikhail Gerasimov, *The Face Finder* (London, 1971), pp. 184-189.

4. *Russia at the Dawn of the Modern Age* (New Haven, 1959) and *The Tsardom of Muscovy, 1547-1682* (New Haven, 1969).

5. Robert O. Crummey,*The Formation of Muscovy, 1304-1613* (New York, 1987).

6. R. G. Skrynnikov, *Ivan the Terrible* (Academic International Press, 1981).

7. *The Correspondence between Prince A.M. Kurbsky and Tsar Ivan IV of Russia* (Cambridge, 1955).

8. Edward L. Keenan *The Kurbskii-Groznyi Apocrypha. The Seventeenth-Century Genesis of the "Correspondence" Attributed to Prince A.M. Kurbskii and Tsar Ivan IV* (Harvard, 1971).

9. Charles J. Halperin, "Keenan's Heresy Revisited," *Jahrbücher für Geschichte Osteuropas*, NF 28 (1980), pp. 484-499.

10. As demonstrated in the article by Maureen Perrie, "The Popular Image of Ivan the Terrible," *Slavonic and East European Review*, 56 (1978), pp. 275-286.

11. For an excellent survey of the Soviet historiography of Ivan see the article by Robert Crummey, "Ivan the Terrible," *Windows on the Russian Past. Essays on Soviet Historiography since Stalin* (Columbus, Ohio, 1977).

12. Alexander Yanov, *The Origins of Autocracy. Ivan the Terrible in Russian History* (Berkeley, 1981).

13. *Kronika Polska* (Polish Chronicle) (Cracow, 1597).

14. *Rerum Moscovitarum Commentarii* (Notes on Moscow) (Frankfurt, 1600).

15. *Omnium Regionum Moschoviae descriptio* (Description of all the regions of Muscovy) (Cracow, 1578).

16. *Liefländische Historia* (Livonian History) (Reval, 1695).

17. The short title generally given to *The Chronicles of the Reign of Tsar Ivan Vasilievich from the Year 7042 [1534] to the Year 7061 [1553]* (St. Petersburg, 1769).

18. *The Ancient Russian Library Containing a Collection of Russian Antiquities Pertaining to Russian History, Geography and Genealogy* (Moscow, 1790).

19. The edition used by Soloviev was *The Russian Chronicle, Nikonian Version* (St. Petersburg, 1791). There have been several more recent editions of this chronicle.

20. *The Russian Chronicles from the Coming of Riurik to the End of Tsar Ivan Vasilievich,* published by N.A. Lvov (St. Petersburg, 1792).

21. Richard Hakluyt, *Early Voyages,* Vol. 1 (London, 1809, originally published 1589).

22. *Collection of State Charters and Treaties, Held in the State College for Foreign Affairs* (Moscow, 1819); *Acts Collected in the Archives and Libraries of the Russian Empire by the Imperial Archeographical Commission* (St. Petersburg, 1836); *Monumenta Livoniae Antiquae* (Monuments of Ancient Livonia) (Riga, Dorpat and Leipzig, 1837); *Historical Acts Collected and Edited by the Archeographical Commission* (St. Petersburg, 1841); *Historical Acts Pertaining to Russia, Drawn from Foreign Archives and Libraries by A.I. Turgenev* (St. Petersburg, 1841).

23. *The Tale of Prince Kurbsky,* ed. N.G. Ustrialov (2nd ed., St. Petersburg, 1842).

24. *The Complete Collection of Russian Chronicles,* which began publication in St. Petersburg in 1848 and is still ongoing, known as PSRL from its Russian initials.

25. *Acts Pertaining to the History of Western Russia, Collected and Edited by the Archeographical Commission* (St. Petersburg, 1848); *The Ambassadorial Book of the Grand Principality of Lithuania* (Moscow, 1843): *Scriptores Rerum Livonicarum* (Writers on Livonian Affairs) (Riga and Leipzig, 1848).

26. *Stoglav* (Hundred Chapters) (St. Petersburg, 1863).

27. See, for example, Edward L. Keenan, "Muscovy and Kazan," *Slavic Review,* 26 (1967), pp. 548-558.

28. Enaley in Russian sources, brother of the Kasimov khan, Shah Ali. See Chapter I, Notes 10 and 21, below.

29. For a brief account of Russian-Tatar relations between 1539 and 1549, see Soloviev, *History,* Vol. 9, pp. 228-236.

30. See Chapter I, Note 53, below.

CHAPTER I

1. See Introduction.

2. Yury, sometimes Georgy, Vasilievich, prince of Uglich, Ivan's younger brother, was born in 1532, only a year before the death of his father Vasily III. He played an insignificant role in government, according to some sources because he was witless and dumb. In 1548 he married a princess of the Paletsky family. No doubt because of his apparent mental disabilities he was not considered a contender for the throne in 1553, unlike his father's first cousin Prince Vladimir of Staritsa (see following note). Yury died in 1563 aged thirty-one, apparently without children.

3. Prince Vladimir of Staritsa (1533-1569) was the son on Prince Andrei Ivanovich, the brother of Ivan's father Vasily III. As the inheritor of the family estates around Staritsa, Vladimir until his death in 1569 was the most powerful appanage prince during Ivan's reign. As such he exercised his princely right to have his own retinue, known as the Ertoul Regiment. Relations between the tsar and his cousin were amicable for a while. Vladimir was charged with several important military and governmental responsibilities. In 1553 Vladimir inevitably became a claimant to the Muscovite throne, and later a rival to Ivan's infant son Dmitry during Ivan's serious illness, when he was put forward as a preferred choice by several powerful boyars (see Chapter III, below). Vladimir made protestations both written and oral of loyalty to Ivan and his descendants. Although the tsar did restrict somewhat Vladimir's independence and authority, he also continued to give him responsible positions in his government. In 1563 Vladimir and his mother, the ambitious Princess Evfrosinia, were accused of slandering the tsar and were tried before Metropolitan Makary (see Note 4, below) They were found guilty as charged. Vladimir was pardoned, but his mother was forced to take the veil. The following year Ivan appropriated Vladimir's principality of Staritsa, including it in his oprichnina, or personal estates, granting Vladimir in exchange less important lands in various locations. In 1567 Ivan's suspicions about Vladimir's loyalty began to get the better of him. In 1569 he finally condemned him and the other male members of his family, and even his mother in her convent, to death by drinking poison. The historical evidence suggests that Vladimir was at best a slow and pliant individual, caught up in Ivan's deadly politics by accident of birth rather than ambition. For more information, see the entry by Hugh H. Graham, "Staritskii, Vladimir Andreevich," *Modern Encyclopedia of Russian, Soviet and Eurasian History* (58 vols., Gulf Breeze, Fla.: Academic International Press, 1976-) (hereafter MERSH), Vol. 37, pp. 86-88.

4. Makary (1481-1563) was one of Ivan's closest advisers and most influential supporters. He was a product of the "Josephite" tradition, named after the famous and influential Russian churchman, Joseph of Volokolamsk (1440-1515). Makary was appointed metropolitan, head of the Russian Orthodox church, in 1542, having been archbishop of Novgorod since 1526. He proved his "Josephism" in the way he attempted to establish the Orthodox church, cleansed of its "heresies," as

signified by the trials of Maxim the Greek and Vassian Patrikeev in 1525 and 1531. He was not only the sole voice for the spiritual life of the Russian people but also the loyal spokesman and apologist for the authority of the Muscovite grand prince until his death on the last day of December, 1563. It is likely that his constant attempts to intercede with Ivan in favor of churchmen and others who incurred the tsar's notorious wrath would have led to Makary's removal as head of the church. The Josephite theocratic notion of keeping the secular ruler subordinate to the head of the church conflicted with Ivan's nature and secularizing outlook. After the death of Ivan's wife Anastasia in 1559, Makary was said to be the only individual able to restrain the tsar's terrible anger. The extreme measures Ivan adopted in 1564 may have been a consequence of the removal of these two influences from Ivan's personal life. For more information on this remarkable churchman, see the entry "Makarii" by David B. Miller, MERSH, Vol. 21, pp. 1-4.

5. The complex system of precedence is referred to in Russian as *mestnichestvo,* the traditional system of hierarchical ranking within Muscovite government and society. The system allocated ranks and precedence in direct proportion to the length of a family's loyal service to the Muscovite throne, its pedigree. Since it ensured that the members of the most loyal families, but not necessarily the most able candidates, rose to the highest positions of service, the tsars began to declare certain important expeditions exempt from the normal system of precedence in order to be able to appoint various talented officers temporarily to positions of greater responsibility than they normally would have been allowed. It is a mark of the respect— and authority—that Ivan wielded, that his suspensions of *mestnichestvo* were respected on this and on several other military ventures during his reign. It should be remembered that declaring exemption from *mestnichestvo* was more an attempt to graft a modern solution onto an older, generally proven and useful system than a campaign to destroy the old system altogether. For more information, see the entry "Mestnichestvo" by Graham, MERSH, Vol. 22, pp. 8-13.

6. On the history of the reign of Vasily III, see the preceding volume (Vol. 9) *The Age of Vasily III* (1976). For more general modern accounts, see the relevant sections in Vernadsky, *Russia at the Dawn of the Modern Age* (New Haven, 1959), and Robert Crummey, *The Formation of Muscovy, 1304-1613* (New York, 1987).

7. Vasilsursk was a fortress town founded higher up the Volga at the debouchure of the Sura river. For details, see Soloviev, Vol. 9, pp. 85-87. See map of Ivan's campaign to Kazan.

8. Ivan Vyrodkov (died 1564), a military engineer and government official, was a specialist in siege warfare. His talents were well used in the campaigns against Kazan. The Sviiazhsk fortress was constructed in the record time of four weeks thanks to Vyrodkov's methods of prefabrication. The wooden towers, gates, and complicated parts of the walls were constructed in advance and floated down the river. Ivan also put Vyrodkov's construction skills to work later on in the Livonian campaign. In 1557 he was ordered to construct a fortress and port at the mouth of the Narva river, and a fortress in Galich. In 1563 he served as a commander in the successful attack on Polotsk but for unspecified reasons was executed shortly thereafter.

9. Junior boyars, or *deti boiarskie,* literally "boyar sons" because traditionally most serving boyars' sons began their service in this rank, were actually low-ranking, mainly military, servitors of the Muscovite tsars, considerably below the boyars in status and responsibilities, even below the courtiers (dvoriane). All three groups together could be considered to comprise the sixteenth-century Muscovite aristocracy. For more information see the entry "Deti Boiarskie" by Robert D. Givens, MERSH, Vol. 9, pp. 101-103.

10. Shah Ali (1506-1567), referred to as Shig-Aley in Russian sources, was the Tatar khan of Kasimov (see Note 21, below). He was a descendant of Chinghis Khan and the khans of the Golden Horde and a pretender to the Kazan throne. An able commander, his career demonstrates the open-mindedness of the later Mus-covite tsars—particularly Ivan IV—who needed and welcomed genuine govern-ing and leadership ability from any quarter. Significantly, the Muscovite elite also accepted the granting to non-Russians of high rank, boyar in Shah Ali's case, and concomitant social status. The practice of finding talented and adaptable non-Russians and training them to carry on the tsar's government, particularly in their native territory, became a dominant pattern over the next four centuries of Russia's imperial development.

11. Yury Mikhailovich Bulgakov, son of one of Vasily III's leading command-ers, was sponsored by the head of the Belsky boyar clan and promoted to boyar status in 1540 during Ivan IV's minority. In 1541 he saw active service against the Crimean Tatars. In 1549 he was sent by Ivan IV on a peace-keeping mission to Kazan. His relations, the Golitsyns and Patrikeevs, were old boyar princely fam-ilies with long records of service as high officials under the Muscovite grand princes. One of the Patrikeevs, Prince Vasily Ivanovich, was involved in the anti-Josephite movement of Non-Possessors. As the monk Vassian he and Maxim the Greek symbolized the Orthodox Reformation; in their defeat and condemnation at the hands of the Josephite Metropolitan Daniel they symbolized the failure of the Reformation and the continuation of theocratic, caesaropapist attitudes. For more information on this topic, see MERSH entries "Daniil, Metropolitan" by S.M. Kashtanov, Vol. 8, pp. 170-171, "Maksim Grek," Vol. 21, pp. 26-28, "Nil Sorskii," by David Goldfrank, Vol. 25, pp. 11-14 and "Patrikeev, Vassian," by Nicholas Lupinin, Vol. 27, pp. 60-62. On the involvement of the Golitsyns with the Belsky and Shuisky boyar clans during Ivan's regency in the 1530s, see Soloviev, Vol. 9, pp. 207-208.

12. Daniel Romanovich (died 1571) was a member of a leading Muscovite boyar family, the Zakharin-Koshkins, in service to the Muscovite princes since the fourteenth century. His father, Roman Yurievich (died 1543), was a lord-in-waiting in the late years of Vasily III's rule and the early years of that of Ivan IV. His sister, Anastasia Romanova (died 1560), became the tsaritsa when she married Ivan IV shortly before his coronation in 1547. Daniel's wife Anna was killed in the 1571 attack of the Crimean khan Devlet Girey on Moscow. According to the Brockhaus Encyclopedia, Daniel also died in 1571. His younger brother Nikita Romanovich (died 1586) took an active part in the Livonian War (1558-1581) and ruled the council of regents for a short time following Ivan's death in 1584.

Nikita's son Fedor (1557-1633) became Patriarch Filaret and played a leading role both during the Time of Troubles (1605-1613) and afterwards until his death as adviser to his son Mikhail Fedorovich, elected the first "Romanov" tsar in 1613.

13. Peter Obolensky-Serebriany, son of one of Vasily III's leading boyar-commanders, rose in military service under the young Ivan IV. He was promoted boyar in 1551 following his successful activity against Kazan and played a leading role in its capture in the 1552 campaign.

14. St. Sergius the Miracle Worker refers to Sergius of Radonezh, one of Russia's most beloved saints. Born in Rostov around 1317, son of a boyar of the Rostov appanage princes, he moved with his impoverished family to Radonezh and the protection of the Muscovite prince's younger brother. At twenty Sergius became a monk and soon founded a retreat in the northern forests on the Konshur river, forty-five miles northwest of Moscow. Other monks, hearing tales of Sergius's learning, simplicity and spirituality, moved to join him and soon the collection of cells became a fully-fledged monastery with institutional buildings, consecrated in the name of the Holy Trinity. In the 1370s Sergius lent his by then considerable influence in the church to Grand Prince Dmitry of Moscow in his struggle against the Tatars of the Golden (Kipchak) Horde. When in 1380 Dmitry won his famous victory over the Tatars at Kulikovo on the Don (see Note 43, below), the church's position in Muscovite society and politics became unassailable. Sergius died in 1391 or 1392, and in 1448 or 1449 he was declared an all-Russian saint by the metropolitan. It was not long before many churches and monasteries were dedicated to him. His original foundation, known after his death as the Trinity-St. Sergius monastery, became Russia's leading monastery and seminary, a position it maintains to this day. For more information, see MERSH entries "Sergii of Radonezh," by Faith Wigzell, Vol. 34, pp. 77-80, and "Trinity-St. Sergius Monastery," by Emily V. Leonard, Vol. 39, pp. 213-216.

15. The Volga in its upper course winds its way through the North Russian forested plain. In its lower course it carves a path almost due south to the Caspian Sea through the open steppe of the great Eurasian plain. Its middle course thus consists of a long curve through the transition zone, where the river skirts a huge uplifted landmass. Kazan was situated on the outside of the curve, on the Volga's "plains side" (lugovaia storona, literally "meadow side"). The inside of the curve—the uplifted side, consisting of steep bluffs, high hills and some deep valleys—was the Volga's "highland side" (gornaia storona, literally the "mountain side"). The Muscovites realized that they must secure the allegiance and pacification of various highland tribes (Cheremiss, Chuvash, Mordvinians), nominally subject to the khanate, before they could hope for a lasting conquest of the entire Kazan khanate.

16. The tribute was the *yasak,* usually furs, demanded of natives who agreed to Muscovite subjection and protection; at first it was simply taken over from the tribute originally imposed by the Tatars. Indeed the Russians themselves paid a yasak to the Tatars of the Golden Horde. Payment of yasak classified a subject of the tsar as a "native subject" rather than a "peasant subject." For more information, see the entry by Edward D. Sokol, "Yasak," MERSH, Vol. 45, pp. 12-16.

17. Adashev, one of Ivan's closest advisers, was in charge of Muscovy's eastern, and indeed all diplomatic, affairs. A skillful administrator and diplomat, he in particular realized the importance of Kazan to Muscovy in terms of the consolidation of its eastern boundary and, ultimately, the control of the Eurasian steppe. For more information on Adashev, see the entry "Adashev, Aleksei Fedorovich" by Graham, MERSH, Vol. 1, pp. 28-30. For a suggestive view of the rivalry of the Golden Horde's three main successor states (Kazan, the Crimea, and Muscovy) over the inheritance of its Eurasian steppe kingdom, see the article by Edward L. Keenan, "Muscovy and Kazan," *Slavic Review*, 26 (1967), pp. 548-558.

18. It was a clever move. The slaves managed much of the economy of the Kazan khanate, acting as business managers and estate stewards for the Tatar magnates. Their removal threatened the collapse of Kazan's economy and society. Many of the Russian slaves did not wish to be freed, having found life as servants for Muslim masters preferable to life as Russian peasants—which says as much about the Tatars' treatment of slaves as it does about conditions in Muscovy.

19. For mention of Khabarov's part in the politics of the boyar regency, see Vol. 9, pp. 208-209.

20. For mention of Paletsky's part in the politics of the boyar regency, see Vol. 9, pp. 209-210.

21. Kasimov, originally Gorodets-Meshchersky, was granted to Khan Kasim, brother of the khan of Kazan and descendant of Chinghis Khan and the khans of the Golden Horde, as a sort of "Kazan khanate-in-exile." Theoretically Kasimov, situated about a third of the way from Moscow to Kazan, was an autonomous kingdom within the Muscovite realm with Shah Ali presently its sole ruler. In practice, Shah Ali's authority rested on his loyal service to the Muscovite tsar, and he was seldom at home. Over the previous century the "khanate" of Kasimov served its purpose well as a rallying point for pro-Muscovite Kazan Tatars. For more information, see the entry by Sokol, "Kasimov, Principality of," MERSH, Vol. 16, pp. 54-56.

22. He used the word *denga*, which was a small silver coin, the basic monetary unit in Muscovite Russia.

23. The Nogay were nomadic horsemen of Turkic origin inhabiting the steppe region between and to the east of the Kazan and Crimean khanates. Their warriors were often used in the increasingly vicious struggle for control of the steppes—sometimes by the Tatars, sometimes by the Muscovites, and sometimes by both at once. For more information, see the entry "Nogay Horde" by Sokol, MERSH, Vol. 25, pp. 38-42.

24. Prince Ivan Sheremetev the Elder (he had a younger brother with the same name who was also one of Ivan IV's boyar-commanders) was promoted boyar in 1550 on his return from the Kazan campaign in that year. He was wounded in the fighting against the Crimean Tatars in 1555, recovered, and commanded the leading regiment in the invasion of Livonia in 1558. Wounded again, he returned to Moscow where he became a member of the boyar estates (zemshchina) and the Assembly of the Land (zemsky sobor) (see Chapter III, below). In 1570, under suspicion of wrongdoing by the irascible tsar, he quit his rank as boyar and entered the

St. Cyril monastery of Beloozero, taking vows under the monastic name of Jonah. He died in 1577.

25. A large lake, the Lower Kaban, was situated just south of the city walls.

26. The Mikulinskys were serving princes originally from Tver who entered the service of the Muscovite princes. In 1537 Prince Simeon commanded a force that defeated Tatars from Azov and the Crimea. In 1548 he defeated Safa-Girey, the khan of Kazan, in a skirmish outside the walls of Kazan. He later took part in the Livonian War and died in 1562.

27. The Romodanovskys were serving princes from Starodub. Prince Ivan's father, Vasily, served as Ivan III's ambassador to Lithuania.

28. Alexander Gorbaty was a relative of the Shuisky family and a son of Prince Boris Gorbaty, a leading commander under Vasily III and a boyar since 1533. He himself became a boyar in 1544. As we shall see, he played a leading role in the conquest of Kazan in 1552 and was appointed its first viceroy. He and his son Peter were executed, although apparently innocent of the charges, on Ivan's orders in 1564.

29. Prince Peter Shuisky, a leader of the Shuisky boyar clan in the political struggle with Prince Belsky and Metropolitan Ioasaf during Ivan IV's minority, became one of Ivan IV's military commanders and was killed in battle in Livonia in 1564. For more information on the Shuiskys, see the entry "Shuiskii Family" by Graham, MERSH, Vol. 35, pp. 53-58.

30. "Putting razors to their beards, making themselves up like women … fornicating with the young men … seducing the good-looking women and honest girls who were captured and freed in the name of God." (Soloviev's note)

31. Kolychevo is a village in Serpukhov district, province of Moscow, and Golutvin a monastery five versts from Kolomna. (Soloviev's note)

32. During Ivan IV's minority Prince Peter Shcheniatiev belonged to the party of Prince Ivan Belsky and Metropolitan Joseph in the internecine strife among the aristocrats at court, and was jailed at Yaroslavl for his part. By 1544 he was freed and back in service. In 1549 he was promoted boyar and the following year accompanied Ivan on campaign to Kazan. He distinguished himself in the successful 1552 campaign and later in the fighting against the Crimean Tatars, the Swedes and the Lithuanians. A close friend of Prince Andrei Kurbsky, he nevertheless remained loyal to Ivan when Kurbsky deserted to Lithuania in 1564 (see following note). In spite of his demonstrated loyalty and protested innocence he became the subject of Ivan's terrible anger four years later. He attempted to quit service and become a monk, but Ivan had him tracked down, dragged back to Moscow, and put to death in a particularly gruesome ceremony involving a giant frying pan. His story illustrates Ivan's increasingly irrational behavior in the 1560s, lashing out in frustration at his very friends and supporters.

33. Prince Andrei Kurbsky, who as we shall see played a significant role not only in the capture of Kazan but also in the Livonian war, was a scion of the ruling princes of Smolensk and Yaroslavl. Well educated in both Russian and Western culture, highly literate, only two years older than Ivan IV, in 1549 at the age of

twenty-one he was called to be groom-in-waiting to the young tsar. The two became close friends. He appears to have been an occasional member of Ivan's "chosen council" which advised the tsar in governmental affairs for the first seventeen years of his reign, though the existence of this "chosen council" has been disputed. See A.N. Grobovsky, *The "Chosen Council" of Ivan IV. A Reinterpretation* (Brooklyn, N.Y., 1969). Mostly Kurbsky devoted himself to his military career, beginning with the Kazan campaign of 1549. He was promoted boyar in 1556; in 1558 he was appointed a senior commander for the Livonian campaign. His proud desertion to the enemy in 1564, as we shall see, signified a serious division in the Muscovite structure of government and society. Kurbsky's relationship with Ivan exemplifies the sharply increasing struggle in sixteenth-century Russia between the forces for "modernization," meaning increased centralization and greater government efficiency and those for "conservatism," meaning the traditionally decentralized political and social structure.

34. Prince Ivan Pronsky-Turuntay (died 1569) was a leading military commander during Ivan's reign. In 1541 he successfully defended Muscovy against an attack by the Crimean Tatars under Khan Sahin-Girey at the Oka river. A friend of the Shuisky boyars, Pronsky suffered banishment in the 1540s as Ivan IV took control of the government out of the boyars' hands, but was restored to favor when he was invited to the tsar's coronation in 1547. Satisfying himself about Pronsky's trustworthiness, Ivan promoted him boyar in 1549 and gave him a leading command in the campaign against Kazan in that year. In 1553 Pronsky was one of the boyars who, in their dislike for the Zakharin-Romanovs, hesitated to take the oath of allegiance to Ivan's infant son Dmitry, yet Ivan when he recovered appeared to forgive Pronsky for his wavering loyalty. From 1554 to 1568 Pronsky commanded various regiments in engagements both in Livonia and against Crimean Tatars. After Ivan's division of the Muscovite government into the oprichnina (crown estates) and the zemshchina (the land) in 1565, Pronsky took a leading governing role in the latter. In 1569 Ivan's wrath descended upon him and he was executed for a litany of disloyalties.

35. Prince Dmitry Khilkov served in various military positions during Ivan's minority. In 1550 he took part as a commander in Kazan operations. In 1551 he was ordered to help Shah Ali to construct Fort Sviiazhsk and then sent to to defend Kolomna against an attack by Crimean Tatars. During the operations against Kazan in 1552, Khilkov is said to have shown great bravery and real leadership. He was promoted boyar in 1556 after successfully putting down a riot and restoring order in Kazan. He led several successful military operations in the Livonian campaign, but eventually ran afoul of Ivan and was executed in 1564.

36. Prince Mikhail Vorotynsky (1510-1573) was another of Ivan's foremost commanders. As a young officer he served in Muscovy's southern regions, defending the state against the incursions of Crimean Tatars. For his part in the the victory at Kazan, Vorotynsky was promoted boyar, but as one of Adashev's supporters (see Note 17) he fell into disfavor and banishment following Adashev's disgrace in 1560. Restored to favor after a few years, Vorotynsky used his

experience fighting Tatars to draw up regulations rationalizing the defenses of Muscovy's southeastern borders. In 1572, following the disastrous sack and burning of Moscow in 1571 by the Crimean Tatar army of Khan Devlet-Girey, Vorotynsky led the Russian force that convincingly defeated the Crimeans at Molodi as they attempted to repeat their victory of the previous year. Testifying to the vicissitudes of service to the Terrible Tsar, Vorotynsky was executed in 1573 following accusations of treasonable negotiations with Khan Devlet-Girey. For information on Devlet-Girey and Russian-Crimean relations during Ivan's reign, see the entry "Devlet-Girei" by Graham, MERSH, Vol. 9, pp. 104-106.

37. Prince Temkin until 1550 was in service among the junior boyars under Prince Vladimir Andreevich of Staritsa, Ivan's cousin (see Note 3, above). In 1551 he was appointed commander of the garrison in Tula and became the hero of its defense in 1552.

38. The Shivorona river is located in the Bogoroditsky district of the province of Tula and flows into the Upa river. (Soloviev's note)

39. See map of Ivan's campaign to Kazan in 1552.

40. See map of the siege of Kazan in 1552.

41. As an appanage prince, Vladimir had the right to have his own retinue. Elsewhere it is referred to as the Ertoul Regiment.

42. *Nerukotvorennyi obraz,* an icon of Christ said to have descended miraculously from heaven.

43. The cross depicted a horizontal crescent moon, points upward, near the foot of the cross, depicting the victory of Christianity over Islam. Grand Prince Dmitry Donskoy (1350-1389), Ivan's great-great-great-grandfather, ruled Muscovy from 1359 to 1389. His most-remembered achievement, for the Muscovites, was his victory in 1380 over the Tatars of the Golden Horde led by Mamay Khan at Kulikovo on the Don river, hence the title Donskoy, "of the Don." Although the hegemony of the Golden Horde subsequently was re-established over Muscovy, the victory broke the legendary—indeed, all too real throughout the preceding century and a half—invincibility of the Tatars in battle. As a ruler, Dmitry is judged to have been a shrewd political realist who accepted the realities of Tatar rule and acted successfully within that framework to the benefit of his patrimonial Muscovy. For more information, see the entry "Dmitrii Ivanovich Donskoi" by Goldfrank, MERSH, Vol. 9, pp. 170-177.

44. Soloviev uses the term *bezbozhnyi,* literally "godless." The Tatars were hardly "godless," having adopted Islam in 1260. Indeed the Russians were hardly more "God-fearing" than the Tatars. Christianity since its official adoption at the end of the tenth century made slow headway against the paganism of the Eastern Slavs. Only in the fifteenth century can we consider the Russians thoroughly Christianized. Nevertheless to the Orthodox proselytizers—and chroniclers— Muslims were godless and, at least on the battlefield, despicable unless, of course, like Shah Ali they were on the Russian side.

45. See Note 8, above.

46. Prince Andrei Kurbsky tells it differently. "When the living captives were brought to our tsar, he ordered them led out in front of the trenches and tied to posts.

Then he sent word into the city that if Kazan were given over to the Christian tsar, the tsar would grant them all—townsmen as well as captives—their lives and their freedom. They listened to these words without reply, and then began firing from the town walls, not at our men but at their own, crying 'It is better that we see you dying at our own Muslim hands than to let these faithless dogs cut you down.'" (Soloviev's note)

47. See Note 13, above.

48. Simeon Sheremetev (died 1561) was one of four Sheremetev brothers who served as military commanders under Ivan IV in his various campaigns. The Sheremetev family was an old Muscovite boyar family, related to the Zakharins. Despite the fact that Ivan "called off" mestnichestvo (see Note 5, above) for the 1552 campaign against Kazan, all four Sheremetevs exercised the highest military commands. Simeon successfully commanded troops against the Nogay (1550), the Kazan Tatars (1552), and the Swedes (1555-1556); in 1557 he and Prince Semeon Ivanovich Mikulinsky (see Note 26, above) were made the military commanders of Kazan. Sheremetev took monastic vows as Stefan on his deathbed in 1561 and was buried in the St. Joseph monastery of Volokolamsk.

49. Vyrodkov also prefabricated this tower. (See Note 8, above.)

50. See Note 41, above.

51. According to Kurbsky's testimony, the first to mount the walls was his brother Prince Roman Kurbsky. (Soloviev's note)

52. The tsarevich, Dmitry Ivanovich, died a year later in June 1553, but not before the scene at Ivan's sickbed when the tsar forced his reluctant boyars to swear allegiance to the tsarevich. (See Note 34, above.) It reflected the young, twenty-three-year-old tsar's anxiety about securing the succession to his Muscovite throne. The succession actually was secured the following year when Anastasia gave birth to a second son, Tsarevich Ivan Ivanovich, who lived to the age of twenty-seven; he only died then, in 1581, ironically at the hands of his enraged father who once again thereby jeopardized the all-important dynasty.

53. St. Vladimir is credited with bringing Christianity to Russia at the end of the tenth century. On Dmitry Donskoy, see Note 43, above. Alexander Nevsky was a Russian warrior-prince of the thirteenth century celebrated for his victories as prince of Novgorod over the Teutonic knights, but more important historically for his diplomacy at the court of the Tatar khan, the new ruler of the Russians, which resulted in his becoming the khan's official viceroy for Russia and thus its ruler in internal affairs.

54. In this translation the term "khan" has been used consistently to refer to a Tatar ruler, "tsar" to refer to the Russian ruler. Russians, including Soloviev, often referred to a khan as "tsar." In his answer to Shah Ali's congratulations after Kazan fell, for example, Ivan addressed him as "tsar." The term was derived from the Latin word caesar, *tsezar'* in Slavonic, but it first was applied by the Russians to the "supreme khan," the ruler of the Golden horde. Both "supreme khan" and "grand prince" implied "first among equals." When the Tatars' "supreme khan" became the Russians' sovereign and absolute ruler, the "grand prince," like Alexander Nevsky, was technically first among equal Russian princes, yet still

subservient to the khan. A new term was needed to describe this subservience, so the Old Slavonic word for emperor—*tsar'*—was adopted to refer to the Russians' absolute ruling khan, despite the fact that in the minds of many Tatars that khan was still only first among equals. The courtiers of Ivan III and Vasily III used the term tsar for their own monarch, but those cautious rulers refused to adopt it officially. The temptation became irresistible to the young Ivan IV at the age of seventeen. We should bear in mind that had his bid for domination of the Kazan Tatars failed in this last all-out attack, he probably would have had to revert to being merely a "grand prince," unable to force his pretensions on contemporaries.

55. Bulgars, a people of Asian Turkic ancestry, moved to the middle Volga region in the late seventh century. They were the predominant element in the Volga Bulgar state that dominated the area and often opposed the Muscovites to the west of them until the Mongol invasion in 1236.

56. Novgorod proper until the end of the fifteenth century was the undisputed economic center of Northwestern Russia. "Lower" (Nizhny) Novgorod became the economic clearinghouse of Northeastern Russia for an east-west trade that under the Tatar domination came to rival that of the older city.

57. Tax-farming privileges were known as *kormlenie* in Muscovy and allowed, indeed required, boyars or other high officials to derive their own salaries from the revenues of their constituents, turning over stipulated amounts to the treasury. The privileges undoubtedly mollified some boyars and ex-appanage princes, unhappy at losing their independence by being forced to agree to serve the Muscovite tsar, as a sort of temporary fiefdom. This practice may even have served to keep the tsar's highest officials in closer touch with the population of the realm than if they merely were granted official salaries. Although there were complaints of abuses, the system was probably the most economical and effective way to administer Muscovy in this period, a stepping stone to the institutionalization of centralized government. For more information, see the entry "Kormlenie" by N.E. Nosov, MERSH, Vol. 17, pp. 189-190.

58. "The tsar soon returned to Moscow. He entrusted boyars in his absence to carry out the organization of Kazan and then to allocate the tax farms; but they soon grew tired of such a great task, they made very little effort, they did not carry the work on to completion, and they only concerned themselves with riches. They began to divide up the tax farms, and the work of running of Kazan was neglected." Quoted from the *Tsarstvennaia kniga* chronicles, pp. 337-338, by Soloviev.

59. Perekop is the narrow isthmus controlling access to the Crimea from the mainland.

60. Astrakhan and Tmutorokan are not synonymous. Astrakhan lies at the mouth of the Volga whereas Tmutorokan was situated on the Taman peninsula.

61. Ivan IV, of the Danilov dynasty, was descended from St. Vladimir, grand prince of Kiev from 980 to 1015 and the Christianizer of Russia, through his great-great-grandson Yury Dolgoruky, grand prince of Vladimir-Suzdal (1125-1155), great-grandfather of Alexander Nevsky, the father of Daniel, prince of Moscow and founder of the Danilov dynasty.

62. Pronsky-Shemiakin (died 1554 or 1555) was the descendant of princes serving Muscovy since the early fifteenth century. His father, Prince Ivan Vasilievich Pronsky-Neliubov-Shemiakin, was an important military commander whose forces defended Muscovy from the Crimean Tatars in the years of Ivan's minority, for which he was promoted boyar in 1547. The son served with distinction in the Kazan campaigns from 1548 to 1552, commanded a regiment at the conquest of the citadel, and as a result was put in charge of the campaign against Astrakhan, although he was killed before the final capture in 1556.

63. That is to say, the Feast of St. John (Ioann or Ivan), his patron saint. August 29 is the feast day of the beheading of St. John the Baptist. The principal feast, commemorating his birth, is on June 24.

64. Mansurov was a member of a family of servitors at the Moscow court, descended from a Tatar of the Golden Horde who entered the service of Grand Prince Ivan I in 1328 and converted to Christianity, adopting the name Boris. The family produced a number of diplomats for the Muscovite rulers.

65. Artsybashev asks, "Were they not perhaps Chechens?" (Soloviev's note) N.S. Artsybashev was the author of a work entitled *Narrative about Russia,* published in Moscow in 1838. See Introduction.

66. Tarki, ruled by a "shamkhal," was Kabarda's eastern neighbor and traditional foe. The rulers of each sought alliances with the states on the far side of their foes: Kabarda with the Astrakhan khanate, Tarki with the Crimean khanate. Now that Muscovy assumed control over Astrakhan, it was being pressured to take part in the intricate wickerwork of Caucasian diplomacy.

67. As Kurbsky expressed it. (Soloviev's note)

68. See Note 24, above.

69. Rzhevsky distinguished himself as a commander in the capture of Kazan. He also participated in the Livonian campaign, among other things defending Polotsk against attack by Stefan Bathory's army in 1578-1579. He is said to have been a particularly skillful writer, which probably explains why he also held the high civil rank of crown secretary.

70. Islam-Kermen (or Kyzy-Kermen), situated on the left bank of the Dnieper about fifty-four miles upriver from its mouth and about forty-three miles upriver from the site of the ancient Greek city of Chersonesos (Kherson in Russian), was one of a series of Turkish forts constructed to protect Crimean territory; it finally was captured by the army of Peter the Great in 1696, and under Catherine II in 1784 it was re-named Berislav.

71. The Turkish name of the fort was Ozi.

72. Vishnevetsky, Polish spelling Wisniowiecki, was a leading Ukrainian cossack courted by both Muscovy and Poland-Lithuania. Pledging his allegiance to the Russian tsar in 1556, he transferred his loyalty back to the Polish king at the start of the Livonian war. In 1563 he was taken prisoner by the Turks and executed in Istanbul. In some accounts he is credited with founding the cossack headquarters known as the Zaporozhian Sich.

73. On Hetman Dashkovich, see Vol. 9, pp. 82-86.

74. Khortitsa was the original home of the Zaporozhian Cossack Host.

75. Zagriazhsky belonged to a family of court aristocracy that served the Muscovite rulers ever since their ancestor, a Tatar aristocrat from the Golden Horde, converted to Christianity and entered Muscovite service.

76. On Mehmet-Girey, khan of the Crimea and son of Mengli-Girey, see the preceding volume.

77. Luckily the Russian forces had just returned for a brief respite from the fighting in Livonia. See the following chapter.

78. *Nenasytitskii porog* in the original.

79. Not all historians agree with Soloviev's estimate. See for example Alexander Yanov, *The Origins of Autocracy* (Berkeley, 1981), especially pp. 13, 200-202.

80. See Volume 25, pp. 180-183, 197-202.

81. Burchard Christoph von Münnich was born in Oldenburg in 1683, the son of an officer of the Danish army. After serving with the armies of France, Hesse and Poland, he entered Russian service in 1721. Peter I entrusted him with supervising the building of the Ladoga canal. He was created a count by the Supreme Privy Council that ruled for five years after Peter's death. In 1730, after the succession of Empress Anna, he was made governor-general of St. Petersburg. In 1732 he was made field marshal and commander of the Russian armies, in which position he sent Russian troops against the Turks in the Crimea and the Danubian lowlands. In 1741 he was arrested and exiled to Siberia, victim of the anti-German sentiment of Empress Elizabeth's supporters. At seventy-eight he was granted amnesty by Emperor Peter III and allowed to return to St. Petersburg, where he died in 1767.

CHAPTER II

1. Gustav I Eriksson Vasa (1496-1560), king of Sweden from 1523 to 1560, ascended the throne at the age of twenty-seven following the expulsion of the Danes and the restoration of an independent Sweden. A reforming monarch, his energies were taxed severely by the lack of reliable native assistants. Four serious peasant rebellions occurred during his reign, nearly forcing him to abdicate and emigrate. His break with Rome, although primarily a political rather than a dogmatic act, forcibly established a Protestant Lutheran hierarchy in Sweden, which partly explains the pro-Catholic peasant rebellions. A devout, moral and essentially cheerful man by nature, he was also irritable and suspicious and could be violent and tyrannical. In foreign affairs, he saw Denmark as more of a threat to his country than Russia, although in the last two years of his reign he became increasingly nervous about Russian and Polish involvement in Livonia after 1558, which he saw generally as a threat to Swedish trade in the Baltic and specifically as a threat by Ivan IV, whose power and resources he tended to exaggerate, to extend his empire to the Baltic.

2. Bytowns, or *prigorody,* were smaller towns near a larger town or city on which they were administratively dependent.

3. The leading merchants, or *gosti,* were wholesale merchants licensed to do business for the tsar, chosen on the basis of their success as private merchants. See Samuel H. Baron, "Who Were the Gosti?" *California Slavic Studies,* 7 (1973), pp. 1-40

4. See Soloviev, Vol. 9, p. 241; also p. 250, Note 29, on "Friazin" not being a surname as such, but rather a Russian designation of a West European.

5. Dorpat was the German name of the Livonian capital, Yuriev the Russian name, Tartu the Estonian name.

6. From Schlitte's papers it is evident that he was concerned more about himself than about the tsar, and acted more according to his own preferences than the tsar's. For example, he recruited four theologians in his group. (Soloviev's note). Soloviev implies in this note that Ivan had no interest in theologians, a doubtful proposition. To judge by the evidence of his education, curiosity, and argumentativeness, Ivan doubtless took delight in confronting and questioning Western theologians. See, for example, the testimony of the papal envoy Antonio Possevino, who attempted to convert Ivan to the Roman faith in 1581, in *The MOSCOVIA of Antonio Possevino, S.J.* tr. and ed. H.F. Graham (Pittsburgh, 1977).

7. Plettenberg was elected master of the Order of Livonian Knights at the end of the fifteenth century and became a powerful and important leader. The treaty in 1503, which stipulated peace for fifty years, concluded an unsuccessful attack on Livonia by Ivan III in 1502. In 1527 Plettenberg was recognized as a prince of the Holy Roman empire by Charles V.

8. According to the Russian chronicles, the Livonians requested and concluded a treaty for fifteen years; according to Livonian sources, fifty years. (Soloviev's note). The latter were surely correct, which would explain why the Livonians were back just fifty years later.

9. This is how Nyenstädt told it. Russow—and following him Hiarn—tells how the mayor of Dorpat, Henck, advised dealing directly [with the Muscovites] and not agreeing to the tribute for the sake of gaining time. (Soloviev's note). For more on Russow, see W. Urban. "The Nationality of Balthasar Russow," *Journal of Baltic Studies,* 12 (1981), pp. 160-172.

10. The Ivangorod kremlin was constructed in the reign of Ivan III, directly facing the fortress of Narva across the Narva river. Designed and built by the inhabitants of Pskov for service rather than show, it affords an instructive contrast between the spare, solid, native Russian style of stone-fortress construction and the ornate, elegant, imported Italianate style as seen in the contemporary walls and towers of Ivan III's new Moscow Kremlin.

11. The Cherkess, or Circassians, were Caucasians from the cis-Caucasian area between Astrakhan and the Crimea. See Chapter I, section on "Caucasian politics."

12. We have no reason to doubt the statement of the Livonian chroniclers that the ambassadors were sent with sixty-six thousand thalers to Moscow, for a

contemporary, Nyenstädt, wrote, "The city of Dorpat contributed ten thousand thalers, which I myself helped to count. Thus some sixty thousand thalers were collected, and I myself helped do it." This information is in agreement with the information contained in the report of the ambassadors, for the latter speaks only of a tribute from Dorpat. (Soloviev's note)

13. Now Viljandi.

14. Gotthard von Kettler was the last master of the independent Livonian Order. When he appealed to his western neighbors to save him from Russia, his realm was quickly partitioned among Poland, Denmark, and Sweden.

15. According to Kurbsky, Nyenstädt only remembered two hundred soldiers. (Soloviev's note)

16. Nyenstädt merely says "the nobles" in general. I have written "most of the nobles" because later, when the bishop was setting conditions for something, he said "those nobles who wished to remain under the grand prince were able to remain in Livonia with their lands and people and all their things." (Soloviev's note)

17. That is, their Protestant belief. The "Confession of Augsburg" was drawn up in 1530 on the initiative of the emperor, Charles V, in the city of Augsburg and enunciated the principles of the Lutheran reformation of the church.

18. Reval is the German name for Livonia's northern fortified seaport; the Russian name is Kolyvan, the Estonian Tallinn.

19. Estimates of the number of Ringen's defenders varies. According to the Pskov chronicles there were only a hundred and forty. According to Kurbsky, the Livonians captured three hundred men in the town, almost all of whom died in dungeons of hunger or cold. According to Livonian witnesses, four hundred Russians were killed in the siege. The commander of the garrison was the chief musketeer Rusin Ignatiev. (Soloviev's note)

20. John was the eldest son of King Gustav I's second marriage, and second in line for the Swedish throne after his half-brother Erik, who became King Erik XIV. In 1562, still duke of Finland, John married Katarzyna Jagiellonica, sister of Sigismund II, king of Poland. Their son, Sigismund, became king of Poland in 1587. When Erik died in 1568 John became king of Sweden and ruled as John III until 1592. He was known as a learned man, a theologian, and a successful ruler.

21. Christian III (1503-1559), king of Denmark and Norway, presided over the Reformation in Denmark. His tutors were Lutheran reformers; he married Anne of Brandenburg. He attended the Diet of Worms in 1521 where he was deeply impressed by Martin Luther's behavior, and throughout his reign he allied himself with the German Evangelical princes. He is considered to have been a good ruler, having found Denmark in ruins and having led it to historic strength and wealth.

22. Frederik II (1534-1588), king of Denmark and Norway in 1559-1588, was Christian III's son. His mother, Dorothea of Saxe-Lauenburg, was the older sister of Catherine, Gustav I of Sweden's first wife. Thus Frederik and Erik XIV were first cousins and also lifelong rivals, since much of Frederik's reign was spent at war with Sweden. He is known for having discovered and employed several great statesmen, to whom he granted large responsibilities. He died in 1588, beloved by his Danish subjects.

23. Yury is the Russian version of Georgy, which was the baptismal name of Yaroslav the Wise, whose reign as grand prince of Kiev (1019-1054) is considered to be the high point of Kievan Russia. He extended and consolidated Kiev's rule over the Eastern Slavs, and presided over a striking religious revival, consolidating his father Vladimir's efforts to introduce Christianity to the Slavs. His reign was also a period of great cultural advancement in law, education, architecture, and art. His wife was a Swedish princess. The Teutonic Knights renamed Yuriev Dorpat.

24. Sigismund I (1467-1548) was elected grand duke of Lithuania in 1505 and king of Poland in 1506. A giant of a man, he was a leader of great governing ability and sound business instincts. His second wife, Queen Bona Sforza, introduced an extravagant Italian flavor into the severe court at Cracow but later generally was hated for being greedy and corrupt. Much of his reign he spent fighting his neighbors: the Livonians (until 1525), the Russians, the Tatars and the Prussians. Although a Roman Catholic himself, he upheld the rights of his Orthodox and other non-Catholic subjects throughout his realm, particularly in Lithuania. He had little sympathy for the new men and new ideas about him in this turbulent age yet did little to stem the rising tide of Protestantism. His daughter Katarzyna married King John III of Sweden; another daughter, Anna, married King Stefan Bathory.

25. Sigismund II Augustus (born 1520, reigned 1548-1572) was the only son of King Sigismund I. Considered by some a diplomat of genius, he engineered the Union of Lublin, which finally made Poland and Lithuania one body politic. His reign was a period of external expansion and domestic turmoil, witnessing the incursion of the Reformation into Poland and the democratic takeover of the king's power by the Polish gentry or *szlachta*. He was the last male of the descendants of Jagailo, grand prince of Lithuania in the fourteenth century, and himself died childless. Sigismund II, unlike his stern and majestic father, was elegant and refined, and a great statesman.

26. Sardanapalus was the last king of Assyria who died childless in 880 BC; he was considered to be the most effeminate and corrupt of a line of similar princes.

27. Vladimir Monomakh, generally considered to be the last great Kievan prince, ruled Kievan Russia from 1113 to 1125. The beautiful, fur-trimmed crown (shapka) that was said to have been his, inherited from his ancestor, the Byzantine emperor Constantine IX Monomachos, was in fact made long after his death, probably for a potentate in Central Asia. Like the fabricated genealogy "proving" the descent of the Muscovite tsars from the Roman emperors, the claim to have inherited the crown of the Kievan grand princes gave an authoritative tone to the tsar's assertions of dynastic legitimacy, as well as to his pretensions to "gather" older Kievan territories under his rule. The crown was worn by Russian rulers until the eighteenth century, and is preserved in the Moscow Kremlin Armory.

28. Gomel, or Homel, was founded in the twelfth century. Situated in present-day Belarus, over time it has suffered the fate of a border city between often-warring countries.

29. See Chapter I, Note 53, above.

30. Mikhail Morozov was one of Ivan leading boyar-commanders. At Kazan he was in command of the artillery. He scored important victories in the Livonian

campaign and in 1561 warred against the Crimeans. In 1564 he ran afoul of the tsar and was imprisoned.

31. Grand prince of Lithuania from 1492 to 1506. See Volumes 7, 8 and 9.

32. Mikhail Bulgakov-Golitsa, a member of an old family of serving princes at the Moscow court, was descended from the fourteenth-century Lithuanian ruler, Grand Prince Gedymin (Gediminas). Mikhail's son Yury was a leading commander in the Kazan campaign. See Chapter I, Note 11, above.

33. Little is known of Fedor Obolensky, except that his father was a leading boyar in the reign of Vasily III and a Shuisky supporter during Ivan's regency.

34. Nicholas (Mikolaj) the Red (1512-1584) was the brother of Barbara, the queen of King Sigismund Augustus. He was made grand hetman of the Lithuanian army. A Calvinist, he was opposed to union of Lithuania with Poland. Nicholas the Black (1515-1565), his cousin and commander of Wilno, was an even more outspoken opponent of union with Poland, but his death in 1565 weakened the separatist position and four years later the diets of the two lands unanimously voted for union. The Radziwill family maintained its power in Poland-Lithuania over the following centuries, at times exercising an extraordinary independence, even having its own army.

35. Prince Ivan Mikhailovich Shuisky, member of the powerful Shuisky family, reached boyar status in 1535 and was made commandant of Moscow; after 1547 he served in Ivan's court in Moscow and died in 1559. On his relationship to the other members of the Shuisky family, see entry by Graham, "Shuisky Family," MERSH, Vol. 35, pp. 53-58.

36. See Chapter I, Note 12, above.

37. Tishkevich's name in Polish would have been transliterated as Tyszkiewicz.

38. St. John Chrysostom (345-407) was perhaps the most famous Greek Father. Born into a noble family at Antioch, the capital of Syria, and a student of noted brilliance, he became a Christian in about 370. He was ordained in 381. As a presbyter in Antioch and later archbishop of Constantinople he won renown for his eloquent and moralistic preaching and writings. In Constantinople he spurned the luxury of his predecessors and turned his income to the establishment of hospitals. The zeal and eloquence he employed to cleanse the church of corruption, while ensuring his popularity, also gained him many enemies both in the church and at court; he even thundered against Empress Eudoxia from his pulpit in the cathedral of the Holy Wisdom. His enemies finally found a pretext to have him deposed and eventually banished to the desert where he died in 407. His voluminous writings, particularly his homilies, were immensely popular for their wisdom, style, and great humanity. Translated into Slavonic they became an integral and ever popular part of Slavonic Orthodoxy.

39. Sir Hugh Willoughby (died 1554), scion of an old English aristocratic family, served as a soldier on the Scottish borders before going to sea. In this expedition in 1553 he was appointed captain of the three ships. Their purpose was not so much to explore northern areas of the world as to discover a northeast passage to China and India, a project much talked about in England since the time

of Henry VIII. The ships became separated in a gale. Willoughby and two of the ships were forced to land for repairs and spend the winter on the northern coast of the Kola peninsula. Although he and the rest of the crew died of cold and starvation, he kept a journal of the voyage that later was found and published in the first volume of R. Hakluyt's *Principal Navigations* in London in 1589, together with Chancellor's journal of his voyage to Muscovy. For a modern edition of Chancellor's journal see Lloyd E. Berry and Robert O. Crummey, eds., *Rude and Barbarous Kingdom. Russia in the Accounts of Sixteenth-century English Voyagers* (Madison, 1968), pp. 3-41. He was more fortunate on this particular expedition, as related below. As Soloviev also relates, he perished three years later in a shipwreck off the northern coast of Scotland on the return voyage of his second expedition to Russia.

40. The Russia Company, also known as the Muscovy Company or the Association of Merchant Adventurers, obtained a charter from Queen Mary in 1555. The two agents were Richard Grey and George Killingworth. Anthony Jenkins, who was appointed captain-general of the Russia Company's outward bound fleet in 1557 and who remained the Company's agent in Moscow for three years thereafter, also kept a journal of his experiences, also published in Hakluyt in 1589. A modern edition of that journal can be found in Berry and Crummey, pp. 43-58.

41. Osip Nepeia (dates unknown) was Russia's first ambassador to England. A native of the northern city of Vologda, little is known of his service background before his appointment. After the shipwreck in 1556 he finally was received at Queen Mary's court on March 25, 1557 and returned to Russia a few months later. See entry by G. Edward Orchard, "Nepeia, Osip Grigor'evich," MERSH, Vol. 24, pp. 146-147, and Samuel H. Baron, "Osip Nepea and the Opening of Anglo-Russian Commercial Relations," *Oxford Slavonic Papers,* New Series, Vol. 11 (1978), pp. 42-63.

CHAPTER III

1. See Vol. 9, pp. 218-223.

2. The *Household Manager* (Domostroi) is a set of guidelines for the proper running of a good Orthodox household, the earliest written versions dating from the sixteenth century. Although the document appears to have originated in Novgorod, the best known version is the one Sylvester re-drafted and published around 1556. His version, the official, church-and-state-approved version, is a fascinating and instructive piece of Muscovite literature of Ivan's time. In form it was written to instruct the head of a family of that time in the correct upbringing of children and in the proper way to treat a wife and servants. In tone it reflects the Josephite ideal of monastic discipline and asceticism. Its sixty-three chapters of instruction reveal the patriarchal character of sixteenth-century Russian society— and the strictness, the ritualism, and the piety that was thought by some to be acceptable. We must be cautious before assuming that the *Manager* tells us what Muscovite society was really like, in spite of its constant reference to "ancient

Russian customs." As with many historical documents, it may reveal the very opposite of what it says. Sylvester's version, unlike its more "democratic" Novgorod prototype, strongly emphasizes absolute obedience to the tsar and his officials—including the church hierarchs. See entry "Domostroi" by George P. Majeska, MERSH, Vol. 9, pp. 212-214. The very fact of its publication at the time as well as its extreme didacticism probably indicates the concerns among the establishment, particularly the religious establishment, that morals were changing as a result of the new ideas being introduced from abroad, and that the old conservative values needed reiterating.

3. See Chapter I, Note 12, above.

4. See Chapter I, Note 3, above.

5. See Vol. 9, p. 210.

6. See Vol. 9, p. 210.

7. See Vol. 9 , pp. 209-210.

8. See Chapter II, Note 38, above.

9. See Chapter I, Note 34, above.

10. The right of "departure" (otezd) from the realm of the grand prince, especially with appanage lands, was a traditional right of appanage princes; it was the ability and good fortune of the Muscovite grand princes over the preceding century or more to prevent such departures and "gather" those appanage lands permanently within the Muscovite realm.

11. See Vol. 9, p. 182.

12. See Vol, 9, pp. 178-87.

13. See Chapter I, Note 4, above. The "pupil" referred to here, as we shall see, was Vassian Toporkov. Joseph's most famous, or notorious, student was Daniel, who became metropolitan in 1521 but was deposed in 1539 and died in 1547; Daniel's most famous student was Makary, who became metropolitan in 1542 and died in 1563. The St. Joseph monastery of Volokolamsk, it has been determined, provided more hierarchs than any other monastery throughout the sixteenth century, testimony to the legacy of its politically powerful founder.

14. See Chapter I, Note 11, above.

15. See Vol. 9, p. 155.

16. For the parable of the talents see Matthew 25:14-30 and Luke 19:11-27.

17. Vasilia, like Vasily, were Russian names derived from the Greek word for emperor, Basileus.

18. Melchisidek is an Old Testament figure, a descendant of Noah and one-time king of Salem, or Jerusalem, who welcomed and fed Abraham after he defeated the four kings who captured his nephew Lot.

19. That is, the Josephite tradition of involvement in politics and supportive of the intimate, "caesaropapist" form of theocratic rule that prevented the Reformation from entering Russian religious and intellectual life. See Chapter I, Notes 4 and 11, above. Soloviev does not mention that Vassian and Maxim met previously as protagonists in the latter's famous trial in 1525; nor that Vassian was Joseph's nephew. Vassian carried on his uncle's political work with devotion, helping

Metropolitan Daniel bring Maxim to trial in 1525. It was presumably for this political favor that he received the bishopric of Kolomna, whence he continued to support the Josephite church leaders, who in turn preached utter devotion to the tsar. Among other things, this illustrates well how the church as an institution served as a ladder for those members of Muscovite society born outside the aristocracy who were yet ambitious for political power.

20. See Vol. 9, pp. 207-208.

21. See Vol. 9, pp. 208-210.

22. *Prince A. M. Kurbsky's History of Ivan IV*, edited and translated by J.L.I. Fennell (Cambridge, 1965) (hereafter cited as Kurbsky, *History*), p. 153. As well as Kurbsky's history of Ivan, his celebrated correspondence with him also has been translated and edited by Fennell, *The Correspondence between Prince A.M. Kurbsky and Tsar Ivan IV of Russia, 1564-1579* (Cambridge, 1963) (hereafter cited as *Correspondence*). Soloviev tends to abridge and even amend the text, often without indicating that he has done so. We have indicated with ellipses (…) where original phrases or passages have been left out of his account. Readers are recommended to consult these works for a full translation of these significant documents in their entirety. An American scholar, Edward L. Keenan, published a work entitled *The Kurbskii-Groznyi Apocrypha* (Harvard, 1971), in which he attempted to show, not only that there is no hard evidence to prove the Kurbsky-Ivan letters actually were written by Kurbsky and Ivan, but that indeed it is possible to hypothesize their forgery in the following century. Keenan's work set off a major scholarly battle, the last shots of which probably still have not been fired. For a guide to and commentary on the first decade of this important controversy, see Charles J. Halperin, "Keenan's Heresy Revisited," *Jahrbücher für Geschichte Osteuropas,* 28 (1980), pp. 481-499.

23. Cf. Kurbsky, *History*, p. 155.

24. A monk from the Volokolamsk monastery.

25. Cf. Kurbsky, *History*, pp. 157, 159.

26. Cf. Kurbsky, *History*, p. 159.

27. The Solovetsk monastery was founded in the 1420s and 1430s on the shore of the island of Solovetsk (Island of the Nightingales) in the White Sea by monks from the St. Cyril monastery of Beloozero, closer to Moscow. The monks constructed massive walls, towers, and other fortifications around the monastery, turning it into a veritable frontier fortress as well as a favorite place of banishment and imprisonment. Through the fifteenth and sixteenth centuries it increased its land-holdings along the mainland shores of the White Sea, developing handcrafts and commerce in various items such as salt, mica, iron and pearls. Its abbot answered directly to the tsar and the metropolitan in Moscow, independent of all local secular and ecclesiastical authorities. As a result it became a powerful economic and political center of the entire White Sea region. It employed many secular workers in its wide-ranging enterprises and in Ivan's time was reckoned to contain six to seven hundred servants and workers for three hundred and fifty monks. It retained its relative independence in the next century, becoming a

stronghold of the Old Believers, even raising the flag of revolt against Moscow in 1668-1676. For more information see V.I. Buganov, "Solovetskii Monastery," MERSH, Vol. 36, pp. 140-141.

28. "... a monastery, which lies a hundred miles from Moscow." Kurbsky elsewhere described the St. Cyril monastery at Beloozero in exactly the same terms. (Soloviev's note)

29. Soloviev has taken this passage almost verbatim from Kurbsky's history of Ivan's reign. See Kurbsky, *History*, p. 181.

30. Alessandro Guagnini, *Omnium Regionum Moschoviae Monarchae subiectarum, morum et religionis descriptio et desta tyrannis Johannis Basilidis* (Description of the Subjects, Morals and Religion of All Regions of the Muscovite Monarchy and of the Ruler Ivan Vasilievich) (Frankfurt, 1600), Chapter V, pp. 182-206. (Soloviev's citation)

31. About eighteen pounds. See Table of Weights and Measures.

32. A grivenka, a measure of weight, was equivalent to about seven ounces; ten grivenki thus amounted to about four and a half pounds.

33. See Vol. 9, pp. 209-210.

34. In Kievan Rus the *druzhina* was the prince's retinue. They accompanied him on campaigns and tribute-gathering expeditions and constituted his permanent body of advisors. For more information see Soloviev, *History*, Vol. 1.

35. The passage referred to is, in our bible, 2 Samuel 24. In the Slavonic bible there are four books of Kings, corresponding to our books 1-2 Samuel and 1-2 Kings.

36. Rehoboam was the son and successor of Solomon. He rejected the counsel of his older mentors who advised the easing of the people's tax burden. As a result the northern tribes revolted against his rule, and the united monarchy of the Jewish nation became divided between the kingdoms of Judea and Israel. See 1 Kings 12.

37. Fedor "the Black" Rostislavich (died 1299), prince of Smolensk and Yaroslavl in the late thirteenth century, was a descendant of Prince Rostislav Mstislavich (died 1167), the grandson of the Kievan grand prince Vladimir Monomakh. Under the rule of Rostislav in the twelfth century Smolensk became an autonomous principality and continued to grow even after Rostislav left for Kiev to become grand prince himself (1159-1167). Fedor the Black received the principality of Yaroslavl by virtue of having married the daughter of its previous ruler, Prince Vasily Vsevolodovich. Fedor died in 1299 and was canonized in 1463.

38. Tver was Moscow's most serious and long-standing rival for political leadership of Russia under Mongol rule in the thirteenth, fourteenth and fifteenth centuries. Prince Mikhail Yaroslavich (1271-1319; ruler of Tver 1285-1319, also grand prince of Vladimir from 1304) came closest to wresting power from his rival and cousin Prince Yury Danilovich of Moscow (ruled 1303-1325). Yury accused Michael of poisoning his (Yury's) wife, who happened to be the sister of Khan Uzbek of the Golden Horde. The situation signifies who was the real arbiter of Russian politics. Uzbek finally sided with Yury. He called both princes to Saray and had Mikhail put to death in Yury's presence. Tver under its successor princes,

however, remained defiant of Mongol rule, opposing Moscow's policy of concili-
ation and cooperation; indeed, it continued to be known as a locus of opposition
sentiment throughout Russian history. For more information on Prince Mikhail,
see the entry by Graham, MERSH, Vol. 22, pp. 55-77; on Tver, see the entry by
Joseph L. Wieczynski, MERSH, Vol. 40, pp. 111-114.

39. The principality of Uglich was practically destroyed by the Mongols in the
mid-thirteenth century. It became an appanage of Muscovy in the late fourteenth
century, losing its autonomous status under Ivan IV. In 1491 Ivan III's brother
Prince Andrei of Uglich together with his two sons were imprisoned for refusing
to participate in a campaign against the Golden Horde. Andrei died in prison in
1493. "The Yaroslavichi" refers to the descendants of Yaroslav Vladimirovich,
son of Prince Vladimir Andreevich "the Brave," hero of the battle of Kulikovo
under Dmitry Donskoy and great-grandson of Ivan I. Vasily Yaroslavich, prince
of Serpukhov, served Grand Prince Vasily II but was arrested on the latter's orders in 1456 and exiled to Uglich; he was transferred to Vologda where he died in
prison in 1483; three of his sons died soon after his arrest. Fennell, *Correspondence*, p. 210, Note 3.

40. Dmitry was Ivan III's eldest grandson, son of Ivan Ivanovich, who pre-
deceased his father, and Princess Elena, and thus a contender for the position of
successor to the Moscow throne during Ivan III's final years; eventually he was
ousted by his step-uncle Vasily, Ivan's son by his second wife Sophia. Vasily became grand prince (Vasily III) in 1505.

41. Kurbsky and Tsaritsa Anastasia had the same great-great-grandfather, the
boyar Boris Ivanovich Morozov.

42. Prince Vladimir of Staritsa was married for a second time in 1558, to Princess Evdokia Romanovna Odoevskaia whose mother was a Kurbsky. On Vladimir,
see Chapter I, Note 3, above.

43. That is, the right to transfer their allegiance from the Muscovite grand
prince to other appanage princes, supposedly without consequences or fear of retribution. See also Chapter III, Note 10, above.

44. See Matthew 10:23.

45. See Chapter I, Notes 8 and 69, above.

46. The "Angelic Form" refers to the monastic tonsure.

47. That Kurbsky did in fact have pretensions to the title of prince of Yaroslavl
is demonstrated in his correspondence with several persons in Lithuania in which
he called himself, grandly, Prince Andrei Yaroslavsky. (Soloviev's note)

48. Ivan refers to the fall of Constantinople to the Turks in 1453; in Russian eyes
the fall was the result of a sell-out by the Greeks, particularly their church leaders.

49. See Exodus 32 and Numbers 12.

50. Dathan and Abiram were members of the tribe of Reuben who rebelled
against Moses, claiming that it was they who led the exodus in order to rule over
the Israelites (Numbers 16). According to Deuteronomy 11:16 the earth swallowed
them up alive.

51. See Numbers 20:25-28.

52. Theophilus (reigned 829-842) was the last of the iconoclast emperors of Byzantium.

53. Ivan referred to Crispus, eldest son of Emperor Constantine the Great. Suspected of plotting to overthrow his father, he was killed in 326 on Constantine's orders.

54. This particular event has gone unrecorded elsewhere.

55. He referred here to the Jebusites, one of the peoples of Canaan. The Israelites' capture of Jerusalem and its conversion into the capital of David's kingdom at the beginning of his reign put an end to the autonomy of the Jebusite kingdom. Not all Jebusites were destroyed. David apparently integrated many Jebusite craftsmen and officials into his service. Ivan referred to the fact that whereas the Jebusites' opposition was open, that of his boyars was secret.

56. Abimelech, a Old Testament figure, was the male offspring of Gideon the Abiezrite by his Shechemite concubine (see Judges 7:31). During the period of the Judges, Abimelech became the ruler of Shechem through the support of his mother's family and the local magnates, who financed the hiring of the regiment with which Abimelech murdered all but one of the seventy sons of Gideon in order to eliminate possible claims to the leadership of Shechem.

57. Prince Mikhailo Karamysh Kurbsky was Kurbsky's paternal grandfather. We have no other source about the treachery that Ivan accuses him of having plotted.

58. Prince Andrei of Uglich, third son of Grand Prince Vasily II, quarreled regularly with his brother Grand Prince Ivan III. His chief act of independence occurred in 1479-1480 when, together with his younger brother Boris, prince of the appanage of Volok, he attempted to obtain military aid from Lithuania against Moscow. In 1480 he became reconciled with Ivan III in the face of a threatened Tatar invasion; in 1491, however, as a result of his refusal to send commanders to aid Ivan's ally at the time, the khan of Crimea, Andrei was arrested and thrown into prison where he soon died. Prince Boris, meanwhile, maintained his appanage independence from Moscow; in 1479 he entertained an outspoken dissident churchman and persuaded him to move to his appanage and set up a monastery to aid him in his opposition to the ecclesiastical and secular authorities in Moscow. The monastery rapidly became one of Russia's most prestigious and its head the most powerful and influential churchman of his time, Joseph of Volokolamsk. See Chapter I, Note 4, above.

59. We know little about Kurbsky's father, Prince Mikhailo Kurbsky, and nothing about any plot against the life of Vasily III in which he might have been involved. He may have been an adherent of the Dmitry-Elena faction in the struggle for succession to the throne (see Note 40, above), since the Patrikeevs (who were tonsured forcibly by Ivan III) were also friends of the Kurbsky family and known supporters of Dmitry and Elena.

60. We know nothing about any activities of Kurbsky's Tuchkov great-grandfather Vasily or the latter's brother Ivan.

61. See Chapter I, Note 14, above.

62. Alexandrov Village (Aleksandrovskaia Sloboda), a small village on the Sherna tributary of the Kliazma, about sixty miles northwest of Moscow, is first mentioned in the testament of Grand Prince Ivan I in the fourteenth century. Presently the town of Alexandrov, it contains an interesting tent-roofed church dating from the first half of the sixteenth century, before Ivan made it his residence. Having set up a press in Moscow under master printer Ivan Fedorov, Ivan had another set up in Alexandrov Village, this one run by master printer Andronik Nevezha.

63. *Oprichnina* was derived from the words *oprich'* (apart) and *oprichnyi* (private). In other volumes of Soloviev's *History* the terms *oprichnina* and *zemshchina* are translated. In this volume, since they constitute a major part of the subject matter, they are left untranslated.

64. An oprichnik was a member of the oprichnina.

65. See Vol. 9, pp. 219-220.

66. See Vol. 9, p. 210.

67. Archbishop German (died 1568) was born Grigory Fedorov early in the sixteenth century in Staritsa. In the late 1530s he entered the St. Joseph monastery at Volokolamsk and as a monk took the name German (pronounced Gherman). He studied with Maxim the Greek during the latter's incarceration, until he was called by the archbishop of Tver to run the Dormition monastery in Staritsa, into which German introduced the strict monastic living style characteristic of the Volokolamsk monastery, to which German returned after two years. In 1554 German was called to Moscow to sit on a church council to judge a heretic; the following year he was appointed to head the Sviiazhsk monastery by Gury, the new (and first, following the Russian conquest) archbishop of Kazan who was at the Volokolamsk monastery with German. At Sviiazhsk he began construction of a number of new buildings, and he became known as an effective proselytizer among the Muslim and other natives in the Sviiazhsk area. When Gury died in 1564, Ivan IV and Metropolitan Afanasy named German to replace him. He served for two years as archbishop of Kazan, where he became known for building schools in the monasteries to educate the baptized natives. In 1566 at the height of the oprichnina Ivan appointed him the new metropolitan, over German's protests, but Ivan fell out with him and had him replaced in 1568 by Philip (see Note 68, below). Philip did not last even that long in the position, and German was executed for attempting to defend him against Ivan's charges.

68. Philip (1507-1569) was born Fedor Stepanovich Kolychev. The Kolychev family was an old boyar family in service of the Muscovite ruler, some of whose members had connections with the appanage house of Staritsa. Following the abortive revolt of Prince Andrei of Staritsa against Ivan's mother the regent Elena, young Fedor became a monk in the Solovetsk monastery, taking the monastic name of Philip, and eventually (in 1548) became its head. Under his leadership the monastery was completely rebuilt and became one of the chief economic and political centers of northern Russia. (See Note 27, above.)

69. See below, pp. 165-170.

70. Grigory Lukianovich Maliuta-Skuratov (sometimes Skuratov-Belsky; died 1573) appears to have belonged to the lesser Russian provincial aristocracy. He joined Ivan's oprichnina when first it was set up and, by marrying into Ivan's family, rapidly advanced in responsibilities. By 1569 he became one of its chief directors, responsible for carrying out Ivan's extensive investigations and summary executions. He died in battle during the operation to recapture the Livonian fortress of Weissenstein in 1573. In Russian folklore, Maliuta-Skuratov is characterized as personifying the brutality and excesses of Ivan's reign.

71. See Vol. 9, p. 99.

72. Soloviev here refers to a work by Christian Kelch entitled *Liefländische Historia* published in Reval in 1695.

73. The Russian chronicles give no details about Vladimir's death. The non-Russian sources are contradictory. In one, he was poisoned; in another, he was knifed; in a third, he had his head cut off. In one his wife and children were poisoned with him. According to one genealogy, Vladimir had one son, Vasily, who had no children; according to another, Vladimir had three sons: Vasily, Ivan and Yury. If we accept as true the foreign sources, which agree with Kurbsky that two sons died with the father, a third must have remained alive, for Tsar Ivan mentions him in his testament of 1572, "Let us re-examine at this time those towns and districts and villages that were given to Prince Vladimir Andreevich in exchange for the towns and districts that were taken from him because of his crimes before me, to see which are the most suitable for Prince Vladimir's son Vasily and his daughter." Thus Vasily at the time of his sister's wedding was already married. Why would the younger brothers have been killed when the eldest was pardoned? (Soloviev's note)

74. Novgorod's vast territory stretching to the northeast as far as the Urals was divided administratively into "fifths" (piatiny). Thus Novgorod's colonial territories came to be called "the Fifths."

75. This refers to the horrifying invasion of Russia in 1238-1240 by the Tatars and Mongols under Batu Khan, Chinghis Khan's grandson.

76. Ivan wrote his testament in Novgorod in 1572 following his fourth marriage while waiting anxiously for news of the approaching battle with the Crimean Tatars, who invaded Russia in force. The battle was decided at Molodi, a significant moment in Russian history. (See Chapter IV, Note 31, below.) Ivan undoubtedly wrote other testaments, but this is the only one that has survived. See Robert Craig Howes, *The Testaments of the Grand Princes of Muscovy* (Cornell, 1967), pp. 307-360.

77. See Soloviev, *History,* Vol. 2.

78. The early Slavs' name for Constantinople was Tsargrad, or "City of the Tsars," rather than "City of Constantine."

79. "Although the wording of this paragraph is obscure, it means that Fedor is to receive a patrimonial principality, but is not to consider it an *udel* in the traditional sense." Howes, p. 360, Note 200.

80. The Christianized Tatar khan of Kasimov. (Soloviev's note). Simeon was a prince of royal Mongol blood, the great-grandson of Khan Akhmet of the Golden

Horde and a descendant of Chinghis Khan (see Chapter IV, Note 29, below; on Kasimov, see Chapter I, Note 21, above). The event probably took place in 1575 rather than 1574. For more information on the crisis that led to these executions and the connection to Bekbulatovich's enthronement, see the article by J.M. Culpepper, "The Kremlin Executions of 1575 and the Enthronement of Simeon Bekbulatovich," *Slavic Review,* 24 (1965), pp. 503-506.

81. Torzhok was a city near Tver; if Ivan did indeed award such an appanage to Prince Simeon Bekbulatovich in 1576, it shows that he did not abandon entirely the idea of appanages in spite of his railing against the aristocrats.

82. That court men (dvorovye) and the oprichniks were one and the same, see the following remark from a church manuscript in the Volhynia library, "Whichever princes and boyars and gentry be needed, he called them oprichniks, that is to say, court men." (Soloviev's note)

83. This is probably an allusion to Ivan's third marriage, to Marfa Vasilievna Sobakina. Apparently the bride's mother gave her a potion to induce fertility, with disastrous effects. At the wedding, on October 28, 1571, she was deathly pale and died within a few weeks, on November 14.

CHAPTER IV

1. The island of Øsel, now known as Saaremaa, with an Estonian population, is about 45 miles long and situated in the Eastern Baltic across the mouth of the Gulf of Riga. In 1227 it was conquered by the Order of Livonian Knights and governed by its own bishop until this point in 1561.

2. See Chapter II, Note 22, above. Soloviev incorrectly calls him Frederik III, who in fact ruled Denmark and Norway from 1648 to 1670.

3. Prince Magnus, Frederik II's younger brother, thus became lord of the island of Øsel. Being ambitious but with little hope of succeeding to the Danish throne he sought his fortune in Livonian politics as a client of the Russian tsar and an opponent of the Danes' traditional enemy, the Swedes.

4. Arensburg, situated on the south coast of Øsel, was its chief town and trading port.

5. Pernau was founded in 1255 by one of the bishops of Øsel on the Livonian mainland on the northern shore of the Gulf of Riga.

6. See Chapter II, Notes 1, 20, and 22, above.

7. The Western Dvina (Düna in German, Daugava in Estonian) flows westward from Russia near the Volga headwaters through Belarus and present-day Latvia, entering the Baltic in the Gulf of Riga at the city of that name. It was Livonia's chief waterway.

8. See Chapter II, Note 25, above.

9. Algirdas (Olgerd) was co-ruler of Lithuania with his brother Kestutis (Keistut) from 1345 to 1377. Vytautas (also Vitautas, Vitovt, or Witold, 1350-1430), Kestutis's son and Algirdas's nephew, was grand duke of Lithuania from 1392 to 1430. Earlier, hoping to gain the Lithuanian throne from his cousin and

rival Jagailo (Algirdas's son), he promised his daughter Sophia to Vasily, son of the Muscovite grand prince Dmitry Donskoy, who was making his way back to Moscow in 1387 after his escape from the Golden Horde. After 1392, when Jagailo became king of now-united Poland-Lithuania, until his death in 1430 Vytautas gradually consolidated his rule as grand prince of Lithuania and increased substantially the territory's prosperity. Historically, Vytautas is considered the builder of Lithuanian autonomy within the Polish-Lithuanian union and a far-sighted statesman. For more information, see Leopold Sobel, "Vitovt," MERSH, Vol. 42, pp. 139-144, and "Lithuania," MERSH, Vol. 20, pp. 63-69.

10. The emperor of the Holy Roman empire at the time was Ferdinand I (1503-1564) who succeeded his brother Charles V when the latter abdicated in 1558. By this time the empire had lost its earlier meaning. There was no empire left to speak of except in Germany, and even in Germany it was merely a convenient legal conception. The Reformation, by destroying the spiritual unity of western Christendom, swept away its political unity and thus the earlier significance of the empire. It was, as Voltaire cynically observed, "neither holy, nor Roman, nor an empire (*Essai sur les Moeurs,* 1769). From the mid-sixteenth century on, until its final liquidation by Napoleon in 1806, the Holy Roman empire is best thought of as a loose federation of different princes of Germany under the presidency—theoretically elected but in practice hereditary—of the Habsburg dynasty.

11. In the negotiations with Szimkowicz, Ivan gave orders to say to the envoy among other things, "Smolensk is recorded as being on our side in the final settlement between Grand Prince Simon Ivanovich and Algirdas." (Soloviev's note)

12. Kestutis was co-ruler of Lithuania with his brother Algirdas from 1345 to 1377 and sole ruler after that until 1382.

13. Peter, abbot of a monastery in Southwest Russia, was appointed metropolitan of the Russian church in 1305 by the patriarch of Constantinople and became an influential figure in Muscovite theocratic politics. Primarily because of his siding with the Danilovichi in Moscow and moving his residence there in 1325, those princes managed to wrest the grand principality from other rivals and secure it for Muscovy.

14. See Chapter I, Note 72, above.

15. This of course refers to the Tatar-Mongol attack on Russia in 1238-1240 led by Batu Khan, grandson of Chinghis Khan.

16. Fedor Ivanovich Kolychev-Umnoy (died 1567) was a boyar from a family long in service to the Muscovite throne. He participated in the Kazan campaign. In December 1563 he accompanied the tsar in the Polotsk campaign. In 1565 he was appointed ambassador to Poland. He left on this mission on March 28 and returned to Moscow, empty-handed, on August 19.

17.   Johann Taube and Ehlert Kruse were the authors of the document *Erschreckliche, greuliche und unerhörte Tyranney Iwan Wasilowitz, jtzo regierenden Großfürst in der Muscow* (The Frightful, Gruesome and Unprecedented Tyranny of Ivan Vasilievich, the Grand Prince Presently Reigning in Moscow). Kruse was a member of the 1557 delegation sent by the Order of

Livonian Knights to Moscow to negotiate a settlement. Ivan demanded tribute, which was promised but not paid, whereupon in 1558 he began the war by invading Livonia. Kruse was captured in 1560 and spent the next four years cooling his heels in a Moscow dungeon. Taube was attending the bishop of Dorpat when both were captured in 1559. The bishop died in Moscow in 1563, possibly of foul play in which Taube was implicated. He managed to clear himself and was invited to enter Muscovite service. He joined with Kruse and both became part of Ivan's intimate oprichnina circle, as well as serving as his expert counsellors on Livonian affairs. They received titles and estates, as well as farming the lucrative government liquor monopoly. As related here, they promoted the idea of the vassal kingdom of Livonia. When this plan misfired with the failure of the siege of Reval in 1571, Taube and Kruse entered into communication with the Polish authorities and subsequently staged an abortive anti-Muscovite uprising in Dorpat. Being obliged thereafter to flee ignominiously to Poland, and not surprisingly being regarded there with a jaundiced eye, they composed for Hetman Jan Chodkiewicz a selective account of their experiences in Muscovy. This document became an important primary source when it was rediscovered in 1816 and used by Karamzin in the ninth volume of his *History of the Russian State*. For further details see the entry by Graham, MERSH, Vol. 38, pp. 203-208.

18. See Chapter II, Note 17, above.

19. The two sisters were the daughters of Vladimir of Staritsa, who was executed two years earlier on Ivan's orders. See Chapter I, Note 3, above.

20. See Chapter I, Note 69, above.

21. Suleiman I "the Magnificent" (1494-1566) became sultan of Turkey in 1520, succeeding his father Selim I and inheriting from him a well-organized state, a disciplined army, and a healthy treasury. He possessed the gift of finding and using the talents of able military and civil officials and became famous for his civilian and military achievements. His reign is considered the high point of Turkish history. His armies conquered Belgrade, Budapest, Temesvar, Rhodes, Tabriz, Baghdad, Nakshivan, Aden and Algiers. He reorganized the clerical class, the ulema, in hierarchical fashion. He reformed and improved both the civil and the military administration of the country, inaugurated a new system of feudal tenure, improved the lot of his Christian subjects and even achieved some fame as a poet. Soloviev uses the style Suleiman II, customarily applied by those who acknowledge the sultanate of Bayezid's eldest son, who reigned in Adrianople 1402-1410.

22. See the article by A.N. Kurat, "The Turkish Expedition to Astrakhan' in 1569 and the Problem of the Don-Volga Canal," *Slavonic and East European Review*, 40 (1961-1962), pp. 7-23, which discusses this canal project and points out the power imbalance that existed between Russia and Turkey at the time in Turkey's favor. For the Turkish sultan, Astrakhan was of minor importance; for the Muscovite tsar, Astrakhan was crucial to his empire and his hold on the Eurasian steppe. Realization of the imbalance led Ivan and his successors to avoid confrontation with the Ottoman empire for a century.

23. See Chapter I, Note 23, above.

24. Titles of Tatar political and military leaders.

25. Temriuk was a Cherkess chieftain from Kabarda who entered the tsar's service in 1557 following the fall of Astrakhan (see Chapter I, Note 66, above). In 1561 Temriuk paid a visit to Ivan in Moscow to apply for special recognition as Ivan's representative in his part of Caucasia. He was accompanied by his beautiful daughter Kucheney, whose hand he offered to Ivan. The tsar, whose beloved Anastasia had died the previous year, accepted the gift. Temriuk's daughter was baptized Maria, and she became Ivan's second wife. Her father became Prince Temriuk, and soon discovered the considerable advantages in being the Muscovite tsar's father-in-law. As Moscow's client he became the most powerful chieftain in Kabarda. He led several successful expeditions for Moscow against his enemies in Tarku and Daghestan to the east and appears to have served Ivan faithfully. Maria's brother Salnuk also entered Ivan's service and like her, but unlike their father, converted to Christianity, taking the name Prince Mikhail Cherkassky. He became one of the most influential men in the oprichnina. Maria died in 1569. Ivan imagined that she was poisoned, either by his or her brother's enemies, which prompted him to execute, possibly by forcing to drink poison, his cousin Prince Vladimir of Staritsa together with Vladimir's wife and youngest daughter (see Chapter I, Note 3 and Chapter III, Note 73, above); a few days later he had Vladimir's mother, Princess Evfrosinia, executed by strangling. Then in 1571 Ivan had Maria's brother Mikhail executed, acting on reports, false as it turned out, that his father, old Prince Temriuk in Kabarda, had betrayed him and joined Devlet-Girey with some other Kabardan chieftains. Although Soloviev does not make the point, the zeal with which Russianized natives such as Prince Temriuk and his son Prince Michael, like Khan Shah Ali and Prince Simeon Bekbulatovich and countless others, served their Russian sovereign demonstrates the extraordinary imperial dynamic that made the Russian empire grow and prosper in the centuries to follow.

26. See Chapter I, Notes 10 and 21, above.

27. Selim II (born 1524, reigned 1566-1574) was the son and incapable successor of Suleiman I. His disastrous campaign against Astrakhan marked the beginning of the slow decline of Ottoman power. October 1571 marks the great defeat of the Turkish fleet at Lepanto, which destroyed the notion of the invincibility of the Turkish navy. He is known in history as "Selim the Sot."

28. That is, Muslims and Roman Catholics.

29. Sain-Bulat (died 1616) was Shah Ali's successor on the Kasimov throne on his death in 1567. In 1573 Sain-Bulat was baptized and took the name Simeon Bekbulatovich, at which time he was required to quit the Islamic Tatar throne of Kasimov. He became the Tsar Simeon that Ivan produced in 1575 (Chapter III, Note 76, above). Simeon was succeeded at Kasimov by Mustafa Ali, grandson of the khan of Astrakhan, who served in that position until 1600. Soloviev incorrectly renders his name as Saip Bulat.

30. Dmitry Donskoy (see Chapter I, Note 43, above), following his much-touted victory at Kulikovo over the Tatars of the Golden Horde in 1380, faced severe retribution in the next few years under the new khan of the Golden Horde,

Tokhtamysh. When the Tatars launched a surprise attack in 1381 Dmitry left Moscow, ostensibly to raise troops. While he was regrouping his forces in Kostroma the Tatars by a ruse sacked Moscow, killing twenty-four thousand citizens and burning books and churches before returning home. His son and successor Vasily I also had to flee from a Tatar attack in 1408, when Khan Edigey attacked Moscow. Vasily fled to Kostroma, leaving the Tatars free to sack some important Russian cities such as Pereiaslavl, Rostov, Klin and Riazan.

31. The battles at Molodi marked a significant moment in the sixteenth century. The rout of the Crimean Tatars dealt a major blow to the military power of the Crimea. Combined with the defeat of the Turkish army at Astrakhan in 1569, it limited Turkish and Tatar expansion in Eastern Europe. On the domestic front, the victory was won by the combined armies of the oprichnina and the zemshchina and therefore hastened the abolition of the oprichnina, already decided on in principle in 1571 following the burning of Moscow.

INDEX

THE EDITOR AND TRANSLATOR

Anthony Rhinelander was born a New Englander and is now a Canadian Maritimer. As an undergraduate at Yale University in the early 1960s he began Russian area studies under such outstanding teachers as Firuz Kazemzadeh, Frederick Barghoorn and Nina Berberova. After receiving his BA in 1963 he continued his studies in Russian history and literature at Trinity College, Cambridge, under the inspiring guidance of Nikolay Andreyev and Elizabeth Hill, receiving a second BA in 1965. He pursued his Ph.D in history at Columbia University where he had the great fortune to have mentors like Marc Raeff, Michael Cherniavsky, John Meyendorff, Loren Graham, Leo Haimson and George Nakashidze. Thus he has been able to study in some depth nearly all periods of Russian history, particularly the fascinating if scantily evidenced Muscovite age of the Josephites and Ivan the Terrible. His doctoral dissertation investigated the incorporation of Georgia into the Russian empire. He has visited and studied in Finland, Russia and Georgia several times, including three times, in 1976-1977, 1979 and 1990, as a Visiting Fellow of the Soviet Academy of Sciences and participant on the Canada-USSR Academic Exchange. In 1986-1987 he was a Visiting Fellow at the University of London School of Slavonic and East European Studies. He visited Georgia most recently in 1995.

Rhinelander has written articles and reviews for such journals as *Canadian Slavonic Papers, Slavonic and East European Review, Canadian-American Slavic Studies, Germano-Slavica* and *International History Review;* several entries for the *Modern Encyclopedia of Russian and Soviet History;* and contributions for various edited collections. Recently he has published a full-length biography of a leading Russian official, *Prince Michael Vorontsov. Viceroy to the Tsar* (Montreal: McGill-Queen's, 1990). He is presently researching the topic "the discourse of Russian imperialism."

Since 1970 he has worked in congenial surroundings at St. Thomas University, a small, undergraduate liberal arts college, teaching and researching and writing history with his students and colleagues at St. Thomas and its sister institution the University of New Brunswick, in Fredericton. He lives with his wife Linda Neilson, a socio-legal scholar, and their two children Jason and Lila on a farm outside Fredericton.